BARRON'S

IELTS®
Writing

D1567567

SECOND EDITION

Lin Lougheed, Ed.D.

Teachers College
Columbia University

Published by Kaplan, Inc., d/b/a Barron's Educational Series
750 Third Avenue
New York, NY 10017
www.barronseduc.com

ISBN: 978-1-5062-6817-0

10 9 8 7 6 5 4 3 2 1

Kaplan, Inc., d/b/a Barron's Educational Series print books are available at special quantity
discounts to use for sales promotions, employee premiums, or educational purposes. For
more information or to purchase books, please call the Simon & Schuster special sales
department at 866-506-1949.

CONTENTS

Introduction

WHAT IS IELTS?

IELTS, the International English Language Testing System, is an English language proficiency exam that tests listening, reading, writing, and speaking skills. There are over 1,000 test centers in more than 140 countries around the world. Over 9,000 organizations, including universities, government agencies, and private companies, accept IELTS test scores.

There are two versions of the test—Academic and General Training. The Academic version is for students who want to pursue a university education in an English-speaking country. The General Training test is for people who need to demonstrate English language proficiency for work, training programs, secondary education, or immigration to certain countries.

HOW TO USE THIS BOOK

This book will help you prepare for the writing section of the IELTS test whether you are planning to take the Academic or the General Training version. Both versions of the test include a writing section with two tasks.

The organization of this book follows the criteria IELTS examiners use to score your writing. If you study everything in this book, you will score well.

- Task Achievement/Task Response
- Coherence and Cohesion
- Lexical Resource
- Grammatical Range and Accuracy

In the **Task Achievement/Task Response** chapter, you will learn to follow a three-step model for creating an essay:

(STEP 1) **Plan**
(STEP 2) **Write**
(STEP 3) **Revise**

You will learn how to apply this model to each of the IELTS writing tasks. Study the sections of this chapter that focus on the version of the test that you plan to take—Academic or General Training.

Each section leads you step by step through the process of writing an essay in response to that particular task. Therefore, you should work your way through each section from beginning to end. As you study a section, you will become familiar with the types of questions you will have to respond to on the IELTS. You will also learn to complete your responses within the time limits of the test.

When you respond to the IELTS writing tasks, you must write clearly, coherently, and correctly. The next three chapters of this book will help you do that. They will help you develop skills you will need for both the Academic and General Training versions of the test.

In the **Coherence and Cohesion** chapter, you will practice organizing your writing and connecting your ideas. In the **Lexical Resource** chapter, you will learn how to develop your vocabulary and use it correctly. In the **Grammatical Range and Accuracy** chapter, you will review grammar rules and practice applying them to your writing.

You can work through these chapters in order. Or, you can focus first on the parts that address your weakest areas. Then, you can use the rest for review and practice.

In the Appendix you will find a **More Writing Practice** section with a selection of essays written in response to IELTS writing tasks. You can study the essays as models of good writing. You can also use this section for further practice by writing your own responses to the tasks included in the section.

IELTS WRITING SCORES

Scores for the IELTS writing tasks are reported in a scale of bands, ranging from Band 0 to Band 9. Each band represents a level of ability. Scores are based on the following criteria.

TASK ACHIEVEMENT (TASK 1): To achieve a high score, you must write a well-developed report that completely addresses all parts of the task.

TASK RESPONSE (TASK 2): To achieve a high score, you must address all parts of the task in a well-developed essay that presents a clear position supported with relevant ideas.

COHERENCE AND COHESION: To achieve a high score, your ideas and information must follow a logical organization (coherence), and you must use a range of cohesive devices skillfully.

LEXICAL RESOURCE: To achieve a high score, you must use a wide range of vocabulary fluently with few errors.

GRAMMATICAL RANGE AND ACCURACY: To achieve a high score, you must use a wide range of grammatical structures fluently and accurately with few errors.

For a complete description of the writing task bands, visit the IELTS website: *http://www. ielts.org/researchers/score_processing_and_reporting.aspx#Writing*

TIPS

Before the test

- Practice writing within time limits. You can use the tasks in the More Writing Practice section of the Appendix for practice. Give yourself 20 minutes to complete a Task 1 response and 40 minutes to complete a Task 2 response.
- Become familiar with word count. If you take the paper-based test, you will write your essays by hand. You will have to write a minimum of 150 words for Task 1 and 250 words for Task 2, but you won't be able to take the time to count your words. As you practice writing essays at home, count your words. You will become familiar with what 150 words and 250 words look like in your handwriting. If you take the computer-based test, the computer will count the words for you as you type. You still need to be aware of word count as you practice for the test so that you can write a good essay with the proper word count within the time limits of the test.
- To prepare for Academic Task 1, take some time to study a variety of graphs, charts, and tables. You can find many on the Internet. Practice reading them and interpreting the information.

During the test

- Read the task carefully and make sure you understand exactly what it asks you to do.
- Do not copy complete sentences from the task. Paraphrase and use synonyms. You will learn how to do this in Chapters 1 and 3.
- Write in complete sentences. You can make notes in abbreviated form when you plan, but your finished essay must have complete sentences and paragraphs.
- Vary your sentences. Use sentence structures that you know you can use correctly, but do not write the same type of sentence over and over. In Chapter 4, you will get practice with different sentence types.
- Learn and use the three-step model presented in this book—**plan**, **write**, **revise**. It will help you write a complete and organized response to both tasks. Following a model will give you confidence.

Task Achievement/ Task Response

1

ACADEMIC WRITING TASK 1: CHARTS, GRAPHS, TABLES

TIME

You will have 60 minutes to complete the writing part of the test. You should allow 20 minutes for Task 1. Divide your time as follows:

Total time   20 minutes

STEP 1	**Plan**	5 minutes
STEP 2	**Write**	12 minutes
STEP 3	**Revise**	3 minutes

LENGTH

You must write at least 150 words. You can write more.

TIPS

- Use only the information provided in the task. Do not include outside information or your own opinion.
- Ask yourself questions to focus on the task:
  - What is this graphic about?
  - Which are the most important details?

SCORE

To receive a good score,

- Address all parts of the task
- Accurately summarize the information
- Make meaningful comparisons
- End with a brief overview of the information
- Use correct grammar, spelling, and punctuation
- Write in complete sentences
- Use your own words; do not copy exact sentences from the task

STEP 1: PLAN

Spend about 5 minutes on planning before you start writing. Planning will make sure you include all the necessary information.

Address the Task

In Task 1, you will see a graphic. This graphic may be a graph, chart, or table. (The graphic might also be a diagram describing a process. See the following section [page 47] for information on process diagrams.) You will be asked to describe the information shown in the graphic and make comparisons. You must immediately recognize the type of graphic and its features. This will help you address the task.

PRACTICE 1

Look at the following tasks and graphics. Write the letter of each graphic or set of graphics next to the corresponding task.

Tasks

1   ....

> The bar graph below shows the number of tourists visiting two different cities by season.
>
> Summarize the information by selecting and reporting the main features, and make comparisons where relevant.

2   ....

> The pie charts below show the form of transportation to work normally used by workers in a particular city.
>
> Summarize the information by selecting and reporting the main features, and make comparisons where relevant.

3   ....

> The line graph below shows the number of single-family homes constructed in the United States by region over a period of six years.
>
> Summarize the information by selecting and reporting the main features, and make comparisons where relevant.

4   ....

> The table below shows the number of hours per week people of different ages spend using the Internet for different types of activities.
>
> Summarize the information by selecting and reporting the main features, and make comparisons where relevant.

5   ....

> *The pie charts below show enrollment in different fields of study at a particular university.*
>
> *Summarize the information by selecting and reporting the main features, and make comparisons where relevant.*

Graphics

A

New Residential Construction

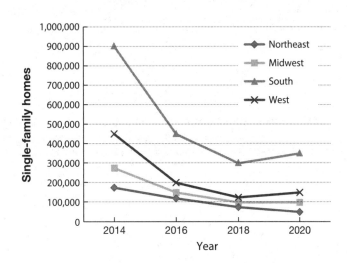

B

Number of Tourists by Season

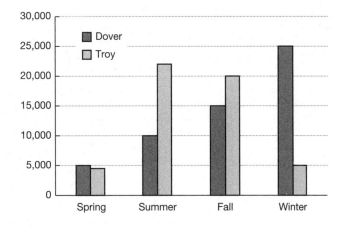

C   Clydesdale University Enrollment

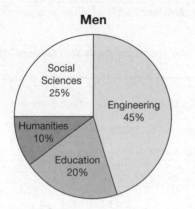

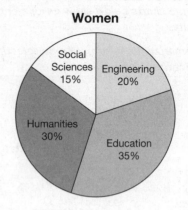

D   Hours per Week Spent on the Internet, by Age

	Teens	20s	30s	40s	50s	60s +
Studying/working	15	50	45	40	40	17
Leisure activities	20	18	17	10	11	18

E   Rockingham, Transportation

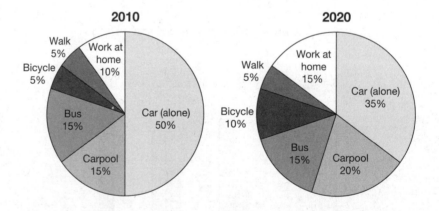

Determine the Topic

In Task 1, you will be asked to summarize the information on the graphic *by selecting and reporting on the main features.* The main features will help you determine the details of the topic of the graphic.

To identify the main details of the graphic, first read the task and identify the type of graphic. Second, read the title of the graphic and scan the features. To focus your thoughts, ask yourself *Who? What? When?* and *Where?* Use this information to determine the details of the topic.

Details

> Task
> Type of graphic
> Title of graphic
> Features
>> Who
>> What
>> When
>> Where

Topic: ....

Look at these examples.

I

> *The graph below shows the average daily sales of selected food items at the Vista Café, by season.*
>
> *Summarize the information by selecting and reporting the main features, and make comparisons where relevant.*

Average Daily Sales, by Number of Servings

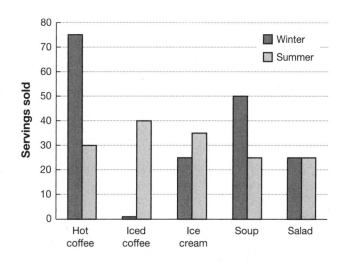

Graphic type: bar graph

Title: Average Daily Sales, by Number of Servings

What? average daily sales

When? winter and summer

Topic: the average number of servings of certain food items sold daily in the winter and in the summer

II | *The graph below shows the number of cell phone subscribers in a particular city, by gender.*

Summarize the information by selecting and reporting the main features, and make comparisons where relevant.

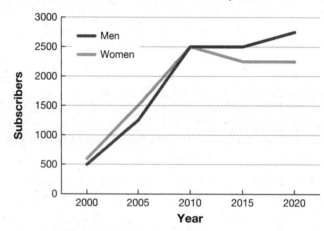

Cell Phone Subscribers, Marysville

Graphic type: line graph

Title: Cell Phone Subscribers, Marysville

What? number of cell phone subscribers

Who? men and women

When? 2000-2020

Where? Marysville

Topic: The number of men and women cell phone subscribers in Marysville from 2000-2020

PRACTICE 2

Determine the topics of the graphics in Practice 1 (pages 7–8) by completing the information.

Graphic A

Graphic type: ....

Title: ....

What? ....

When? ....

Where? ....

Topic: ....

Graphic B

Graphic type: ....

Title: ....

What? ....

When? ....

Where? ....

Topic: ....

Graphic C

Graphic type: ....

Title: ....

Who? ....

What? ....

Where? ....

Topic: ....

Graphic D

Graphic type: ....

Title: ....

Who? ....

What? ....

When? ....

Topic: ....

Graphic E

Graphic type:	....
Title:	....
Who?	....
What?	....
When?	....
Topic:	....

Make Notes About Comparisons

In Task 1, you will be asked to *make comparisons where relevant*. When you look at a graphic, look for things you can compare. The graphic might show, for example, different places, types of people, types of activities, products, and/or changes over time. Look for similarities and differences among these things.

In Practice 2 (page 11), you asked yourself *Who? What? When?* and *Where?* about the graphics. Use this same information to find comparisons.

Look at these examples.

I

Average Daily Sales, by Number of Servings

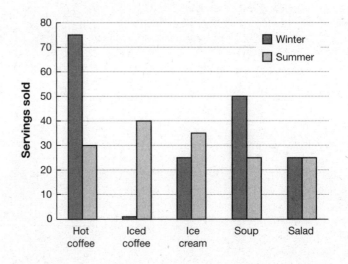

Graphic type:	bar graph
Title:	Average Daily Sales, by Number of Servings
What?	average daily sales
When?	winter and summer
Topic:	the average daily sales of selected food items in the winter and in the summer

When we write about Graphic I, we can make two kinds of comparisons:

1   the average daily sales of selected food items in winter
2   the average daily sales of selected food items in summer

II   **The line graph below shows the number of cell phone subscribers in a particular city, by gender.**

Summarize the information by selecting and reporting the main features, and make comparisons where relevant.

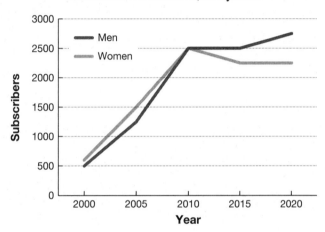

Cell Phone Subscribers, Marysville

Graphic type:	line graph
Title:	Cell Phone Subscribers, Marysville
What?	number of cell phone subscribers
Who?	men and women
When?	2000-2020
Where?	Marysville
Topic:	The number of men and women cell phone subscribers in Marysville from 2000-2020

When we write about Graphic II, we can make two kinds of comparisons:

1   the number of men cell phone subscribers in different years
2   the number of women cell phone subscribers in different years

PRACTICE 3

Look at the information you completed in Practice 2 (page 11). Use this information to determine the comparisons you can make for each of the graphics from Practice 1 (pages 7–8).

Graphic A

Comparisons

1 ....

2 ....

Graphic B

Comparisons

1 ....

2 ....

Graphic C

Comparisons

1 ....

2 ....

Graphic D

Comparisons

1 ....

2 ....

Graphic E

Comparisons

1 ....

2 ....

Make Notes About Details

In Practice 3 (page 14) you determined the possible comparisons in a graphic. Now, you will look for the details that describe the comparisons.

Look for where things change. Look for where numbers go up or down. Look for where the biggest differences are.

For Graphic I on page 12, we determined these two comparisons:

1   the average daily sales of different food items in winter

2   the average daily sales of different food items in summer

The relevant details will be about *how many* servings of each item were sold. Look at the following details for Graphic I.

Comparison

1   the average daily sales of different food items in winter

Details

A   highest number of sales—hot coffee—75

B   second highest number of sales—soup—50

C   salad and ice cream sales—25 each

D   lowest number of sales—iced coffee—almost 0

Comparison

2   the average daily sales of different food items in summer

Details

A   highest number of sales—iced coffee—40

B   second highest number of sales—ice cream—35

C   hot coffee sales—30

D   lowest number of sales—soup and salad—25 each

PRACTICE 4

Look at the graphics in Practice 1 (pages 7–8). Use the comparisons you determined for each of the graphics in Practice 3 (page 14) to determine the relevant details for each graphic. Find between two and four details for each comparison.

Graphic A

Comparison

1 ....

Details

A ....

B ....

C ....

D ....

Comparison

2 ....

Details

A ....

B ....

C ....

D ....

Graphic B

Comparison

1 ....

Details

A ....

B ....

C ....

D ....

Comparison

2 ....

Details

A ....

B ....

C ....

D ....

Graphic C

Comparison

1 ....

Details

A ....

B ....

C ....

D ....

Comparison

2 ....

Details

A ....

B ....

C ....

D ....

Graphic D

Comparison

1 ....

Details

A ....

B ....

C ....

D ....

Comparison

2 ....

Details

A ....

B ....

C ....

D ....

Graphic E

Comparison

1 ....

Details

A ....

B ....

C ....

D ....

Comparison

2 ....

Details

A ....

B ....

C ....

D ....

STEP 2: WRITE

After you plan, you are ready to write. You will use your notes about the task, topic, comparisons, and details as a guide. You should take about 12 minutes to write your essay.

Write the Introduction

The introduction tells what you will write about. In Task 1, you are asked to summarize and compare. In your introduction, tell *what* you will summarize and compare.

Write the Topic Sentence

For the first sentence of the introduction, write a topic sentence that summarizes the information in the graphic. In Practice 2 (page 11), you identified the main features of the graphic and determined the topic. Now you will change those notes into a topic sentence. Do NOT copy exact phrases and sentences from the task and graphic title. Paraphrase by using other phrases and synonyms to express the same ideas. See Chapter 3 (page 187) for more information on synonyms.

Look at these examples.

Graphic I

Task

> *The graph below shows the average daily sales of selected food items at the Vista Café, by season.*
>
> *Summarize the information by selecting and reporting the main features, and make comparisons where relevant.*

Notes

Graphic type: bar graph

Title: Average Daily Sales, by Number of Servings

Topic: the average daily sales of selected food items in the winter and in the summer

Topic sentence

The bar graph shows how many servings of certain food items sold on average every day in two different seasons at the Vista Café.

Discussion

This topic sentence mentions the main features of the graphic. It avoids copying exact phrases and sentences from the task and graphic title by using the phrase *how many* instead of *the number of, certain* instead of *selected,* and *every day* instead of *daily.*

Graphic II

> *The graph below shows the number of cell phone subscribers in a particular city, by gender.*
>
> *Summarize the information by selecting and reporting the main features, and make comparisons where relevant.*

Notes

Graphic type: line graph

Title: Cell Phone Subscribers, Marysville

Topic: The number of men and women cell phone subscribers in Marysville from 2000-2020

Topic sentence

The graph shows how many men and women in Marysville paid for cell phone service from 2000 to 2020.

Discussion

This topic sentence mentions the main features of the graphic. It avoids copying exact phrases and sentences from the task and graphic title by using the words *how many* instead of *the number of* and the phrase *paid for cell phone service* instead of *subscribers.*

PRACTICE 5

Find the synonym for each of the following words and phrases. Write the letter of the synonym in the blank.

Words/Phrases

1 .... construct
2 .... region
3 .... the number of
4 .... visit
5 .... different
6 .... type
7 .... passengers
8 .... on weekdays
9 .... men
10 .... women

Synonyms

A various
B how many
C female
D male
E during the week
F people who ride
G build
H spend time in
I kind
J area

PRACTICE 6

Rewrite the following topic sentences by using synonyms for the underlined sections.

1 The graph shows <u>the number of</u> schools <u>constructed</u> in each <u>region</u> of the country in 2020.

   ....

2 The graph shows <u>the number of</u> people <u>who visited</u> the Palm Island Resort in each of the years from 2015 to 2020.

   ....

3 The charts show the percentages of <u>men and women</u> shoppers who shopped at Mayfield's Clothing Store at <u>different</u> times of the day.

   ....

4 The table shows the <u>different types</u> of career interests reported by students at Bingham University.

   ....

5 The graph shows the number of <u>bus passengers</u> in the city <u>on weekdays</u>.

   ....

Make a Statement About Comparisons

The first sentence of your introduction is the topic sentence. The topic sentence tells what the graphic is about. In the next sentence, tell what comparisons you will make. In Practice 3 (page 14), you made notes about comparisons. Now you will turn those notes into a sentence that tells what comparisons you will make in your essay.

Look at these examples.

Comparisons for Graphic I (page 12):

1   the average daily sales of selected food items in winter
2   the average daily sales of selected food items in summer

Topic sentence

The bar graph shows how many servings of certain food items sold on average every day in two different seasons at the Vista Café.

Second sentence

The average number of sales of each item changed with the season.

Discussion

The second sentence tells what you will compare (*average number of sales of each item*) and how you will compare them (*changed with the season*).

Comparisons for Graphic II (page 13):

1   the number of men cell phone subscribers in different years
2   the number of women cell phone subscribers in different years

Topic sentence

The graph shows how many men and women in Marysville paid for cell phone service from 2000 to 2020.

Second sentence

The number of subscribers of each gender rose at similar rates during the twenty-year period.

Discussion

The second sentence tells what you will compare (*number of subscribers*) and how you will compare them (*rose at similar rates*).

PRACTICE 7

Choose the best sentence to complete the introduction for each graphic.

1

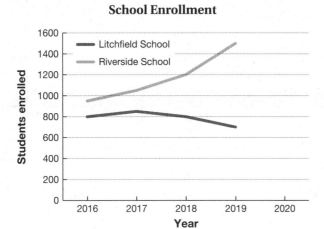

School Enrollment

Comparisons

enrollment in Riverside School

enrollment in Litchfield School

Introduction

The graph shows how many students were registered at Riverside School and Litchfield School in each of the years from 2016 to 2019.

A The number of students at each school changed every year.

B The number of students at Litchfield School went down between 2018 and 2019.

C The number of students at both schools went up between 2016 and 2019.

2

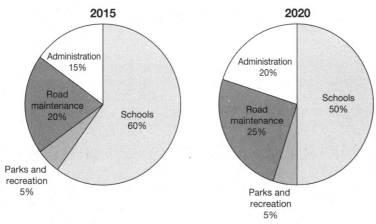

Town Budget—Milford

Comparisons

town spending in Milford in 2015

town spending in Milford in 2020

Introduction

The charts show how the town of Milford spent its money in 2015 and 2020.

A At least half the budget was spent on schools in both years.
B Spending on administration went up in 2015.
C Spending fell in some areas, while it rose in others.

3

Ticket Sales—Springfield Cinema

	3:00	5:00	7:00	9:00
Saturday	100	125	150	150
Sunday	125	100	75	50

Comparisons

Saturday ticket sales
Sunday ticket sales

Introduction

The table shows how many movie tickets were sold at the Springfield Cinema at different times of the weekend.

A One hundred fifty tickets were sold at 9:00 on Saturday.
B On Sunday the fewest tickets were sold in the evening.
C On Saturday sales were highest in the evening, while on Sunday they were highest in the afternoon.

PRACTICE 8

Use your notes from Practice 2 (page 11) and Practice 3 (page 14) to write an introduction for an essay about each of the graphics in Practice 1 (pages 7–8). Include a topic sentence and a statement about comparisons in each introduction.

Graphic A

....
....
....
....
....

Graphic B

....
....
....
....
....

Graphic C

....
....
....
....
....

Graphic D

....
....
....
....
....

Graphic E

....
....
....
....
....

Write the Paragraphs

When you planned your essay, you made notes about comparisons and details. Now you will turn these notes into paragraphs for the body of your essay. You will write one paragraph about each comparison.

Write the Main Idea

Begin each paragraph with a main idea that summarizes the comparison you are making.

Look at these example main ideas.

Graphic I

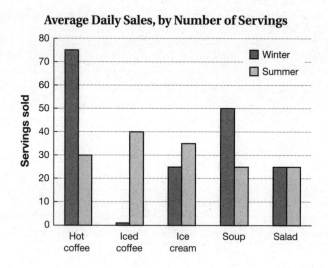

Average Daily Sales, by Number of Servings

Comparison for Paragraph 1
the average daily sales of selected food items in winter

Main ideas
A   Certain food items had much higher sales than others in the winter.
B   People bought different food items at the Vista Café.
C   Iced coffee had the lowest number of winter sales.

Discussion
Statement A is the best main idea for the paragraph. It is a general statement about the difference in sales numbers among the selected food items. Statement B is too general. It doesn't say when people bought the items or how you will compare them. Statement C is too specific. It is only about one item.

Comparison for Paragraph 2
the average daily sales of selected food items in summer

Main ideas

A   People bought both hot coffee and iced coffee.

B   The sales numbers for each food item were different in the summer than they were in the winter.

C   Ice cream sales went up in the winter.

Discussion

Statement B is the best main idea for the paragraph. It is a general statement about what happened to the sales in the café in the summer. Statement A is too general. It doesn't tell when people bought coffee, and it doesn't tell how the sales will be compared. Statement C is too specific. It is only about one particular item.

PRACTICE 9

Choose the best main idea for each of the paragraphs for Graphic II.

Graphic II

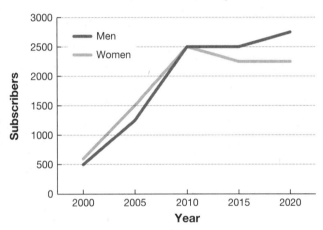

Cell Phone Subscribers, Marysville

Comparison for Paragraph 1

the number of men cell phone subscribers in different years

Main ideas

A   Cell phone subscriptions for men were higher in 2005 than they were in 2000.

B   The number of men subscribers remained the same between 2010 and 2015.

C   The number of men cell phone subscribers rose significantly between 2000 and 2020.

Comparison for Paragraph 2

the number of women cell phone subscribers in different years

Main ideas

A   Cell phone subscriptions for women went up.

B   The number of women subscribing to cell phone service rose in most years between 2000 and 2020.

C   The number of women subscribers went down between 2010 and 2015.

Write the Supporting Details

The main idea of each paragraph is followed by details that support it. Use your notes about details to write statements that support the main idea.

Look at how the notes for the first comparison for Graphic I have been turned into the supporting details of a paragraph.

1   **Notes**

     Comparison

     the average daily sales of different food items in winter

     Details

     A   highest number of sales—hot coffee—75

     B   second highest number of sales—soup—50

     C   salad and ice cream sales—25 each

     D   lowest number of sales—iced coffee—almost 0

     Paragraph 1

     main idea → Certain food items had much higher sales than others in the winter.

Hot coffee had the highest number of sales, with an average of 75 servings sold daily. The item with the second highest number of sales was soup, with an average of 50 servings sold daily. Salad and ice cream had average daily sales of 25 servings each, and iced coffee had the lowest number of sales, with close to zero servings sold daily.

PRACTICE 10

Look at the notes and the following paragraphs for Graphics I and II (pages 25–26). In each paragraph, underline the main idea and cross out the detail that does not support it.

Graphic I

Paragraph 2

Notes

     Comparison

     the average daily sales of different food items in summer

     Details

     A   highest number of sales—iced coffee—40

     B   second highest number of sales—ice cream—35

     C   hot coffee sales—30

     D   lowest number of sales—soup and salad—25 each

The sales numbers for each food item were different in the summer from what they were in the winter. Iced coffee sales rose significantly, to an average of 40 servings sold daily. The item with the second highest number of sales was ice cream, with an average of 35 servings sold daily. Sales of ice cream go up in the summer when the weather is hot. Hot coffee fell to daily sales of just 30 servings. Soup and salad had the lowest number of sales, with 25 servings sold daily on average.

Graphic II

Paragraph 1

Notes

Comparison

the number of men cell phone subscribers in different years

Details

A a little over 500—2000

B rose significantly to 2500 in 2010

C stayed the same—2010–2015

D rose again slightly 2015–2020

The number of male cell phone subscribers rose significantly between 2000 and 2020. In 2000, a little over 500 men subscribed to cell phone service. Women also subscribed to the service at that time. The number increased considerably over the next few years until it reached 2500 in the year 2010. There was no change in the number of subscribers between 2010 and 2015, but then it rose slightly between 2015 and 2020, when there were about 2750 male subscribers.

Paragraph 2

Notes

Comparison

the number of women cell phone subscribers in different years

Details

A 500 subscribers—2000

B increased to 2500 in 2010

C dropped slightly, to about 2250—2010–2015

D stayed steady 2015–2020

The number of women subscribing to cell phone service rose in most years between 2000 and 2020. Before 2000, cell phone use was not very common. In 2000, 500 women subscribed to cell phone service. By 2010, the number of female subscribers had increased to 2500. There was a slight drop between 2010 and 2015, to about 2250 subscribers, and that number stayed steady between 2015 and 2020.

Describe Trends

Use these words to describe the trends shown on a graph, chart, or table.

Nouns/Verbs

Up	Down
increase	decrease
rise	fall
climb	drop
growth/grow	decline
	dip

Adjectives

A lot	A little	No change
significant	slight	steady
sharp		
considerable		

Adverbs

A lot	A little	No change in rate
significantly	slightly	steadily
sharply		
considerably		

PRACTICE 11

Complete the paragraphs about the bar graph using words from the charts above.

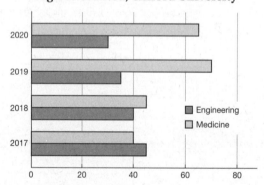

Degrees Granted, Clifford University

The number of medical degrees rose almost every year between 2017 and 2020. It **1** .... slightly between 2017 and 2018 from 40 degrees granted to 45. Then, in 2019, the number of degrees granted rose **2** .... to 70. There was a slight **3** .... in 2020, when about 65 medical degrees were granted at Clifford University.

The number of engineering degrees, on the other hand, dropped steadily from 2017 to 2020. It **4** .... from about 45 degrees granted in 2017 to 40 in 2018. In 2019 there was another **5** .... drop, when just 35 engineering degrees were granted. The number **6** .... again, to 30 degrees granted in 2020.

PRACTICE 12

Use your notes about comparisons and details from Practice 3 (page 14) and Practice 4 (page 16) to write body paragraphs for each of the graphics in Practice 1 (pages 7–8). Write one main idea and three or four supporting statements for each paragraph.

Graphic A

....

....

....

....

....

Graphic B

....

....

....

....

....

Graphic C

....

....

....

....

....

Graphic D

....

....

....

....

....

Graphic E

....

....

....

....

....

Write the Conclusion

In the conclusion, you sum up the ideas you developed in your essay. In the introduction, you made a general statement about the comparisons you planned to make. The conclusion is a restatement of these ideas.

Look at the following introduction and conclusion from an essay about Graphic I on page 26.

Introduction

The bar graph shows how many servings of certain food items sold on average every day in two different seasons at the Vista Café. The average number of sales of each item changed with the season.

Conclusion

In general, the average daily sales of each food item changed depending on the season. Certain items were more popular in the winter and certain others were more popular in the summer.

Discussion

The introduction states the comparisons that will be made in the body of the essay—the average number of sales of each item in different seasons. The conclusion makes a general statement about these comparisons—that some items had higher sales in the summer and others had higher sales in the winter.

Look at the following introduction and conclusion from an essay about Graphic II on page 27.

Introduction

The graph shows how many men and women in Marysville paid for cell phone service from 2000 to 2020. The number of subscribers of each gender rose at similar rates during the twenty-year period.

Conclusion

Overall, while the numbers of both male and female subscribers rose significantly, they rose more for men.

Discussion

The introduction states the comparisons that will be made in the body of the essay—the number of male and female cell phone subscribers. The conclusion makes a general statement about these comparisons—that the rate of increase was higher for men than for women.

PRACTICE 13

On a separate sheet of paper, take the introductions you wrote in Practice 8 (page 24) and put each one together with the corresponding body paragraphs you wrote in Practice 12 (page 31). Then, complete each essay by writing an appropriate conclusion.

STEP 3: REVISE

You should allow at least 3 minutes to revise your essay after you write.

TIP

There is no need to rewrite everything. You can cross out the words you want to change and write in the corrections neatly.

Use the Revision Checklist

When you revise, you check the content and the language of your essay. You also check to make sure the essay is clear and well organized and that you have used correct grammar and spelling. You can use this revision checklist to practice revising.

> ## REVISION CHECKLIST
>
> **Addressing the Task**
> ☐ Thesis Statement
> ☐ Main Ideas
>
> **Coherence**
> ☐ Main Idea—Paragraph
> ☐ Supporting Details
>
> **Cohesion**
> ☐ Introduction—Conclusion
> ☐ Transition Words
>
> **Lexical Resource**
> ☐ Vocabulary Variety
> ☐ Spelling
>
> **Grammatical Range and Accuracy**
> ☐ Sentence Variety
> ☐ Accuracy

Read the following model essay, and note how well it follows the items on the checklist.

> *The graph below shows the average daily sales of selected food items at the Vista Café, by season.*
>
> *Summarize the information by selecting and reporting the main features, and make comparisons where relevant.*

Average Daily Sales, by Number of Servings

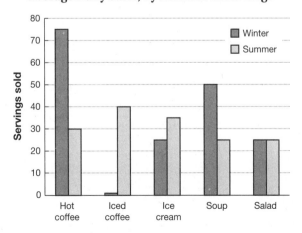

The bar graph shows how many servings of certain food items are sold on average every day in two different seasons at the Vista Café. The average number of sales of each item changed with the season.

main idea 1

Certain food items had much higher sales than others in the winter. Hot coffee had the highest number of sales, with an average of 75 servings sold daily. Following this, the item with the second highest number of sales was soup, with an average of 50 servings sold daily. Salad and ice cream had average daily sales of 25 servings each, and iced coffee had the lowest number of sales, with close to zero servings sold daily.

main idea 2

The sales numbers for each food item were different in the summer from what they were in the winter. Iced coffee sales rose significantly, to an average of 40 servings sold daily. The item that had the second highest number of sales was ice cream, with an average of 35 servings sold daily. Hot coffee sales fell to just 30 servings daily. Soup and salad had the lowest number of sales, with 25 servings sold daily on average.

In general, the average daily sales of each food item changed when the season changed. Certain items were more popular in the winter, but certain others were more popular in the summer.

Check for Thesis Statement

The thesis is a statement of what the essay is about. The first sentence of this essay is the topic sentence. It briefly summarizes the information in the graph and lets the reader know that the essay is about the graph.

Thesis Statement: *The bar graph shows how many servings of certain food items are sold on average every day in two different seasons at the Vista Café.*

Check for Main Ideas

The main ideas support the thesis. The second sentence of this essay tells what comparisons the writer will make—the average number of sales of the food items in two different seasons. These comparisons will become the main ideas of the body paragraphs of the essay—one paragraph will be about sales in the winter season, and the other will be about sales in the summer season.

Check for Supporting Details

The supporting details in an essay give information to support the main ideas. Each body paragraph in this essay has a main idea that matches a comparison introduced in the first paragraph. Each main idea is followed by details that support it.

Paragraph 2

Main Idea

Certain food items had much higher sales than others in the winter.
The sales numbers for each food item were different in the summer from what they were in the winter.

Supporting Details

- *Hot coffee had the highest number of sales*
- *the item with the second highest number of sales was soup*
- *Salad and ice cream had average daily sales*
- *iced coffee had the lowest number of sales*

Paragraph 3

Main Idea

The sales numbers for each food item were different in the summer than they were in the winter.

Supporting Details

- *Iced coffee sales rose significantly*
- *the second highest number of sales was ice cream . . . servings sold daily.*
- *Hot coffee sales fell*
- *Soup and salad had the lowest number of sales*

Check for the Conclusion

The conclusion should sum up the ideas presented in the introduction. In this essay, the introduction states the comparisons that will be made in the body of the essay—the average daily sales of food items in different seasons. The conclusion makes a general statement about these comparisons—that some items sold more in the winter and others sold more in the summer.

Check for Transition Words

Transition words connect ideas. See Chapter 2 (page 166) for more information on transition words. This essay uses appropriate transition words.

Paragraph	Transition Word	Purpose
Paragraph 2	*Following*	Shows sequence
Paragraph 4	*In general*	Summarizes
Paragraph 4	*but*	Shows contrast

Check for Grammar and Spelling

Correct grammar and spelling help keep your ideas clear to the reader. See Chapter 4 for guidance on grammar and Chapter 3 (page 189) for guidance on spelling. There are no grammar or spelling errors in this essay.

Check for Sentence Variety

Using a variety of sentence types in your essay can help you express your ideas more clearly, and it makes your essay more interesting to read. It also shows the range of your writing ability. See Chapter 4 (page 215) for a discussion of different sentence types.

This essay uses a variety of sentence types. Here are some examples.

Paragraph	Sentence Type	Example
Paragraph 2	Simple Sentence	*Certain food items had much higher sales than others in the winter.*
Paragraph 4	Complex sentence	*In general, the average daily sales of each food item changed when the season changed.*
Paragraph 4	Compound Sentence	*Certain items were more popular in the winter, but certain others were more popular in the summer.*

PRACTICE 14

Read the following model essays and answer the questions that follow each one. Use the Revision Checklist to help you answer the questions.

A
> *The line graph below shows the number of cell phone subscribers in a particular city, by gender.*
>
> *Summarize the information by selecting and reporting the main features, and make comparisons where relevant.*

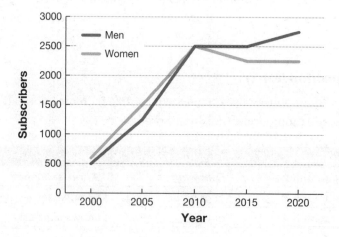

Cell Phone Subscribers, Marysville

The graph shows how many men and women in Marysville paid for cell phone service from 2000 to 2020. The number of subscribers of each gender rose at similar rates during the twenty-year period.

The number of male cell phone subscribers rose significantly between 2000 and 2020. In 2000, a little over 500 men subscribed to cell phone service. The number increased considerably over the next few years until it reached 2500 in the year 2010. There was no change in the number of subscribers between 2010 and 2015. Then, the number rose slightly between 2015 and 2020, when there were about 2750 male subscribers.

Similarly, the number of women subscribing to cell phone service rose in most years between 2000 and 2020. In 2000, 500 women subscribed to cell phone service. By 2010, the number of female subscribers had increased to 2500. There was a slight drop to about 2250 subscribers between 2010 and 2015, and that number stayed steady between 2015 and 2020.

Overall, while the numbers of both male and female subscribers rose significantly, they rose more for men.

REVISION CHECKLIST

Addressing the Task
- [ ] Thesis Statement
- [ ] Main Ideas

Coherence
- [ ] Main Idea—Paragraph
- [ ] Supporting Details

Cohesion
- [ ] Introduction—Conclusion
- [ ] Transition Words

Lexical Resource
- [ ] Vocabulary Variety
- [ ] Spelling

Grammatical Range and Accuracy
- [ ] Sentence Variety
- [ ] Accuracy

Exercises

1   Find the thesis statement, which is the topic sentence that summarizes the graph, and underline it.

2   In the second sentence of the first paragraph, underline the comparisons that will become the main ideas of the body paragraphs.

3   Put a check (✔) next to the main idea in the second paragraph. Mark each supporting detail with the letter: A, B, C, etc.

4   Put a check (✔) next to the main idea in the third paragraph. Mark each supporting detail with the letter: A, B, C, etc.

5   Underline three transition words/phrases in the second and third paragraphs.

6   Check grammar and spelling. Correct any errors.

7   Find and mark one simple sentence (ss), one compound sentence (cm/s), and one complex sentence (cx/s).

B
> *The graph below shows the number of students enrolled in two different schools.*
>
> *Summarize the information by selecting and reporting the main features, and make comparisons where relevant.*

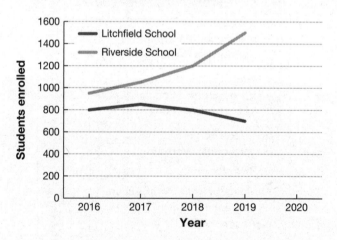

The graph shows how many students were registered at Riverside School and Litchfield School in each of the years from 2016 to 2019. The number of students at each school changed every year.

Enrollment at Riverside School rose steadily over the four-year period shown on the graph. There was a small increase from a little under 1000 students in 2016 to a little over 1000 in 2017. Then, enrollment started to rise more rapidly. In 2018, there were 1200 students enrolled in Riverside School, and in 2019 enrollment was close to 1500.

Enrollment in Litchfield School, on the other hand, mostly fell during the same period. There was a small rise between 2016 and 2017, from 800 students to just over 800. In 2018, enrollment fell back to 800 students. It also fell in 2019, to around 700 students.

While enrollment changed each year at both schools, it increased at Riverside School and fell at Litchfield School.

REVISION CHECKLIST

Addressing the Task
☐ Thesis Statement
☐ Main Ideas

Coherence
☐ Main Idea—Paragraph
☐ Supporting Details

Cohesion
☐ Introduction—Conclusion
☐ Transition Words

Lexical Resource
☐ Vocabulary Variety
☐ Spelling

Grammatical Range and Accuracy
☐ Sentence Variety
☐ Accuracy

Exercises

1   Find the thesis statement, which is the topic sentence that summarizes the graph, and underline it.

2   In the second sentence of the first paragraph, underline the comparisons that will become the main ideas of the body paragraphs.

3   Put a check (✔) next to the main idea in the second paragraph. Mark each supporting detail with the letter: A, B, C, etc.

4   Put a check (✔) next to the main idea in the third paragraph. Mark each supporting detail with the letter: A, B, C, etc.

5   Underline the transition words/phrases in the second, third, and fourth paragraphs.

6   Check grammar and spelling. Correct any errors.

7   Find and mark one simple sentence (ss), one compound sentence (cm/s), and one complex sentence (cx/s).

C | The table below shows the numbers of weekend ticket sales at a certain movie theater.

Summarize the information by selecting and reporting the main features, and make comparisons where relevant.

Ticket Sales—Springfield Cinema

	3:00	5:00	7:00	9:00
Saturday	100	125	150	150
Sunday	125	100	75	50

The table shows how many movie tickets were sold at the Springfield Cinema at different times of the weekend. On Saturday sales were highest in the evening, and on Sunday sales were highest in the afternoon.

On Saturday, the most popular times to see a movie were in the evening. Sales started out relatively low, with 100 tickets sold for the 3:00 show and 125 sold for the 5:00 show. After that, sales rose to 150 tickets sold for both the 7:00 and 9:00 shows.

On Sunday, on the other hand, the most popular time to see a movie was in the afternoon. Sales started out highest for the 3:00 show, when 125 tickets were sold. Then, sales dropped steadily, and they reached their lowest for the 9:00 show, when just 50 tickets were sold.

In general, moviegoers at the Springfield Cinema seem to prefer later shows on Saturday and earlier shows on Sunday.

REVISION CHECKLIST

Addressing the Task
- ☐ Thesis Statement
- ☐ Main Ideas

Coherence
- ☐ Main Idea—Paragraph
- ☐ Supporting Details

Cohesion
- ☐ Introduction—Conclusion
- ☐ Transition Words

Lexical Resource
- ☐ Vocabulary Variety
- ☐ Spelling

Grammatical Range and Accuracy
- ☐ Sentence Variety
- ☐ Accuracy

Exercises

1   Find the thesis statement, which is the topic sentence that summarizes the graph, and underline it.

2   In the second sentence of the first paragraph, underline the comparisons that will become the main ideas of the body paragraphs.

3   Put a check (✔) next to the main idea in the second paragraph. Mark each supporting detail with the letter: A, B, C, etc.

4   Put a check (✔) next to the main idea in the third paragraph. Mark each supporting detail with the letter: A, B, C, etc.

5   Underline the transition words/phrases in the second, third, and fourth paragraphs.

6   Check grammar and spelling. Correct any errors.

7   Find and mark one simple sentence (ss), one compound sentence (cm/s), and one compound-complex sentence (cm-cx/s).

D   *The pie charts below show the highest level of education achieved by people over age 21 in two different countries.*

Summarize the information by selecting and reporting the main features, and make comparisons where relevant.

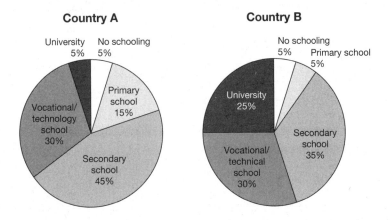

Country A

University 5%   No schooling 5%
Primary school 15%
Vocational/ technology school 30%
Secondary school 45%

Country B

No schooling 5%   Primary school 5%
University 25%
Secondary school 35%
Vocational/ technical school 30%

The charts show the top levels of education reached by adults in two countries. The levels of education reached were different for each country.

In Country A, most adults had at least some schooling. Only five percent of the adult population had not gone to school at all, and just fifteen percent stopped studying after primary school. Forty-five percent of the population ended their studies after secondary school, while thirty percent completed vocational/ technical school. A very small part of the population, five percent, got university degrees.

In Country B, more of the adult population reached higher levels of education than in Country A. Five percent had no schooling. Another five percent did not go beyond primary school. Thirty-five percent of the adult population, on the other hand, stopped studying after secondary school. Thirty percent studied at vocational/technical school, and twenty-five percent got university degrees.

In both countries, most of the adults had at least some education, and many continued studying after secondary school.

REVISION CHECKLIST

Addressing the Task
☐ Thesis Statement
☐ Main Ideas

Coherence
☐ Main Idea—Paragraph
☐ Supporting Details

Cohesion
☐ Introduction—Conclusion
☐ Transition Words

Lexical Resource
☐ Vocabulary Variety
☐ Spelling

Grammatical Range and Accuracy
☐ Sentence Variety
☐ Accuracy

Exercises

1   Find the thesis statement, which is the topic sentence that summarizes the graph, and underline it.

2   In the second sentence of the first paragraph, underline the comparisons that will become the main ideas of the body paragraphs.

3   Put a check (✔) next to the main idea in the second paragraph. Mark each supporting detail with the letter: A, B, C, etc.

4   Put a check (✔) next to the main idea in the third paragraph. Mark each supporting detail with the letter: A, B, C, etc.

5   Underline the transition words/phrases in the third paragraph.

6   Check grammar and spelling. Correct any errors.

7   Find and mark one sentence with a simple sentence (ss), one compound sentence (cm/s), and one complex sentence (cx/s).

PRACTICE 15

Use the Revision Checklist to revise the essays you wrote in Practice 13 (page 32).

PRACTICE 16

Write an essay in response to each of the following tasks. Remember to allow 20 minutes for each essay, dividing the time as follows:

(STEP 1)   **Plan**   5 minutes

(STEP 2)   **Write**   12 minutes

(STEP 3)   **Revise**   3 minutes

A

> *The charts below show agricultural production in two different regions of the country.*
>
> *Summarize the information by selecting and reporting the main features, and make comparisons where relevant.*

Write at least 150 words.

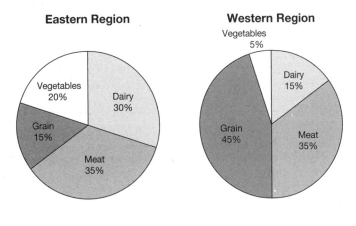

....

....

....

....

....

....

....

....

....

....

....

....

B | *The table below shows the average monthly rainfall in two different cities.*
Summarize the information by selecting and reporting the main features, and make comparisons where relevant.

Write at least 150 words.

Average Monthly Rainfall, in Inches

	Jan	Feb	Mar	Apr	May	June	July	Aug	Sep	Oct	Nov	Dec
Woodsville	5	4	3.75	2.5	1.75	1.5	0.75	1	1.5	3	6	5.5
Blacksboro	3	4	2.5	1	0.25	0.1	0.01	0.04	0.25	0.5	1	2.5

....

....

....

....

....

....

....

....

....

....

....

....

....

....

....

....

....

....

....

....

....

....
....
....
....
....
....
....
....
....
....
....
....
....
....
....
....
....
....
....
....
....
....
....
....
....
....
....

EXTRA PRACTICE

See the More Writing Practice section (page 223) in the Appendix for more Academic Task 1 topics that you can use for further writing practice.

ACADEMIC WRITING TASK 1: PROCESS DIAGRAMS

The process diagram is not as common as a graph, table, or chart on IELTS, but you should be prepared for it. A process diagram may show the steps in a process, or it may show changes in a place over time. You will have to describe the steps in the process or describe the changes.

Remember that you will have 60 minutes to complete the writing part of the test, and to allow 20 minutes for Task 1. Divide the time as follows:

(STEP 1) **Plan** 5 minutes
(STEP 2) **Write** 12 minutes
(STEP 3) **Revise** 3 minutes

LENGTH

You must write at least 150 words. You can write more.

TIPS

- Make sure you understand all parts of the process before you start planning.
- Write only about what you see in the diagram. Do not add extra information.

SCORE

To receive a good score,

- Address all parts of the task
- Accurately describe each step or change
- Use correct grammar, spelling, and punctuation
- Write in complete sentences
- Use your own words; do not copy exact sentences from the task

STEP 1: PLAN

Spend about 5 minutes on planning before you start writing. Planning will make sure you include all the necessary information.

Address the Task

When you see a diagram, determine whether it shows the steps in a process or changes in a place. This will help you address the task.

PRACTICE 1

Look at the following tasks and diagrams. Write the letter of each diagram next to the corresponding task. Decide whether the diagram shows steps in a process or changes in a place. Write "steps" or "changes."

Tasks

1 ....

> The diagram below shows the stages in the life cycle of a dragonfly.
>
> Summarize the information by selecting and reporting the main features, and make comparisons where relevant.

2 ....

> The diagram below shows the process of generating electricity with a wind turbine.
>
> Summarize the information by selecting and reporting the main features, and make comparisons where relevant.

3 ....

> The diagram below shows the area around a river before and after a flood.
>
> Summarize the information by selecting and reporting the main features, and make comparisons where relevant.

4 ....

> The diagram below shows the process of producing cloth and clothes from cotton.
>
> Summarize the information by selecting and reporting the main features, and make comparisons where relevant.

5 ....

> The diagram below shows a neighborhood before and after construction.
>
> Summarize the information by selecting and reporting the main features, and make comparisons where relevant.

Diagrams

A   **Cotton Cloth Production**

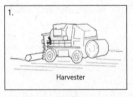
1. Harvester

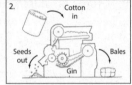
2. Gin (Cotton in, Seeds out, Bales)

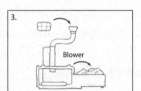
3. Blower

4. Carding Machine

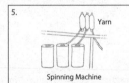
5. Spinning Machine (Yarn)

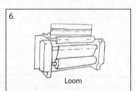
6. Loom

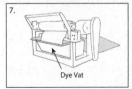
7. Dye Vat

8. Cloth → Clothing

B   Dragonfly Life Cycle

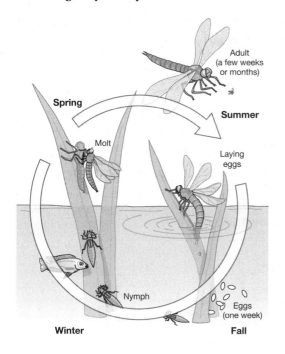

C   Benfield Neighborhood

Before

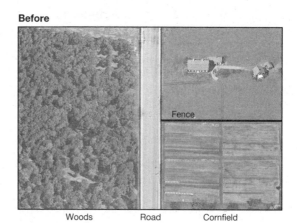

Woods   Road   Cornfield

After

Park   Road

D   Blackstone River

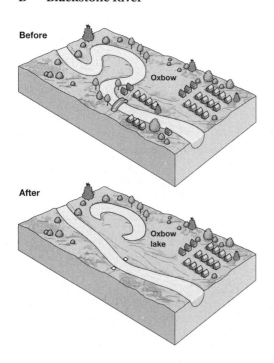

E   Wind Turbine

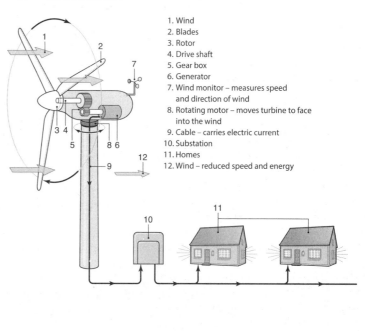

1. Wind
2. Blades
3. Rotor
4. Drive shaft
5. Gear box
6. Generator
7. Wind monitor – measures speed and direction of wind
8. Rotating motor – moves turbine to face into the wind
9. Cable – carries electric current
10. Substation
11. Homes
12. Wind – reduced speed and energy

Determine the Topic

You can find the topic by reading the title of the diagram and the description of the diagram in the task. Make a note of both the title and the description.

Look at these examples.

Diagram I

The diagram below shows the process of producing raisins from grapes.

Summarize the information by selecting and reporting the main features, and make comparisons where relevant.

Raisin Production

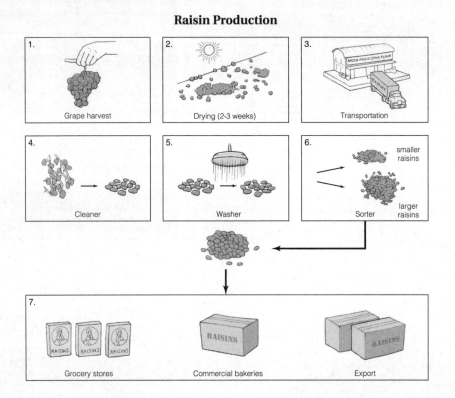

1. Grape harvest	2. Drying (2-3 weeks)	3. Transportation
4. Cleaner	5. Washer	6. Sorter — smaller raisins, larger raisins

7. Grocery stores / Commercial bakeries / Export

Title: Raisin Production

Description: the process of producing raisins from grapes

Diagram II

The diagram below shows a library before and after renovations.

Summarize the information by selecting and reporting the main features, and make comparisons where relevant.

Taftsville Public Library

Before

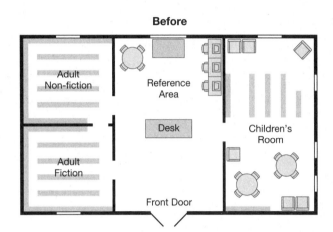

After

Title: Taftsville Public Library

Description: a library before and after renovations

PRACTICE 2

Look at the diagrams in Practice 1 (pages 48–49). Note the title and the description for each one.

Diagram A

Title: ....

Description: ....

Diagram B

Title: ....

Description: ....

Diagram C

Title: ....

Description: ....

Diagram D

Title: ....

Description: ....

Diagram E

Title: ....

Description: ....

Make Notes About Details

For a diagram that shows steps in a process, you will have to determine what happens at each step of a process and the order in which the steps happen.

For a diagram that shows how a place changes, you will have to determine the differences between the before and after pictures.

Most diagrams will have labels to help you identify objects and actions. A diagram may also have arrows to show direction of movement, entering or exiting, etc.

Look at these sample notes for the diagrams on pages 50–51.

Diagram I

Raisin Production ....

Details

1   harvest ....
2   drying ....
3   transporting to processing plant ....
4   cleaning ....
5   washing ....
6   sorting ....
7   packaging for sale ....

Diagram II

Taftsville Library ....

Details

Before

desk in the middle ....
reference area behind desk ....
children's room on the right ....
adult fiction on the left ....
adult nonfiction behind adult fiction ....

After

desk closer to door ....
new reading area ....
old children's area divided—magazines and reference area ....
new children's area ....
new garden ....
adult fiction and nonfiction in same place ....

PRACTICE 3

Look at the diagrams in Practice 1 (pages 48–49). Make notes about details for each one. Not all diagrams will have the same number of steps or changes.

Diagram A
Details

1 ....

2 ....

3 ....

4 ....

5 ....

6 ....

7 ....

8 ....

9 ....

10 ....

Diagram B
Details

1 ....

2 ....

3 ....

4 ....

5 ....

6 ....

7 ....

8 ....

9 ....

10 ....

Diagram C

Details

Before

....

....

....

....

....

After

....

....

....

....

Diagram D

Details

Before

....

....

....

....

After

....

....

....

....

Diagram E

Details

1 ....

2 ....

3 ....

4 ....

5 ....

6 ....

7 ....

8 ....

9 ....

10 ....

STEP 2: WRITE

When you planned, you made notes about the topic and details of the diagram. Now you will use these notes to write your essay. You should take about 12 minutes to write your essay.

Write the Introduction

The introduction tells the topic of your essay. Your essay will be about the diagram. In Practice 2 (page 52), you made notes about the topic of the diagram. Now you will use those notes to write the introduction to your essay.

Write the Topic Sentence

Write one sentence that tells what the diagram is about. Do not copy the title and task exactly. Use synonyms. See Chapter 3 (page 187) for more information on synonyms.

Look at these examples based on the sample diagrams on pages 50–51.

Diagram I

Task

| The diagram below shows the process of producing raisins from grapes. |
| Summarize the information by selecting and reporting the main features, and make comparisons where relevant. |

Notes

Title: Raisin Production

Description: the process of producing raisins from grapes

Topic Sentence

The diagram presents the steps for making raisins from grapes.

Discussion

The topic sentence avoids copying exact phrases and sentences from the task and diagram title by using the word *presents* instead of *shows, steps* instead of *process,* and *making* instead of *producing.*

Diagram II

Task

| The diagram below shows a library before and after renovations. |
| Summarize the information by selecting and reporting the main features, and make comparisons where relevant. |

Notes

Title: Taftsville Public Library

Description: a library before and after renovations

Topic Sentence

The diagram illustrates the changes that were made to the Taftsville Public Library.

Discussion

The topic sentence avoids copying exact phrases and sentences from the task and diagram title by using the word *illustrates* instead of *shows* and *changes* instead of *renovations.*

PRACTICE 4

Choose synonyms from the list for each of the following words and write them on the lines. Some words will have more than one synonym.

Synonyms

1	.... show	A	prior to
2	.... produce	B	changes
		C	illustrate
3	.... process	D	steps
4	.... renovations	E	present
		F	following
5	.... construction	G	make
6	.... before	H	building
7	.... after	I	growth
		J	explain
8	.... development	K	manufacture

PRACTICE 5

Rewrite the following topic sentences by using synonyms for the underlined sections.

1   The diagram shows a housing site <u>before</u> and <u>after construction</u>.

    ....

2   The diagram shows the <u>process</u> for <u>producing</u> boxes from recycled cardboard.

    ....

3   The diagram <u>shows</u> the process for <u>making</u> juice from apples.

    ....

4   The diagram <u>shows</u> the <u>development</u> of a frog from egg to maturity.

    ....

5   The diagram shows the <u>process</u> for <u>producing</u> chocolate from cacao beans.

    ....

Write a General Statement

The topic sentence tells what the diagram is about. In the next sentence, make a general statement summarizing what you will say about the diagram.

    If the diagram shows a process, mention how the process begins and ends.

> It takes a number of steps to go from an apple on a tree to applesauce we can buy in a store.

If there is a pair of diagrams showing changes in a place, mention the overall effect of the changes.

The neighborhood was much busier following the construction of the bridge.

PRACTICE 6

Choose words from the list to complete the general statements about the diagrams in Practice 1 (pages 48–49). There are more words than you will need.

clothes	mature	cotton	generated
washed away	used	an egg	cloth
added	bales	quiet	crowded
distributed			

A   It takes several steps to go from .... in the field to .... you can buy and wear.

B   It goes through several stages from .... in the water to a .... dragonfly in the air.

C   The neighborhood changed from a .... area to a .... place to live.

D   Many things were .... by the floodwaters.

E   The electricity is .... by the turbine and then is .... to people's homes.

PRACTICE 7

Write an introduction for each of the diagrams in Practice 1 (pages 48–49). Use your notes from Practice 2 (page 52) to write the topic sentence, and use the general statements from Practice 6 above.

Diagram A

....

....

....

....

....

....

....

Diagram B

....
....
....
....
....
....
....

Diagram C

....
....
....
....
....
....
....

Diagram D

....
....
....
....
....
....
....

Diagram E

....

....

....

....

....

....

....

Write the Body of the Essay

When you planned your essay, you made notes about details. You identified the steps in a process or the changes between two diagrams. Now you will turn these notes into sentences for the body of your essay.

Use Passive Voice

A Task 1 diagram shows actions. It doesn't usually show the person performing the actions. When you don't know who or what performs an action, use passive voice.

Passive voice is formed with the verb *be* and the past participle form of the main verb. It can be used in any verb tense. In Task 1, you will generally use either present tense or past tense. Look at these examples of passive voice.

The apples <u>are</u> <u>harvested</u>.   (present tense)
         be   past participle

The books <u>were</u> <u>moved</u>.   (past tense)
         be   past participle

See Chapter 4 (page 209) for more information on passive voice.

PRACTICE 8

Change the following sentences to passive voice.

1   Somebody packs the cotton in bales.

....

2   Somebody dyes the cloth.

....

3   Somebody sells the cloth to a factory.

....

4   Somebody dries the raisins in the sun.

....

5   Somebody sorts the raisins.

....

6   Somebody built a new room.

....

7   Somebody painted the walls.

....

8   Somebody placed the desk by the window.

....

PRACTICE 9

Complete the essay about the diagram with the passive form of the verbs in parentheses. Use present tense.

Frozen Orange Juice Concentrate

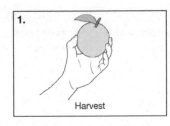

Harvest

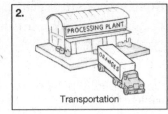

Transportation

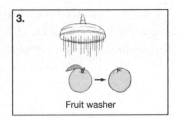

Fruit washer

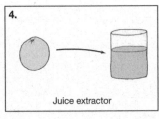

Juice extractor

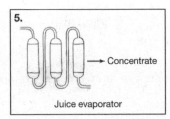

Juice evaporator

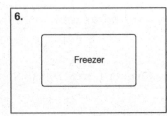

Freezer

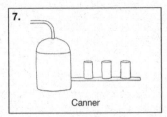

Canner

Grocery store

Consumer

The diagram shows the steps for making frozen orange juice concentrate from fresh

oranges. First, the fruit **1** .... When the oranges are ripe, they

                      (prepare)

2 .... Then, they **3** .... onto trucks. The trucks

     (harvest)   (load)

carry the oranges to the processing plant. There, they **4** .... before

                                        (wash)

the juice **5** .... The washed oranges go though the extractor, which

         (make)

extracts the juice. Next, the juice goes to the evaporator, where it **6** ....

                                         (turn)

into concentrate. The concentrate **7** .... Then, it

                          (freeze)

8 .... in the canner. The cans of juice **9** ....

     (can)   (distribute)

to grocery stores. Customers buy the frozen concentrate and enjoy it at home.

Use Sequence Words and Phrases

When you write about a process diagram, you will write about the steps of the process in the order that they occur. Use sequence words and phrases to show their order in time. See Chapter 2 (page 166) for more information on sequence words and phrases.

Beginning Step

First
To begin
The first step is

Middle Steps

Next
Then
Before
After
The next step

Last Step

Finally
The last step
The final step

Be careful with *before* and *after*. Use *before* with the step that comes later. Use *after* with the step that comes first.

Before *the raisins are put into packages, they are sorted.*

Meaning—First the raisins are sorted; then they are put into packages.

The raisins are taken to the processing plant after *they are dried.*

Meaning—First the raisins are dried; then they are taken to the processing plant.

PRACTICE 10

Complete the paragraphs about the diagram using words from the chart.

Sequence Words
after
before
finally
first
next
then

Recycling Plastic Bottles

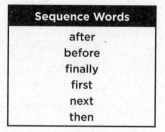

1. Plastic bottle consumer

2. Recycling bin

3. To the recycling plant

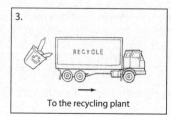

4. Washer

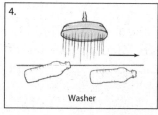

5. Shredder

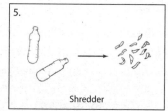

6. Extruder — Pellets

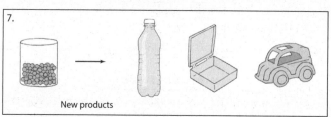

7. New products

The diagram shows the process of recycling plastic bottles to make new products. It takes several steps to go from used bottles to new products made out of the same material. The **1** .... step is to send the used bottles to the recycling plant. **2** .... someone finishes drinking from a bottle, she puts it in a recycling bin with other used bottles. **3** ...., a truck picks up the bottles and transports them to the recycling plant. **4** .... the bottles can be recycled, they have to go through the washer. **5** ...., they are sent to another machine, where they are shredded into small pieces. **6** ...., the shredded pieces go into the extruder. This machine turns the pieces into pellets. **7** ...., the pellets are used to make new plastic products such as bottles, cups, and toys.

Describe the Location

In Task 1, you might see a pair of diagrams that show the changes in a place over time. You will have to describe what you see in each diagram. Use prepositions of place and related expressions to describe the location of objects in the diagram.

Location	
on	on the right
in	on the left
next to	on the other side
beside	in the middle
in front of	across from
behind	

Look at these examples.

Wild River

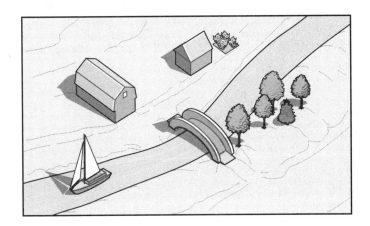

There is a bridge <u>over</u> the river.

There are some trees <u>next to</u> the bridge.

<u>Across</u> the river <u>from</u> the trees there is a house.

Some flowers are growing <u>next to</u> the house.

On <u>the other side</u> of the house there is a barn.

A boat is sailing <u>on</u> the river.

PRACTICE 11

Write sentences describing the location of objects in the diagram. Write at least one sentence about each of the objects on the list.

Lakeside Park

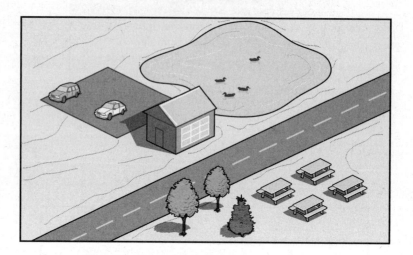

1   nature center

....

2   parking lot

....

3   cars

....

4   picnic area

....

5   trees

....

6   ducks

....

PRACTICE 12

On a separate sheet of paper, write a complete essay for each of the diagrams in Practice 1 (pages 48–49). Begin with the introductions you wrote in Practice 7 (page 59); then use your notes about details from Practice 3 (page 54) to write the body of each essay. Mention each of the steps or each of the changes you identified.

STEP 3: REVISE

You should allow at least 3 minutes to revise your essay after you write.

Use the Revision Checklist

When you revise, you check the content and the language of your essay. Make sure the essay is clear and well organized and that you have used correct grammar and spelling. You can use this revision checklist to practice revising.

REVISION CHECKLIST

Addressing the Task
- [ ] Topic Sentence
- [ ] General Statement

Coherence
- [ ] Process—Sequence of Steps
  or
- [ ] Changes—Before and After

Cohesion
- [ ] Transition Words

Lexical Resource
- [ ] Vocabulary Variety
- [ ] Spelling

Grammatical Range and Accuracy
- [ ] Sentence Variety
- [ ] Accuracy

Read the following model essay, and note how well it follows the items on the checklist.

> *The diagram below shows the process of producing raisins from grapes.*
>
> *Summarize the information by selecting and reporting the main features, and make comparisons where relevant.*

Raisin Production

1. Grape harvest
2. Drying (2-3 weeks)
3. Transportation
4. Cleaner
5. Washer
6. Sorter — smaller raisins, larger raisins
7. Grocery stores / Commercial bakeries / Export

The diagram presents the steps for making raisins from grapes. It takes several steps to go from grapes on the vine to packaged raisins ready for sale.

To begin, the grapes are picked from the vines. After picking, they are laid in the sun to dry. It takes two to three weeks to dry the fruit. When the raisins are dry, they are packed in boxes and taken by truck to the processing plant. At the plant, the raisins go through a cleaner, which removes bits of dirt. Next they are washed in a washer. Before the raisins are packaged, they are sorted by size. Then, the raisins are put in different kinds of packages. Some raisins are put in small packages, and they are sold to grocery stores. Some are put in larger packages to be sold to commercial bakeries or to be exported to other countries.

Check for Topic Sentence

The first sentence of this essay is the topic sentence. It tells the topic of the diagram and lets the reader know that the essay is about the diagram.

The diagram presents the steps for making raisins from grapes.

Check for General Statement

The second sentence of the essay is the general statement. It briefly summarizes the information presented in the diagram. Together with the topic sentence, it introduces the reader to the essay.

It takes several steps to go from grapes on the vine to packaged raisins ready for sale.

Check for Sequence of Steps

This diagram shows the steps in a process, so the essay must describe the steps in sequence.
The essay describes these steps in the sequence they are presented in the diagram.

picked from the vines
laid in the sun to dry
packed in boxes and taken by truck to the processing plant
go through a cleaner
washed in a washer
sorted by size
put in different kinds of packages
sold to grocery stores, commercial bakeries, exported

Check for Transition Words

Transition words connect ideas. This essay describes a sequence of steps and uses sequence words and phrases to connect the steps.

To begin, the grapes are picked
After picking
Next they are washed
Before the raisins are packaged
Then, the raisins are put

Check for Grammar and Spelling

Correct grammar and spelling help keep your ideas clear to the reader. See Chapter 4 for guidance on grammar and Chapter 3 (page 189) for guidance on spelling. This essay contains no grammar or spelling errors.

Check for Sentence Variety

Using a variety of sentence types in your essay can help you express your ideas more clearly, and it makes your essay more interesting to read. It also shows the range of your writing ability. See Chapter 4 (page 215) for a discussion of different sentence types.
This essay uses a variety of sentence types. Here are some examples.

Sentence Type	Example
Simple Sentence	*Next they are washed in a washer.*
Complex Sentence	*Before the raisins are packaged, they are sorted by size.*
Compound Sentence	*Some raisins are put in small packages, and they are sold to grocery stores.*

Read the following model essays. Answer the questions that follow each essay. Use the Revision Checklist to help you answer the questions.

A

> *The diagram below shows the process of recycling plastic bottles.*
>
> *Summarize the information by selecting and reporting the main features, and make comparisons where relevant.*

Recycling Plastic Bottles

1. Plastic bottle consumer

2. Recycling bin

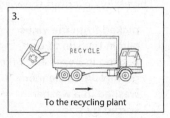

3. To the recycling plant

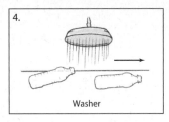

4. Washer

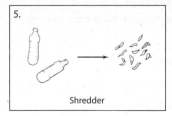

5. Shredder

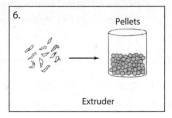

6. Extruder — Pellets

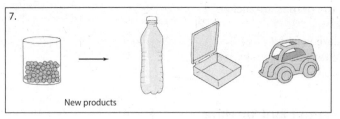

7. New products

The diagram shows the process of recycling plastic bottles to make new products. It takes several steps to go from used bottles to new products made out of the same material.

First, the bottles have to be sent to the recycling plant. After someone finishes drinking from a bottle, she puts it in a recycling bin with other used bottles. Then, the bottles are picked up by truck, and they are transported to the recycling plant. There, they have to be washed before they can go through the recycling process. After washing, they are sent to another machine, where they are shredded into small pieces. Next, the shredded pieces go into the extruder. This machine turns the pieces into pellets. Finally, the pellets are used to make new plastic products such as bottles, cups, and toys, which we can buy and use at home.

REVISION CHECKLIST

Addressing the Task
- ☐ Topic Sentence
- ☐ General Statement

Coherence
- ☐ Process—Sequence of Steps

or
- ☐ Changes—Before and After

Cohesion
- ☐ Transition Words

Lexical Resource
- ☐ Vocabulary Variety
- ☐ Spelling

Grammatical Range and Accuracy
- ☐ Sentence Variety
- ☐ Accuracy

Questions for A

1   Find the topic sentence and underline it.

2   Find the general statement and underline it.

3   In the body of the essay, put a check (✔) next to each step in the process that is shown on the diagram.

4   Circle the transition words and phrases.

5   Check grammar and spelling. Correct any errors.

6   Find and mark one simple sentence (ss), one compound sentence (cm/s), and one complex sentence (cx/s).

B *The diagram below shows a library before and after renovations.*

Summarize the information by selecting and reporting the main features, and make comparisons where relevant.

Taftsville Public Library

Before

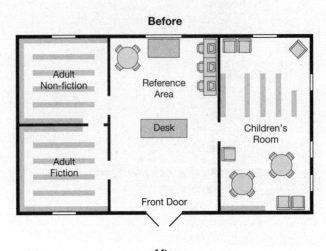

After

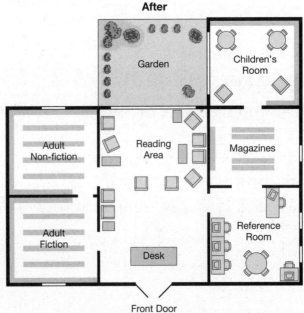

The diagrams illustrate the changes that were made to the Taftsville Public Library. The library was larger and it had more rooms after the renovations were done.

Before the renovations, the desk was in the middle of the library. Behind it was the reference area. There was a large children's room on the right. Additionally, there were two rooms for adults, one nonfiction and the other fiction, on the left.

After the renovations, things were rearranged and the space was made larger. The desk was moved closer to the front door. Behind the desk, in place of the old reference area, was a new reading area. The old children's room was divided into two rooms, one for magazines and one for the new reference area. Behind these rooms, a new children's room was built. Also, a new garden was created next to it. Although changes were made to the other areas of the library, the two adult rooms remained in the same place.

REVISION CHECKLIST

Addressing the Task
☐ Topic Sentence
☐ General Statement

Coherence
☐ Process—Sequence of Steps
or
☐ Changes—Before and After

Cohesion
☐ Transition Words

Lexical Resource
☐ Vocabulary Variety
☐ Spelling

Grammatical Range and Accuracy
☐ Sentence Variety
☐ Accuracy

Questions for B

1   Find the topic sentence and underline it.

2   Find the general statement and underline it.

3   In the body of the essay, put a check (✔) by each different item described in the "before" paragraph.

4   In the body of the essay, put a check (✔) by each change described in the "before" paragraph.

5   Circle the transition words and phrases.

6   Check grammar and spelling. Correct any errors.

7   Find and mark one simple sentence (ss), one complex sentence (cx/s), and one compound-complex sentence (cm-cx/s).

The diagram below shows how a wood pellet boiler heats a house.

Summarize the information by selecting and reporting the main features, and make comparisons where relevant.

Wood Pellet Boiler

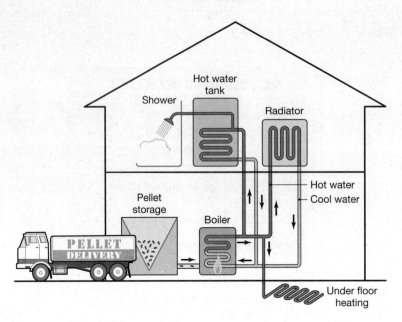

The diagram shows how a wood pellet boiler is used to provide heat and hot water for a house. The pellets are burned to produce heat, which is then distributed through the house.

To begin, a truck delivers wood pellets to the house, and they are stored in a large container. Then, when heat is needed, the pellets move to the boiler, where they are burned to heat up water. Next, the hot water moves to several places in the house. Some of it goes to pipes under the floor for under-floor heating. Some of it also goes to a radiator to heat the rooms of the house. Additionally, some of the hot water goes to a hot water tank, which holds the water for washing and bathing. After the hot water has heated the house, it returns as cool water to the boiler, where it is heated to be used again.

REVISION CHECKLIST

Addressing the Task
- ☐ Topic Sentence
- ☐ General Statement

Coherence
- ☐ Process—Sequence of Steps

  or
- ☐ Changes—Before and After

Cohesion
- ☐ Transition Words

Lexical Resource
- ☐ Vocabulary Variety
- ☐ Spelling

Grammatical Range and Accuracy
- ☐ Sentence Variety
- ☐ Accuracy

Questions for C

1   Find the topic sentence and underline it.

2   Find the general statement and underline it.

3   In the body of the essay, put a check (✔) next to each step in the process that is shown on the diagram.

4   Circle the transition words and phrases.

5   Check grammar and spelling. Correct any errors.

6   Find and mark one simple sentence (ss), one compound sentence (cm/s), and one complex sentence (cx/s).

D   *The diagram below shows how frozen orange juice concentrate is made.*

Summarize the information by selecting and reporting the main features, and make comparisons where relevant.

Frozen Orange Juice Concentrate

1.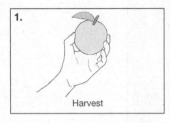
Harvest

2.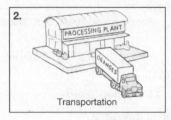
Transportation

3.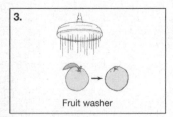
Fruit washer

4.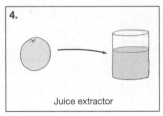
Juice extractor

5.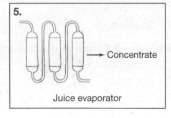
Juice evaporator

6.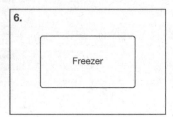
Freezer

7.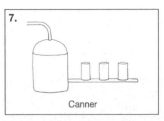
Canner

8.
Grocery store

9.
Consumer

The diagram explains the process of making frozen orange juice concentrate from fresh oranges. It takes several steps to go from oranges on the tree to frozen concentrate that can be mixed and consumed at home.

First, the ripe oranges are harvested. Then, they are loaded onto trucks and transported to the processing plant. After the trucks are unloaded at the plant, the oranges go through a fruit washer. Next, they are sent through an extractor, which squeezes out the juice. Then, the extracted juice goes through the juice evaporator, which concentrates it, and the juice concentrate is frozen in the freezer. Finally, the frozen concentrate is put into cans and is ready for sale. The cans of frozen concentrate are distributed to grocery stores, where customers buy it for use at home. The customer mixes the frozen concentrate with water and enjoys a delicious glass of orange juice.

REVISION CHECKLIST

Addressing the Task
- ☐ Topic Sentence
- ☐ General Statement

Coherence
- ☐ Process—Sequence of Steps

    or

- ☐ Changes—Before and After

Cohesion
- ☐ Transition Words

Lexical Resource
- ☐ Vocabulary Variety
- ☐ Spelling

Grammatical Range and Accuracy
- ☐ Sentence Variety
- ☐ Accuracy

Questions for D

1   Find the topic sentence and underline it.

2   Find the general statement and underline it.

3   In the body of the essay, put a check (✔) next to each step in the process that is shown on the diagram.

4   Circle the transition words and phrases.

5   Check grammar and spelling. Correct any errors.

6   Find and mark one simple sentence (ss), one complex sentence (cx/s), and one compound-complex sentence (cm-cx/s).

PRACTICE 14

Use the Revision Checklist to revise the essays you wrote in Practice 12 (page 67).

PRACTICE 15

On a separate sheet of paper, write an essay in response to each of the following tasks. Remember to allow 20 minutes for each essay, dividing the time as follows:

STEP 1	**Plan**	5 minutes
STEP 2	**Write**	12 minutes
STEP 3	**Revise**	3 minutes

A

> *The diagram below shows how coffee beans are processed.*
>
> *Summarize the information by selecting and reporting the main features, and make comparisons where relevant.*

Write at least 150 words.

Coffee Production

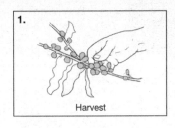

1.

Harvest

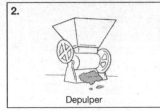

2.

Depulper

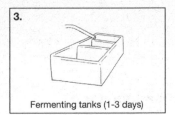

3.

Fermenting tanks (1-3 days)

4.

Drying the beans

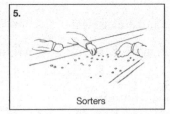

5.

Sorters

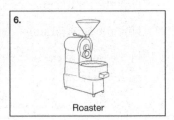

6.

Roaster

7.

Grinder

8.

To the grocery store

9.

Consumer

B   *The diagram below shows City Park before and after a swimming pool was constructed.*

Summarize the information by selecting and reporting the main features, and make comparisons where relevant.

Write at least 150 words.

City Park

Before

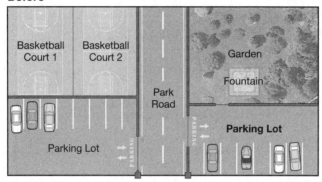

Entrance

After

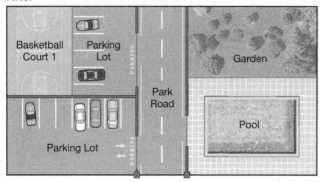

Entrance

EXTRA PRACTICE

See the More Writing Practice section (page 223) in the Appendix for more Academic Task 1 topics that you can use for further writing practice.

TIME

You will have 60 minutes to complete the writing part of the test. You should allow 20 minutes for Task 1. Divide your time as follows:

Total time   20 minutes

(STEP 1)   **Plan**   5 minutes
(STEP 2)   **Write**   12 minutes
(STEP 3)   **Revise**   3 minutes

LENGTH

You must write at least 150 words. You can write more.

TIPS

- Make sure you understand all parts of the task before you start planning.
- Use your imagination to add details, but make sure they are relevant to the task.

SCORE

To receive a good score,

- Address all parts of the task
- Make the purpose of the letter clear
- Include relevant details
- Use correct grammar, spelling, and punctuation
- Write in complete sentences
- Use your own words; do not copy exact sentences from the task

STEP 1: PLAN

Take about 5 minutes to plan before you start writing. This will help you develop your ideas and ensure that you include all the necessary information.

Address the Task

In Task 1, you will see a brief description of a situation. You will be asked to write a letter to a certain person about the situation. You will be given several points to cover in your letter. You must address all the points.

PRACTICE 1

Read the following tasks and determine what each one asks you to do. Circle your choices on the list that follows each task. There may be more than one answer for each task.

1

> *You recently bought a jacket, but when you got home, you discovered it was damaged. When you took it back to the store, you were told that merchandise cannot be returned.*
>
> *Write a letter to the store manager. In your letter*
>
> - *describe the problem with the jacket.*
> - *explain what happened when you tried to return it.*
> - *say what you would like the manager to do.*

Write at least 150 words.

You do **NOT** need to write any addresses.

Begin your letter as follows:

Dear Sir or Madam,

make an invitation	describe a problem	ask for help
describe a thing or place	ask for advice	suggest a solution

2

> *You are planning a business trip to another city. You will have some free time to do some sightseeing while you are there.*
>
> *Write a letter to a friend who lives in the city you will visit. In your letter*
>
> - *explain the purpose of the trip.*
> - *ask about things to do and see in the city.*
> - *invite your friend to do something with you during your visit.*

Write at least 150 words.

You do **NOT** need to write any addresses.

Begin your letter as follows:

Dear _____,

make an invitation	describe a problem	ask for help
describe a thing or place	ask for advice	suggest a solution

3 *You live in a small apartment building with a parking lot in back, and you often cannot find an empty parking space when you get home from work.*

Write a letter to your landlord. In your letter

- *describe the situation.*
- *explain why it bothers you.*
- *suggest something the landlord could do to solve the problem.*

Write at least 150 words.

You do **NOT** need to write any addresses.

Begin your letter as follows:

Dear _____,

make an invitation   describe a problem   ask for help

describe a thing or place   ask for advice   suggest a solution

4 *You have rented a house by a lake for the summer.*

Write a letter to a friend. In your letter

- *describe the house.*
- *describe how you are spending your time there.*
- *invite your friend to come and visit.*

Write at least 150 words.

You do **NOT** need to write any addresses.

Begin your letter as follows:

Dear _____,

make an invitation   describe a problem   ask for help

describe a thing or place   ask for advice   suggest a solution

5   *You rode in a taxi yesterday. When you got home, you realized you had left your bag in the taxi.*

Write a letter to the manager of the taxi company. In your letter

- *explain how you lost your bag.*
- *describe your bag.*
- *ask the manager to help you find it.*

Write at least 150 words.

You do **NOT** need to write any addresses.

Begin your letter as follows:

Dear Sir or Madam,

make an invitation	describe a problem	ask for help
describe a thing or place	ask for advice	suggest a solution

Determine the Topic

Task 1 begins with a brief description of a situation. This tells you the topic of the letter you will write.

PRACTICE 2

Choose the correct topic for each of the tasks in Practice 1 (page 81). Write the letter of the topic next to the number of the corresponding task. You will not use all the topics.

Topics

1   ....   **A**   Looking for a lost bag

2   ....   **B**   Advice about buying a house

               C   A problem finding a parking space

3   ....   **D**   A vacation at a rental house

4   ....   **E**   A bad purchase

               F   A complaint about a driver

5   ....   **G**   Making plans for a trip

               H   Looking for a new job

Make Notes About Main Ideas

Task 1 mentions three points that you must cover in your letter. Look at this example.

> *Write a letter to your friend. In your letter*
> - *explain why you are no longer using your bicycle.*
> - *describe your bicycle.*
> - *explain why you think your friend would like to have it.*

Read the three points and take a minute to brainstorm some ideas for addressing each one. Then, choose one idea for each point to include in your letter. It doesn't matter which ideas you choose; just choose something you can write about.

PRACTICE 3

Read the following tasks. Brainstorm a short list of ideas for addressing each point. The lists have been started for you.

Task

> *You have a bicycle that you are no longer using. You would like to sell it to a friend.*
>
> *Write a letter to your friend. In your letter*
> - *explain why you are no longer using your bicycle.*
> - *describe your bicycle.*
> - *explain why you think your friend would like to have it.*

1   Explain why you are no longer using your bicycle.

no time

want a different kind of bicycle

....

....

2   Describe your bicycle.

racing bike

mountain bike

....

....

3   Explain why you think your friend would like to have it.

friend likes racing bikes

friend needs a good way to get to work

....

....

Task

> *You live in a small apartment building. You are frequently bothered by noise from your upstairs neighbor's apartment.*
>
> *Write a letter to your neighbor. In your letter*
>   - *describe the situation.*
>   - *explain why it is a problem for you.*
>   - *suggest a solution.*

4   Describe the problem.

frequent parties

loud TV

....

....

5   Explain why it is a problem for you.

can't sleep

can't concentrate

....

....

6   Explain what you would like your friend to do.

notify me about parties ahead of time

turn down the TV

....

....

PRACTICE 4

Look at the tasks in Practice 1 (page 81). Brainstorm a short list of ideas for addressing each point in each of the tasks. Then, choose one idea for each point. Later, you will use these as main ideas when you write your letter.

Task 1

1   Describe the problem with the jacket.

....

....

....

....

2   Explain what happened when you tried to return it.

....

....

....

....

3   Say what you would like the manager to do.

....

....

....

....

Task 2

1   Explain the purpose of the trip.

....

....

....

....

2   Ask about things to do and see in the city.

....

....

....

....

3   Invite your friend to do something with you during your visit.

....

....

....

....

Task 3

1   Describe the situation.

....

....

....

....

2   Explain why it bothers you.

....

....

....

....

3   Suggest something the landlord could do to solve the problem.

....

....

....

....

Task 4

1   Describe the house.

   ....
   ....
   ....
   ....

2   Describe how you are spending your time there.

   ....
   ....
   ....
   ....

3   Invite your friend to come and visit.

   ....
   ....
   ....
   ....

Task 5

1   Explain how you lost your bag.

   ....
   ....
   ....
   ....

2   Describe your bag.

   ....
   ....
   ....
   ....

3   Ask the manager to help you find it.

....

....

....

....

Make Notes About Details

After you have come up with a main idea to address each point in the task, think of two or three details to support each main idea. Look at this example.

Task

> *You have a bicycle that you are no longer using. You would like to sell it to a friend.*
>
> *Write a letter to your friend. In your letter*
>
> - *explain why you are no longer using your bicycle.*
> - *describe your bicycle.*
> - *explain why you think your friend would like to have it.*

Main idea *(point 1)*	no time for bicycle
Details	demanding job
	exercise at gym
Main idea *(point 2)*	racing bike
Details	lightweight and fast
	silver
	carrying rack
Main idea *(point 3)*	you like racing bikes
Details	your favorite color
	special price for you

PRACTICE 5

Read the following tasks; then complete the notes with your own ideas. Include two or three details for each main idea.

Task

> *You live in a small apartment building. You are frequently bothered by noise from your upstairs neighbor's apartment.*
>
> *Write a letter to your neighbor. In your letter*
>
> - *describe the situation.*
> - *explain why it is a problem for you.*
> - *suggest a solution.*

A **Main idea** *(point 1)* loud parties ....

  Details ....

  ....

  ....

  Main idea *(point 2)* can't sleep ....

  Details ....

  ....

  ....

  Main idea *(point 3)* solution: notify me about party plans ....

  ....

  ....

  ....

Task

> *You have decided to look for a new job.*
>
> *Write a letter to a friend. In your letter*
>
> - *explain why you are looking for a new job.*
> - *describe the kind of job you would like to have.*
> - *ask your friend to help you find a job.*

B **Main idea** *(point 1)* current job is routine ....

  Details ....

  ....

  ....

Main idea *(point 2)*   would like a more challenging job ....

Details   ....

....

....

Main idea *(point 3)*   can you suggest places to send my résumé ....

....

....

....

PRACTICE 6

Complete the notes for each of the tasks in Practice 1 (page 81). Start with the main ideas you identified in Practice 4 (page 86); then brainstorm two or three details for each main idea.

1   **Main idea** *(point 1)*   ....

    Details   ....

....

....

    Main idea *(point 2)*   ....

    Details   ....

....

....

    Main idea *(point 3)*   ....

    Details   ....

....

....

2   **Main idea** *(point 1)*   ....

    Details   ....

....

....

    Main idea *(point 2)*   ....

    Details   ....

....

....

Main idea *(point 3)* ....

Details ....

....

....

3   **Main idea** *(point 1)* ....

Details ....

....

....

Main idea *(point 2)* ....

Details ....

....

....

Main idea *(point 3)* ....

Details ....

....

....

4   **Main idea** *(point 1)* ....

Details ....

....

....

Main idea *(point 2)* ....

Details ....

....

....

Main idea *(point 3)* ....

Details ....

....

....

5   **Main idea** *(point 1)* ....

      Details ....

        ....

        ....

      Main idea *(point 2)* ....

      Details ....

        ....

        ....

      Main idea *(point 3)* ....

      Details ....

        ....

        ....

STEP 2: WRITE

After you plan, you are ready to write. You will use your notes about the topic, main ideas, and details as your guide. You should take about 12 minutes to write your letter.

Write the Greeting

You will begin your letter with a greeting. The instructions might provide the entire greeting:

Begin your letter as follows:

Dear Sir or Madam,

This is a greeting for a formal business letter when you don't know the name of the person you are addressing, for example, the manager of a store or restaurant.

TIP

Traditionally, *Dear Sir or Madam* has been considered the correct greeting for a formal business letter, although nowadays the custom is changing. If the IELTS task provides you with this or any other specific greeting, you must use it. Outside of the testing situation, however, you could use another type of greeting such as

    Dear Recruiter   *Dear Editor*   *Dear Manager*

The instructions might provide just part of the greeting:

Begin your letter as follows:

Dear _____,

In this case, you will have to provide a name. If the letter is for a person with whom you would have a business relationship, for example, a landlord, use a title such as *Mr., Mrs.,* or *Ms.* and a last name. Some examples are *Mr. Lee, Mrs. Kim,* or *Ms. Wilson.* It doesn't matter what last name you use, just choose any last name that comes to mind. If you can't think of a last name, use your own or a friend's last name.

If the letter is for a friend, use a first name. Again, it doesn't matter what name you use; any name will do.

PRACTICE 7

Choose the best greeting for a letter to each of the following people.

1   Your best friend from school

   A Dear Tom,   **B** Dear Tom Wilson,

2   Your lawyer

   A Dear Sir or Madam,   **B** Dear Ms. Lopez,

3   Your next-door neighbor whom you know well

   A Dear Mr. Lu,   **B** Dear George,

4   Your neighbor whom you have met only once

   A Dear Mrs. Hill,   **B** Dear Sir or Madam,

5   The manager of a bookstore whose name you don't know

   A Dear Sir or Madam,   **B** Dear Mr. or Mrs.,

6   Your cousin

   A Dear Mr. Broussard,   **B** Dear Billy,

Write the Introduction

After you write the greeting, you will write the introduction. This paragraph introduces the ideas that you will develop in your letter.

Write the Topic Sentence

The first sentence of your introduction is the topic sentence. When you planned your letter, you determined the topic. Now you will turn the topic into a topic sentence.

Begin the sentence with a phrase such as the following:

I want to let you know
I want to inform you
I thought you should know
I thought you'd be interested
I am writing about
I am writing to request
I would like to ask

Then briefly explain the topic of the letter. Look at these examples.

Task

You have a bicycle that you are no longer using. You would like to sell it to a friend.

Write a letter to your friend. In your letter

- *explain why you are no longer using your bicycle.*
- *describe your bicycle.*
- *explain why you think your friend would like to have it.*

Topic	selling a bicycle to a friend
Topic Sentence	I thought you'd be interested in the bike I am selling.

Task

You have decided to look for a new job.

Write a letter to a friend. In your letter

- *explain why you are looking for a new job.*
- *describe the kind of job you would like to have.*
- *ask your friend to help you find a job.*

Topic	looking for a new job
Topic Sentence	I want to let you know that I have decided to seek new employment.

PRACTICE 8

Write a topic sentence for each of the following tasks.

Task

> You live in a small apartment building. You are frequently bothered by noise from your upstairs neighbor's apartment.
>
> Write a letter to your neighbor. In your letter
>
> - describe the situation.
> - explain why it is a problem for you.
> - suggest a solution.

1   **Topic**   a noisy neighbor ....

    Topic Sentence ....

Task

> You let a friend stay at your apartment while you were away on a trip. When you returned home, you discovered that a valuable possession was broken.
>
> Write a letter to your friend. In your letter
>
> - describe the broken possession.
> - explain why it is important to you.
> - explain what you would like your friend to do.

2   **Topic**   friend broke valuable possession ....

    Topic Sentence ....

Task

> You have recently moved to a new neighborhood.
>
> Write a letter to a friend. In your letter
>
> - explain why you moved.
> - describe your new neighborhood.
> - invite your friend to visit you.

3   **Topic**   moving to a new neighborhood ....

    Topic Sentence ....

Task

> *You have a problem in your apartment that needs repairs.*
>
> *Write a letter to the building manager. In your letter*
>
> - *describe the problem.*
> - *say what you think should be done about it.*
> - *ask the building manager to visit your apartment to see the problem.*

4 **Topic** <u>repairs needed in apartment</u>

 Topic Sentence

Summarize the Main Ideas

When you wrote your notes, you identified main ideas. Now you will summarize those main ideas in your introduction.

Look at the following notes and introduction for the task about selling a bicycle to a friend.

Notes

 Topic <u>selling a bicycle to a friend</u>

 Main idea *(point 1)* <u>no time for bicycle</u>

 Main idea *(point 2)* <u>racing bike</u>

 Main idea *(point 3)* <u>you like racing bikes</u>

Introduction

I thought you'd be interested in a bicycle I am selling. I just don't have time to use it much anymore. However, it's a really great racing bicycle, and I think you would really like it.

Discussion

- The first sentence of the paragraph is the topic sentence.
- The second sentence, *I just don't have time to use it much anymore* corresponds to the main idea in the notes *no time for bicycle.*
- The third sentence in the paragraph, *However, it's a really great racing bicycle, and I think you would really like it* corresponds to the main ideas *racing bike* and *you like racing bikes.*

PRACTICE 9

Look at these notes and introductions for the tasks in Practice 8 (page 96). Choose the correct sentence to complete each introduction.

1   **Topic**   a noisy neighbor

    Main idea   loud parties

    Main idea   can't sleep

    Main idea   solution: notify me about party plans

I am writing to let you know about a difficulty I am having with noise from your apartment. I know you enjoy entertaining; however, your loud parties are a problem for me.

....:

I hope we can agree on a way to solve this problem.

    A They really make it difficult for me to sleep.
    B I like to sleep late on the weekends.
    C Sleeping is very important for your health.

2   **Topic**   friend broke valuable possession

    Main idea   a porcelain vase

    Main idea   an important possession

    Main idea   pay for repairs

I am writing to ask you about a valuable possession that was broken while you were staying at my apartment last week.

....:

It is one of my more important possessions, and I hope you will agree to pay for it.

    A I bought a porcelain vase for you while I was on my trip.
    B I would like to start a collection of porcelain vases.
    C When I returned home, I discovered that my porcelain vase was broken.

3 **Topic** moving to a new neighborhood

   Main idea closer to job

   Main idea quiet and pretty

   Main idea visit me soon

I wanted to let you know that I have recently moved to a new neighborhood.

....:

It is a quiet and pretty place to live, and I hope you will visit me here soon.

A The reason is that I am looking for a job.
B The reason is that I wanted to be closer to my job.
C The reason is that I wanted to live in a quieter and prettier place.

4 **Topic** repairs needed in apartment

   Main idea leak in the sink

   Main idea replace pipe

I thought you should know about a problem in my apartment that needs some repairs.

....:

I believe that the pipe under the sink should be replaced soon, and I think you should take a look at it yourself.

A I am very good at repairing leaky sinks.
B The kitchen sink has been leaking for some time now.
C The best way to repair a sink is to call a plumber.

PRACTICE 10

Use the notes you wrote in Practice 6 (page 91) to write an introduction for each of the tasks in Practice 1.

Task 1

....

....

....

....

....

....

Task 2

....
....
....
....
....
....

Task 3

....
....
....
....
....
....

Task 4

....
....
....
....
....

Task 5

....
....
....
....
....
....

Write the Paragraphs

Once you have written the introduction, you are ready to write the body paragraphs. Use the main ideas and supporting details from your notes to write the sentences for each paragraph.

Look at the following notes for the first task in Practice 8 (page 96), and the paragraph that follows. Notice how the main idea and supporting details have been turned into sentences.

Notes

Topic	a noisy neighbor
Main idea	loud parties
Details	noise of guests arriving
	loud music
	lasts until late at night

Paragraph

You may not realize it, but often the parties in your apartment are quite loud. From my apartment, which is just below yours, I can easily hear the noise of your guests arriving. Then, the music you play throughout the evening is very loud. The party noise usually lasts until very late at night.

PRACTICE 11

Look at the following notes for the tasks in Practice 8 (page 96). Use each one to write a paragraph.

1	**Topic**	a noisy neighbor
	Main idea	can't sleep
	Details	can't sleep until party is over
		have to get up early for work
		don't get enough hours of sleep

2 **Topic** friend broke valuable possession

 Main idea a porcelain vase in living room

 Details colors = blue and gold

 hand painted with flowers and butterflies

3 **Topic** moving to a new neighborhood

 Main idea closer to job

 Details before—an hour to get to work

 now—15 minutes

 life is easier now

4 **Topic** repairs needed in apartment

 Main idea leak in the sink

 Details damp under sink

 hole in pipe

PRACTICE 12

On a separate sheet of paper, use the notes you wrote in Practice 6 (page 91) to write the body paragraphs for each of the tasks in Practice 1 (page 81). Write one paragraph for each main idea.

Write the Conclusion

After you write the body paragraphs, conclude your letter with one or two sentences suggesting an action, conveying a feeling, or thanking the reader, depending on the topic of the letter.

Here are some examples of ways to conclude the letter.

If the letter **asks for advice or help**, you can write

Thank you for your advice.

Thank you for your help.

I really appreciate any suggestions you can give me.

Let me know if you can help me.

If the letter contains **an invitation**, you can write

Let me know when you can come.

Let me know which dates are best for you.

I hope you can accept my invitation.

I look forward to seeing you.

If the letter **suggests some solutions** to a problem, you can write

Let me know what you think of my ideas.

I hope one of these solutions works for you.

I hope we can meet to discuss these ideas.

I hope we can agree on a solution to these problems.

I hope you are willing to accept my solution.

PRACTICE 13

Choose the best conclusion for each of the following letters.

1   *Dear Roger,*

I am writing to ask you about a valuable possession that was broken while you were staying at my apartment last week. When I returned home, I discovered that my porcelain vase was broken. It is one of my most important possessions.

The vase I am talking about is a porcelain vase that was on the coffee table in the living room. It is mostly blue with gold around the rim. It has flowers and butterflies hand painted all over it.

This vase is very important to me. In the first place, it is handmade and very old, which makes it worth a good deal of money. It is even more valuable to me because it once belonged to my grandmother.

I am very sad that you broke it, but I have a solution to suggest. I know someone who can repair it if you would pay for the cost of the repairs.

A I would appreciate any suggestions you could give me.
B I hope you are willing to accept my solution.
C I look forward to seeing you soon.

2   *Dear Sally,*

I wanted to let you know that I have recently moved to a new neighborhood. The reason is that I wanted to be closer to my job. It is a quiet and pretty place to live, and I hope you will visit me here soon.

I had been looking for some time for a house closer to my job. Before, it took me almost an hour to get to work by bus. Now, I can walk to the office in just 15 minutes. This makes my life easier in many ways.

My new neighborhood is very nice. There are many tall trees and lots of gardens, so it is very pretty. It is also quiet because there is very little traffic.

I hope you will be able to visit me at my new house sometime soon. We could have lunch and then take a walk through the neighborhood. I think you would enjoy seeing the gardens since you are such an avid gardener yourself.

A Let me know when you can come, and we'll make plans.
B I hope we can meet soon to discuss these suggestions.
C If you could help me in any way, I would really appreciate it.

3 *Dear Sam,*

I am writing to ask you for advice about my vacation. I will have some time off of work soon. I would like to spend most of that time at the beach, and I hope you have some suggestions for me.

I will have the entire month of August off of work. I am looking forward to this because I haven't had a vacation in a long time. We have been very busy at the office for most of this year, so I am glad to have the opportunity to relax now.

I would like to spend my month off at a nice beach resort. I am hoping to stay at a hotel that is right next to the beach and that provides all meals. I would also prefer a place that is peaceful and quiet.

I hope you can suggest a good place for my vacation. I know you travel a lot and have stayed at many resorts. If you could let me know the names of some of your favorite ones, I would appreciate it.

A Let me know which dates are best for you.
B I hope we can agree on the best way to solve this.
C Thank you so much for your help.

4 *Dear Mr. Smith,*

I thought you should know about a problem in my apartment that needs some repairs. The kitchen sink has been leaking for some time now. I believe that the pipe under the sink should be replaced soon.

The leak in the kitchen sink is causing a serious problem. Because the area under the sink has become very damp, the wood is beginning to rot. Unfortunately, it appears that the cause of the dampness is a hole in the drainpipe.

In my opinion, the drainpipe should be replaced as soon as possible. Otherwise, the problem will only get worse, and the entire cabinet will have to be replaced.

I suggest that you come to my apartment and look at the leaky sink with me. Then, we can discuss the best action to take.

A Let me know what you think of my idea.
B I hope you can accept my invitation.
C Thank you very much for your advice.

Write the Signature

After you write the conclusion, sign the letter. There are several ways to do this, depending on the type of letter.

For a formal or business letter, write

Sincerely,
Yours sincerely,

For a letter to a friend, write

Yours truly,
Your friend,
Best wishes,

Then, sign a name. If it is a formal or business letter, use a first and last name. If it is a letter to a friend, use a first name only. For the test, it doesn't matter what name you use. It can be your own name or another name.

PRACTICE 14

Choose the best signature for a letter to each of the following people.

1   Your best friend from school

    A Sincerely,   **B** Best wishes,
       Mary   Mary

2   Your lawyer

    A Sincerely,   **B** Yours sincerely,
       Paul Wilson   Paul

3   Your next-door neighbor whom you know well

    A Yours truly,   **B** Yours sincerely,
       Martha   Martha

4   Your neighbor whom you have met only once

    A Your friend,   **B** Sincerely,
       Jane Scott   Jane Scott

5   The manager of a bookstore whose name you don't know

    A Sincerely,   **B** Yours sincerely,
       George L. Smithers   George

6   Your cousin

    A Yours truly,   **B** Best wishes,
       Samantha Stern   Sam

PRACTICE 15

On a separate sheet of paper, write a complete letter for each of the tasks in Practice 1 (page 81). Begin with the introductions you wrote in Practice 10 (page 99) and put each one together with the corresponding paragraphs you wrote in Practice 12 (page 103). Then, complete each letter by writing an appropriate conclusion and adding a greeting and a signature.

STEP 3: REVISE

You should allow at least 3 minutes to revise your letter after you write.

Use the Revision Checklist

When you revise, you should check the content and the language of your letter. You check to make sure the letter is clear and well organized and that you have used correct grammar and spelling. You can use this revision checklist to practice revising.

REVISION CHECKLIST

Addressing the Task
- [ ] Thesis Statement
- [ ] Main Ideas

Coherence
- [ ] Main Idea—Paragraph
- [ ] Supporting Details

Cohesion
- [ ] Introduction—Conclusion
- [ ] Transition Words

Lexical Resource
- [ ] Vocabulary Variety
- [ ] Spelling

Grammatical Range and Accuracy
- [ ] Sentence Variety
- [ ] Accuracy

Read the following task and model letter and note how well the letter follows the items on the checklist.

Task

> *You have decided to look for a new job.*
>
> *Write a letter to a friend. In your letter*
>
> - *explain why you are looking for a new job.*
> - *describe the kind of job you would like to have.*
> - *ask your friend to help you find a job.*

Write at least 150 words.

You do **NOT** need to write any addresses.

Begin your letter as follows:

     Dear _____,

    Dear Eric,

    I want to let you know that I have decided to seek new employment. My current job is no longer interesting to me. I would like to find more challenging work soon, and I am hoping that you can help me.

    My current job at a small accounting firm has become very routine. When I started here five years ago, everything about the work interested me. I had little experience at the time, and I had a lot to learn. But now the work has become boring. It seems that every new client we get is the same as the last.

    I would like to find a more challenging position at a larger accounting firm. Then, I would have the opportunity to work with a wider variety of clients. I would also have more chances to advance at a larger firm.

    I hope you don't mind if I ask you for some help. Perhaps you can suggest some larger firms to which I could send my résumé. I know you have many contacts in accounting since you have worked in this field for years.

    I would really appreciate any suggestions you might have for me.

    Yours truly,
    Elisabeth

Check for Thesis Statement

The thesis is a statement of what the writing is about. The first sentence of this letter is the topic sentence. It tells what the letter is about—seeking new employment.

Check for Main Ideas

The main ideas support the thesis. The first paragraph of this letter mentions three ideas that expand on the topic. These will become the main ideas of the paragraphs in the body of the letter. One paragraph will be about the uninteresting current job, one will be about the challenging work the writer would like to have, and one will be about asking for help.

Check for Supporting Details

The supporting details give information to support the main ideas. In this letter, the body paragraphs each have a main idea and supporting details. Each main idea matches a topic introduced in the first paragraph.

Paragraph 2

Main Idea

My current job at a small accounting firm has become very routine.

Supporting Details

- *When I started here . . . the work interested me.*
- *I had little experience at the time, and I had a lot to learn.*
- *But now the work has become boring.*

Paragraph 3

Main Idea

I would like to find a more challenging position at a larger accounting firm.

Supporting Details

- *Then, I would have the opportunity to work with a wider variety of clients.*
- *I would also have more chances to advance at a larger firm.*

Paragraph 4

Main Idea

I hope you don't mind if I ask you for some help.

Supporting Details

- *Perhaps you can suggest some larger firms to which I could send my résumé.*
- *I know you have many contacts in accounting*
- *you have worked in this field for years.*

Check the Conclusion

The conclusion should suggest an action, convey a feeling, or thank the reader, depending on the topic of the letter. This letter asks for suggestions and appropriately thanks the reader: *I would really appreciate*

Check for Transition Words

Transition words connect ideas. See Chapter 2 (page 166) for more information on transition words. This letter uses appropriate transition words.

Paragraph	Transition Word	Purpose
Paragraph 2	But	Shows contrast
Paragraph 3	Then	Shows a result
Paragraph 3	also	Adds information

Check for Grammar and Spelling

Correct grammar and spelling help keep your ideas clear to the reader. See Chapter 4 for guidance on grammar and Chapter 3 (page 189) for guidance on spelling. There are no grammar or spelling errors in this letter.

Check for Sentence Variety

Using a variety of sentence types in your writing can help you express your ideas more clearly, and it makes your letter more interesting to read. It also shows the range of your writing ability. See Chapter 4 (page 215) for a discussion of different sentence types.

This letter uses a variety of sentence types. Here are some examples.

Paragraph	Sentence Type	Example
Paragraph 1	Simple Sentence	*My current job is no longer interesting to me.*
Paragraph 2	Complex Sentence	*When I started here five years ago, everything about the work interested me.*
Paragraph 2	Compound Sentence	*I had little experience at the time, and I had a lot to learn.*

PRACTICE 16

Read the following model letters. Answer the questions that follow each letter. Use the Revision Checklist to help you answer the questions.

A

> *You have a bicycle that you are no longer using. You would like to sell it to a friend.*
>
> *Write a letter to your friend. In your letter*
>
> - *explain why you are no longer using your bicycle.*
> - *describe your bicycle.*
> - *explain why you think your friend would like to have it.*

Write at least 150 words.

You do **NOT** need to write any addresses.

Begin your letter as follows:

Dear _____,

Dear Armand,

I thought you'd be interested in a bicycle I am selling. I just don't have time to use it much anymore. However, it's a really great racing bicycle, and I think you would really like it.

I used to enjoy riding my bicycle frequently, but these days I usually don't have time for it. My new job is very demanding, and I am working many more hours a week than I used to. Another reason I don't use the bicycle much is that we have a gym at the office, and I try to get my regular exercise there.

The bicycle is a really nice ten-speed racing bicycle. It's lightweight and fast. Also, it has a rack for carrying packages. In addition, it is a very nice silver color.

I think you'd like it because it's a great bicycle for racing, and I know racing is what you like to do. Also, I know silver is your favorite color. I can let you have it at a special price.

Let me know if you are interested, and we'll discuss the price.

Best wishes,
Robert

REVISION CHECKLIST

Addressing the Task
- ☐ Thesis Statement
- ☐ Main Ideas

Coherence
- ☐ Main Idea—Paragraph
- ☐ Supporting Details

Cohesion
- ☐ Introduction—Conclusion
- ☐ Transition Words

Lexical Resource
- ☐ Vocabulary Variety
- ☐ Spelling

Grammatical Range and Accuracy
- ☐ Sentence Variety
- ☐ Accuracy

Questions for A

1   Find the thesis statement, which is the topic sentence that tells what the letter is about, and underline it.

2   In the first paragraph, find the three ideas that expand on the topic. Number them. They will become the main ideas of the body of the letter.

3   Put a check (✔) next to the main idea of the second paragraph. Mark each supporting detail with the letter: A, B, C, etc.

4   Put a check (✔) next to the main idea of the third paragraph. Mark each supporting detail with the letter: A, B, C, etc.

5   Put a check (✔) next to the main idea of the fourth paragraph. Mark each supporting detail with the letter: A, B, C, etc.

6   Find and underline three transition words.

7   Check grammar and spelling. Correct any errors.

8   Find and mark one simple sentence (ss), one compound sentence (cm/s), and one compound-complex sentence (cm-cx/s).

B

> *You have recently moved to a new neighborhood.*
>
> *Write a letter to a friend. In your letter*
>
> - *explain why you moved.*
> - *describe your new neighborhood.*
> - *invite your friend to visit you.*

Write at least 150 words.

You do **NOT** need to write any addresses.

Begin your letter as follows:

     Dear _____,

Dear Sally,

I wanted to let you know that I have recently moved to a new neighborhood. The reason is that I wanted to be closer to my job. It is a quiet and pretty place to live, and I hope you will visit me here soon.

I had been looking for some time for a house closer to my job. Before, it took me almost an hour to get to work by bus. Now, I can walk to the office in just 15 minutes. This makes my life easier in many ways.

My new neighborhood is very nice. There are many tall trees and lots of gardens, so it is very pretty. It is also quiet because there is very little traffic.

I hope you will be able to visit me at my new house sometime soon. We could have lunch and then take a walk through the neighborhood. I think you would enjoy seeing the gardens since you are such an avid gardener yourself.

Let me know which dates are best for you.

Your friend,
Janet

REVISION CHECKLIST

Addressing the Task
- ☐ Thesis Statement
- ☐ Main Ideas

Coherence
- ☐ Main Idea—Paragraph
- ☐ Supporting Details

Cohesion
- ☐ Introduction—Conclusion
- ☐ Transition Words

Lexical Resource
- ☐ Vocabulary Variety
- ☐ Spelling

Grammatical Range and Accuracy
- ☐ Sentence Variety
- ☐ Accuracy

Questions for B

1   Find the thesis statement, which is the topic sentence that tells what the letter is about, and underline it.

2   In the first paragraph, find the three ideas that expand on the topic. Number them. They will become the main ideas of the body of the letter.

3   Put a check (✔) next to the main idea of the second paragraph. Mark each supporting detail with the letter: A, B, C, etc.

4   Put a check (✔) next to the main idea of the third paragraph. Mark each supporting detail with the letter: A, B, C, etc.

5   Put a check (✔) next to the main idea of the fourth paragraph. Mark each supporting detail with the letter: A, B, C, etc.

6   Find and underline three transition words.

7   Check grammar and spelling. Correct any errors.

8   Find and mark one simple sentence (ss), one compound sentence (cm/s), and one complex sentence (cx/s).

C

> *You are planning a vacation and want some advice.*
>
> *Write a letter to a friend. In your letter*
>
> - *explain why you are taking a vacation.*
> - *describe the kind of vacation you want.*
> - *ask your friend for help with your plans.*

Write at least 150 words.

You do **NOT** need to write any addresses.

Begin your letter as follows:

Dear _____,

Dear Sam,

I am writing to ask you for advice about my vacation. I will have some time off of work soon. I would like to spend most of that time at the beach, and I hope you have some suggestions for me.

I will have the entire month of August off of work. I haven't had a vacation in a long time. Therefore, I am really looking forward to this. Since we have been very busy at the office for most of this year, I am glad to have the opportunity to relax now.

I would like to spend my month off at a nice beach resort. I am looking for a hotel next to the beach that provides all meals. Also, I prefer a quiet atmosphere. I can't spend too much money, but I would like a comfortable place to stay.

I hope you can suggest a good place for my vacation. I know you travel a lot and have stayed at many resorts. If you could let me know the names of some of your favorite ones, I would appreciate it.

Thank you for your help.

Your friend,
Lee

REVISION CHECKLIST

Addressing the Task
☐ Thesis Statement
☐ Main Ideas

Coherence
☐ Main Idea—Paragraph
☐ Supporting Details

Cohesion
☐ Introduction—Conclusion
☐ Transition Words

Lexical Resource
☐ Vocabulary Variety
☐ Spelling

Grammatical Range and Accuracy
☐ Sentence Variety
☐ Accuracy

Questions for C

1   Find the thesis statement, which is the topic sentence that tells what the letter is about, and underline it.

2   In the first paragraph, find the three ideas that expand on the topic. Number them. They will become the main ideas of the body of the letter.

3   Put a check (✔) next to the main idea of the second paragraph. Mark each supporting detail with the letter: A, B, C, etc.

4   Put a check (✔) next to the main idea of the third paragraph. Mark each supporting detail with the letter: A, B, C, etc.

5   Put a check (✔) next to the main idea of the fourth paragraph. Mark each supporting detail with the letter: A, B, C, etc.

6   Find and underline three transition words.

7   Check grammar and spelling. Correct any errors.

8   Find and mark one simple sentence (ss), one compound sentence (cm/s), and one complex sentence (cx/s).

D

> *You have a problem in your apartment that needs repairs.*
>
> *Write a letter to the building manager. In your letter*
>
> - *describe the problem.*
> - *say what you think should be done about it.*
> - *ask the building manager to visit your apartment to see the problem.*

Write at least 150 words.

You do **NOT** need to write any addresses.

Begin your letter as follows:

Dear _____,

Dear Mr. Smith,

I am writing about a problem in my apartment that needs some repairs. The kitchen sink has been leaking for some time now, and I believe the drainpipe should be replaced. I think you should take a look at it.

The leak in the kitchen sink is causing a serious problem. Because the area under the sink has become very damp, the wood is beginning to rot. Unfortunately, it appears that the cause of the dampness is a hole in the drainpipe.

In my opinion, the drainpipe should be replaced as soon as possible. Otherwise, the problem will only get worse. If we ignore it, the entire cabinet will have to be replaced eventually.

I suggest that you come to my apartment and take a look at the leaky sink with me. I can show you the damaged area, and we can discuss the best action to take.

I hope you agree with my suggestion. Let me know when you can come by and look at the pipe.

Sincerely,
Ethel Wilson

REVISION CHECKLIST

Addressing the Task
- ☐ Thesis Statement
- ☐ Main Ideas

Coherence
- ☐ Main Idea—Paragraph
- ☐ Supporting Details

Cohesion
- ☐ Introduction—Conclusion
- ☐ Transition Words

Lexical Resource
- ☐ Vocabulary Variety
- ☐ Spelling

Grammatical Range and Accuracy
- ☐ Sentence Variety
- ☐ Accuracy

Questions for D

1   Find the thesis statement, which is the topic sentence that tells what the letter is about, and underline it.

2   In the first paragraph, find the three ideas that expand on the topic. Number them. They will become the main ideas of the body of the letter.

3   Put a check (✔) next to the main idea of the second paragraph. Mark each supporting detail with the letter: A, B, C, etc.

4   Put a check (✔) next to the main idea of the third paragraph. Mark each supporting detail with the letter: A, B, C, etc.

5   Put a check (✔) next to the main idea of the fourth paragraph. Mark each supporting detail with the letter: A, B, C, etc.

6   Find and underline three transition words.

7   Check grammar and spelling. Correct any errors.

8   Find and mark one simple sentence (ss), one compound sentence (cm/s), and one complex sentence (cx/s).

PRACTICE 17

Use the Revision Checklist to revise the letters you wrote in Practice 15 (page 107).

PRACTICE 18

Write a letter in response to each of the following tasks. Remember to allow 20 minutes for each letter, dividing the time as follows:

STEP 1	**Plan**	5 minutes	
STEP 2	**Write**	12 minutes	
STEP 3	**Revise**	3 minutes	

A

> *You recently spent the night at an expensive hotel. There was a problem with your room, but the hotel staff was unable to do anything about it.*
>
> *Write a letter to the hotel manager. In your letter*
>
> - *describe the problem.*
> - *explain what happened when you asked the hotel staff for help.*
> - *say what you would like the manager to do.*

Write at least 150 words.

You do **NOT** need to write any addresses.

Begin your letter as follows:

Dear Sir or Madam,

....

....

....

....

....

....

....

....

....

....

....

....

....

....

....

....

B

> *You are looking for an apartment to rent in a certain neighborhood.*
>
> *Write a letter to a friend who lives in that neighborhood. In your letter*
>
> - *explain why you want to live in that neighborhood.*
> - *describe the type of apartment you are looking for.*
> - *ask your friend to help you find an apartment.*

Write at least 150 words.

You do **NOT** need to write any addresses.

Begin your letter as follows:

Dear _____,

....

....

....

....

....

....

....

....

....

....

....

....

....

....

....

EXTRA PRACTICE

See the More Writing Practice section (page 223) in the Appendix for more General Training Task 1 topics that you can use for further writing practice.

TIME

You will have 60 minutes to complete the writing part of the test. You should allow 40 minutes for Task 2. Divide your time as follows:

Total time   40 minutes

(STEP 1)	**Plan**	10 minutes
(STEP 2)	**Write**	25 minutes
(STEP 3)	**Revise**	5 minutes

LENGTH

You must write at least 250 words. You can write more.

TIPS

- Read the task carefully, and make sure you understand what it is asking for.
- You can make planning notes on the question paper; they will not be scored.

SCORE

To receive a good score,

- Address all parts of the task
- Use correct grammar, spelling, and punctuation
- Write in complete sentences
- Use your own words; do not copy exact sentences from the task
- Explain your own opinion

STEP 1: PLAN

Take 10 minutes to plan before you write. A good essay is a well-planned essay.

Address the Task

In Task 2, you will read a statement and a question asking your opinion. The question may be stated in one of several ways. You may be asked to

A Agree or disagree
B Describe advantages and disadvantages
C Discuss two points of view and give your own
D Suggest solutions to a problem
E Answer two questions

PRACTICE 1

Read the following tasks. Determine what the question asks you to do. Write the corresponding letter from the above list next to each task.

1 .... Obesity is an increasing public health problem in some parts of the world.

Explain some possible reasons for this problem, and suggest some solutions.

2 .... People should never eat meat because raising animals for human consumption is cruel.

To what extent do you agree or disagree with this opinion?

3 .... Some people say that physical education classes are an important part of a child's education. Others believe that it is more important to focus on academics during school time.

Discuss both these views, and give your opinion.

4 .... In some educational systems, children are required to study one or more foreign languages. In others, foreign language study is not a requirement.

What are the potential benefits of foreign language study?

Do you think foreign language study is an important part of education?

5 .... A growing number of people rely on restaurants and convenience food (frozen food and packaged meals) rather than home-cooked food to supply most of their meals.

What are the advantages and disadvantages of eating this way?

Write a Thesis Statement

The thesis statement for your Task 2 essay should do two things:

- Address the task—It should do what the task asks for—agree or disagree, describe advantages and disadvantages, etc.
- Present the topic of the essay—It should tell the reader what the essay is about.

There is more than one way to write a thesis statement for any one question, as long as it does the above two things.

Look at these example questions and thesis statements.

1

> *Some parents send their children to preschool when they are three or four years old. Other parents wait until their children are old enough for primary school before they send them to school.*
>
> *Discuss the advantages and disadvantages of sending children to preschool at a young age.*

Give reasons for your answer, and include any relevant examples from your own knowledge or experience.

Write at least 250 words.

Thesis Statement A

While many children start preschool when they are only three or four years old, there are both advantages and disadvantages to this situation.

Thesis Statement B

Sending children to school at an early age has both advantages and disadvantages.

Discussion

Both thesis statements address the task: *Discuss the advantages and disadvantages . . . .* These thesis statements both mention the topic: young children attending preschool. They tell the reader that the essay will discuss the advantages and disadvantages of young children attending preschool.

2

> *Some people say that the best way to discourage smoking is to make smoking illegal in public places. Other people say that this is not enough and that other measures are needed.*
>
> *Discuss both these views, and give your opinion.*

Give reasons for your answer, and include any relevant examples from your own knowledge or experience.

Write at least 250 words.

Thesis Statement A

In my opinion, laws against smoking are an important part of discouraging this bad habit, but I agree that more needs to be done.

Thesis Statement B

In my opinion, it is unpleasant to be in public places where people are smoking.

Discussion

Thesis Statement A addresses the task. It mentions both points of view laid out in the question as well as the writer's opinion. It also mentions the topic: discouraging smoking. It tells the reader that the essay will discuss the two points of view about discouraging smoking and explain the writer's opinion on this topic.

Thesis Statement B does NOT address the task. It does mention the writer's opinion, but it does not mention the two points of view that should be discussed. It also does not correctly describe the topic. The topic is about discouraging smoking, not about whether or not the writer feels that smoking is unpleasant.

A more appropriate Thesis Statement B would be:

In my opinion, laws against smoking in public places will do a lot to discourage this unpleasant and unhealthy habit, and I don't believe any further measures are needed.

From this thesis statement, the reader knows that the essay will discuss the two points of view laid out in the task and defend the writer's opinion.

PRACTICE 2

Choose the thesis statements that are appropriate for each task. There can be more than one possible answer.

1
> *Obesity is an increasing public health problem in some parts of the world.*
>
> *Explain some possible reasons for this problem, and suggest some solutions.*

Give reasons for your answer, and include any relevant examples from your own knowledge or experience.

Write at least 250 words.

A   Obesity is a big problem in many places because it can cause serious health problems.

B   There are several reasons why obesity has become such a widespread issue, but there are also ways we can solve this problem.

C   Obesity has become a serious public health issue for a variety of reasons, but, fortunately, there are ways we can deal with this problem.

2 | *People should never eat meat because raising animals for human consumption is cruel.*
| *To what extent do you agree or disagree with this opinion?*

Give reasons for your answer, and include any relevant examples from your own knowledge or experience.

Write at least 250 words.

A   There are people who believe that we should not eat meat because it involves cruelty to animals, but I completely disagree with this point of view.

B   I never eat meat because I believe that it is bad for my health, but I don't mind if other people eat meat.

C   Some people feel that raising animals for meat is cruel, and I am of the same opinion.

3 | *Some people say that physical education classes are an important part of a child's education. Others believe that it is more important to focus on academics during school time.*
| *Discuss both these views, and give your opinion.*

Give reasons for your answer, and include any relevant examples from your own knowledge or experience.

Write at least 250 words.

A   While there are people who think that school should only be about academics, others believe that physical education is also important, and I agree with this point of view.

B   In my opinion, a child's education should focus on academics.

C   The best schools are the ones that have a strong physical education program.

4

> *In some educational systems, children are required to study one or more foreign languages. In others, foreign language study is not a requirement.*
>
> *What are the potential benefits of foreign language study?*
>
> *Do you think foreign language study is an important part of education?*

Give reasons for your answer, and include any relevant examples from your own knowledge or experience.

Write at least 250 words.

A   Foreign languages can be difficult to learn well, but my opinion is that children should study them.

B   Foreign language study improves children's minds as well as their understanding of the world, and I believe it should be a requirement in all schools.

C   Studying foreign languages has some benefits for children; however, I don't believe it is an essential part of education.

5

> *A growing number of people rely on restaurants and convenience food (frozen food and packaged meals) rather than home-cooked food to supply most of their meals.*
>
> *What are the advantages and disadvantages of eating this way?*

Give reasons for your answer, and include any relevant examples from your own knowledge or experience.

Write at least 250 words.

A   Home-cooked food is much cheaper than convenience food, and it is also better for your health.

B   Convenience food has become very popular, but it has disadvantages as well as advantages.

C   Many people don't know how to cook or they don't enjoy it, so they prefer to eat their meals in restaurants.

PRACTICE 3

Write your own thesis statements for the five tasks in Practice 2 (page 124).

1 ....
....
....
....

2 ....
....
....
....

3 ....
....
....
....

4 ....
....
....
....

5 ....
....
....
....

When you write
your thesis
statement,
don't worry too
much about how
accurately it
represents your
true opinion. The
examiners are
only interested in
seeing how well
you can develop
ideas in written
English. It doesn't
matter what the
actual ideas are.

Make Notes About Main Ideas and Supporting Details

Your thesis statement tells what your essay will be about. Now you will write notes about main ideas and supporting details that will make up the body of your essay. The main ideas support your thesis. The supporting details explain each main idea.

You should have two or three main ideas per essay and at least two supporting details per main idea.

A clear and easy way to organize your ideas is to make notes in outline form. Your outline should show your thesis and the main idea and supporting details for each paragraph. Here is a blank outline.

Thesis ....

Paragraph   **Main idea**   ....

                Supporting details ....

                                        ....

                                        ....

Paragraph   **Main idea**   ....

                Supporting details ....

                                        ....

                                        ....

Paragraph   **Main idea**   ....

                Supporting details ....

                                        ....

                                        ....

Look at the following example outline for a specific task.

Task

> In some parts of the world, the rate of divorce has increased dramatically over the past few decades.
>
> Explain some possible reasons for this problem and suggest some solutions.

Thesis The divorce rate is a problem, but it can be solved. ....

Paragraph   **Main idea**   Breakdown of the extended family ....

                Supporting details Past—family help with child care

                                        Past— family help with expenses

                                        Now—people don't have this support

Paragraph	**Main idea**	Stress in the workplace
	Supporting details	Less time with family
		Feel tired and irritable
		Family life is unhappy

Paragraph	**Main idea**	Ways to solve these problems
	Supporting details	Live closer to extended family
		Find a less demanding job
		Changed lifestyle—a happier life

Compare the outline with the following essay.

The divorce rate is increasing in many places. I believe that the breakdown of the extended family and the stresses of work are the major causes of this situation. Fortunately, although these issues have led to a rise in the divorce rate, there are ways we can solve this problem.

In my opinion, the biggest cause of divorce is the breakdown of the extended family. In the past, a family was made up of parents, grandparents, children, and other relatives. This meant that there was always somebody available to help with child care. It also meant that expenses could be shared in times of financial difficulty. These days, people often don't have this kind of support from their families, and this puts more stress on a marriage.

Stress in the workplace is another cause of divorce. These days, people are often expected to work longer hours than they did in the past. This means they spend less time at home with their families. It also means that when they are at home, they are tired and probably irritable, too. All of this adds up to an unhappy family life.

Fortunately, there are things that can be done to solve some of these problems if people really want to. People can decide to live closer to their extended family. They can invite their elderly parents to live with them or look for a job closer to their relatives' homes. People can also look for less demanding jobs or decide to have one parent stay at home instead of working. These things require changing one's lifestyle in some big ways, but they can lead to a happier marriage and family life.

There are a lot of demands in modern life that place stress on a marriage and lead to divorce. However, people can choose to make changes to their lifestyle that can result in a better, stronger marriage.

When you write your outline, make sure your main ideas support your thesis.

PRACTICE 4

Read each thesis statement and the main ideas that follow. Choose the main idea that does NOT belong.

1   In my opinion, laws against smoking in public places will do a lot to discourage this unpleasant and unhealthy habit, and I don't believe any further measures are needed.

    A Laws can do a great deal to reduce smoking.
    B Laws against smoking are more effective than education, taxes, or anything else.
    C Smoking leads to many diseases in addition to cancer.

2   Sending children to school at an early age has both advantages and disadvantages.

    A In many places there are few or no preschools available.
    B Children can learn a lot by being around other children.
    C Young children feel insecure when they are away from their parents.

3   The Internet is crucial to modern life, and parents and schools can do a lot to make sure children use the Internet safely.

    A Although the Internet is widely available, there are still people who don't use it.
    B Many schools have developed systems that limit the websites children can access.
    C Parents often limit how and when their children can use the Internet.

4   I agree that modern technology has made our lives better in many ways.

    A Cell phones have greatly improved communication in both our private and professional lives.
    B There have always been people who protest any technological change.
    C Cars are now much easier and much safer to drive.

5   Although many products are tested on animals for safety and efficacy, I believe this is a cruel practice as well as being completely unnecessary.

    A Laboratory animals suffer a great deal of pain and discomfort.
    B There are other ways to test products besides using animals.
    C Both drug and cosmetic companies test their products on animals.

When you write your outline, think of two or three details to support each main idea.

PRACTICE 5

Choose the main idea of each group of sentences.

1   **A** Children at this age are ready and eager to learn.
    B This is the time when children need to become independent of their parents.
    C The best time to start school is at the age of three or four.
    D Young children need to be with other children of the same age.

2   A The older you are, the better decisions you will make.
     B Divorces will decrease if people get married when they are older.
     C It is better to be married when you are established in your profession.
     D Young people haven't had enough experience to choose a spouse wisely.

3   A Nonsmokers can get cancer from secondhand smoke.
     B Many people are allergic to cigarette smoke.
     C Smoking is a public health hazard and should be outlawed.
     D Smoking leaves an unpleasant smell in buildings and buses.

4   A Cars have made many good contributions to our way of life.
     B Cars make it easy to become familiar with other towns and cities.
     C Cars give people more choices of where they will work and live.
     D Cars make it easier for people to manage their own schedules.

5   A Cell phones cause drivers to take their eyes off the road.
     B People tend to drive faster when they are talking on cell phones.
     C Drivers aren't aware of surrounding traffic when they are using a cell phone.
     D Cell phone use while driving is very dangerous.

PRACTICE 6

Read each essay. Then, complete the missing parts of each outline.

> *Some parents send their children to preschool when they are three or four years old. Other parents wait until their children are old enough for primary school before they send them to school.*
>
> *Discuss the advantages and disadvantages of sending children to preschool at a young age.*

While many children start preschool when they are only three or four years old, there are both advantages and disadvantages to this situation. Preschool gives children the chance to develop important skills. It also provides a safe place for children while their parents are at work. On the other hand, it takes them away from their parents at a young age.

Preschool gives children an opportunity to develop important skills. They develop social skills when they play with the other children at school. They learn to share, to negotiate disagreements, and to do things as a group. They also learn skills that will prepare them for primary school. They learn about colors, numbers, and letters. They learn to sit and listen to the teacher. These things will help them later when they start first grade.

Preschool also provides a safe place for children while their parents are working. At preschool, children are cared for by trained teachers who understand children and their needs. They also know how to handle emergencies. Parents can feel confident that their children are well cared for at preschool.

There are, however, some disadvantages to sending children to preschool. The biggest one is that it separates them from their parents for a large part of the day. Many children at the age of three or four are not yet ready to spend so much time away from their parents. It can cause them to feel unhappy and insecure. It is often better for young children to be cared for by relatives, if this is possible.

Preschool can be a good experience for many children, but others aren't ready for school at an early age. Parents need to make the decision about preschool based on the personality of each individual child and the family situation.

Thesis		Advantages and disadvantages of preschool
Paragraph	**Main idea**	Chance to develop important skills
	Supporting details	1
		2
Paragraph	**Main idea**	3
	Supporting details	Teachers understand children
		Teachers can handle emergencies
Paragraph	**Main idea**	4
	Supporting details	Separates them from their parents
		Feel unhappy and insecure
		Better to be cared for by relatives

> *Some people say that the best way to discourage smoking is to make smoking illegal in public places. Other people say that this is not enough and that other measures are needed.*
>
> *Discuss both these views, and give your opinion.*

Give reasons for your answer, and include any relevant examples from your own knowledge or experience.

Smoking is a serious public health problem, and it needs to be discouraged. Some people feel that making laws against smoking in public places is a good way to do this. Others believe that more needs to be done. In my opinion, laws against smoking are an important part of discouraging this bad habit, but I agree that more needs to be done.

Laws against smoking in public can go a long way toward discouraging this dangerous habit. If people aren't allowed to smoke in public, that means they can't smoke in restaurants, stores, parks, offices, banks, libraries, and other places. It means that whenever they are not in their own homes or their friends' homes, they can't smoke. This makes it difficult to smoke much of the time, and it makes people think twice before they light a cigarette.

However, I don't feel that such laws are enough. They still allow people to smoke some of the time. I believe that education is also important. This could take several forms. For example, schools could have special programs to teach students about the dangers of smoking. In addition, there could be notices on TV, the radio, and the Internet that give information about the negative effects of smoking. The more information people see about the dangers of smoking, the more they will become aware of it. Then, they will be less likely to choose to smoke, even in their own homes.

Smoking is a serious problem, and we need to do something about it. I believe that laws against smoking in combination with education can do a lot to prevent people from starting or continuing this dangerous habit.

Thesis		Laws against smoking are important, but more needs to be done.
Paragraph	**Main idea**	Laws can discourage smoking
	Supporting details	5
		Difficult to smoke much of the time
Paragraph	**Main idea**	6
	Supporting details	7
		Schools could have programs.
		8

PRACTICE 7

Look at the thesis statements you wrote in Practice 3 (page 127). Create an outline for each one.

1	**Thesis**		
	Paragraph	**Main idea**	
		Supporting details	
	Paragraph	**Main idea**	
		Supporting details	

Paragraph   **Main idea**   ....

                               Supporting details   ....

                                                      ....

                                                      ....

2   **Thesis** ....

Paragraph   **Main idea**   ....

                               Supporting details   ....

                                                      ....

                                                      ....

Paragraph   **Main idea**   ....

                               Supporting details   ....

                                                       ....

                                                      ....

Paragraph   **Main idea**   ....

                               Supporting details   ....

                                                       ....

                                                      ....

3   **Thesis** ....

Paragraph   **Main idea**   ....

                               Supporting details   ....

                                                       ....

                                                      ....

                                                      ....

Paragraph   **Main idea**   ....

                               Supporting details   ....

                                                       ....

                                                      ....

Paragraph   **Main idea**   ....

                               Supporting details   ....

                                                       ....

                                                      ....

4   **Thesis** ....

       Paragraph   **Main idea** ....

                        Supporting details ....

                        ....

                        ....

       Paragraph   **Main idea** ....

                        Supporting details ....

                        ....

                        ....

       Paragraph   **Main idea** ....

                        Supporting details ....

                        ....

                        ....

5   **Thesis** ....

       Paragraph   **Main idea** ....

                        Supporting details ....

                        ....

                        ....

       Paragraph   **Main idea** ....

                        Supporting details ....

                        ....

                        ....

       Paragraph   **Main idea** ....

                        Supporting details ....

                        ....

                        ....

TIP

When you write
your outline,
you can write in
note form with
abbreviated words
and phrases. When
you write your
essay, however,
you will need to
write in complete
sentences.

STEP 2: WRITE

After you plan, you are ready to write. Allow about 25 minutes for this step. Use your outline as a guide to writing your essay.

Write the Introduction

The introduction to your essay states your thesis and tells the reader how you plan to develop your ideas. The main ideas that you develop from your outline should be summarized in the introduction.

Compare these introductions,

Task

> *In many parts of the world, people rely on private cars for transportation.*
>
> *In what ways does reliance on private cars affect the way we live?*
>
> *Do the effects tend to be positive or negative?*

Version A

A lot of people have their own cars, and this affects the way we live. We rely on our cars, and this can be both good and bad.

Version B

In many places, private cars are the most important form of transportation, and this has had a big impact on the way people live. Private cars offer a lot of freedom, but they also cause crowding and pollution, and they encourage isolation. Despite the advantages, I believe they have a negative effect on our lives.

Discussion

Version A presents the topic that private cars affect our lives in both good and bad ways, but it does not tell us much. What are the ways that cars affect our lives?

Version B mentions several ways in which cars affect our lives—they give us freedom but also cause crowding and pollution as well as isolation. This introduction lets the reader know what to expect in the body of the essay—that each one of these effects will be discussed in detail.

Task

> *Using a cell phone while driving is dangerous because it causes the driver to become distracted. Therefore, cell phone use by drivers should be made illegal.*
>
> *To what extent do you agree or disagree?*

Version A

I agree that it is dangerous to drive while talking on a cell phone. This is why we need laws against this practice.

Version B

Some people believe that there should be a law against using a cell phone while driving, but I do not agree with this point of view. I think that often cell phone use by a driver is necessary and that there are ways to make it safe.

Discussion

Version A presents the writer's agreement with the statement, but it does not give any reasons for this opinion. The reader is given no guidance about how the essay will be developed.

Version B also presents the writer's opinion, and then supports it with two reasons—that cell phone use is often necessary and that it can be safe. From this introduction, the reader can expect to see one paragraph in the body of the essay for each of these reasons.

PRACTICE 8

Read the introductions for the following tasks. Determine the thesis of each essay and what the main idea of each paragraph will be. The first one is an example.

1 Task

> *A growing number of people work by telecommuting, that is, the employee works from home, using a computer and the Internet to connect with the office.*
>
> *What are the advantages and disadvantages of working this way?*

Give reasons for your answer, and include any relevant examples from your own knowledge or experience.

Introduction

While telecommuting is becoming increasingly popular, there are both benefits and drawbacks to this way of working. Telecommuting has many conveniences for the employee, and it can help the employer cut costs as well. On the other hand, employers often feel it makes it more difficult to manage their workers.

Thesis	There are both benefits and drawbacks to telecommuting.
Main idea 1	More convenient for the employee
Main idea 2	Employer can cut costs
Main idea 3	More difficult to manage workers

2 Task

> *Some families think the best way to take care of their aging parents is to care for them at home. Others believe that it is better for their parents to live in a special home for the elderly.*
>
> *Discuss both these views and give your opinion.*

Give reasons for your answer, and include any relevant examples from your own knowledge or experience.

Introduction

Caring for aging parents is an issue many families face today. Some families prefer to keep their parents at home because they will get better and less expensive care that way. Others put their parents in a home for the elderly because they don't have the time or resources to care for them in their own homes. While I understand the reasons for special homes for the elderly, I would prefer to have my own family care for my aging parents.

Thesis   ....

Main idea 1   ....

Main idea 2   ....

Main idea 3   ....

3 Task

> *Some people feel that life was better in the past when we had less modern technology because things were simpler and less complicated.*
>
> *To what extent do you agree or disagree with this opinion?*

Give reasons for your answer, and include any relevant examples from your own knowledge or experience.

Introduction

Some people believe that things were better in the past before modern technology complicated our lives, but I do not agree with this point of view. I believe that life was worse in a number of ways. The lack of modern machines meant that people worked harder, the lack of modern medicine meant that they died younger, and the lack of modern transportation meant that they had fewer opportunities.

Thesis   ....

Main idea 1   ....

Main idea 2   ....

Main idea 3   ....

4 Task

> *Traffic congestion is a growing problem in many of the world's major cities.*
>
> *Explain some possible reasons for this problem, and suggest some solutions.*

Give reasons for your answer, and include any relevant examples from your own knowledge or experience.

Introduction

Most of the world's major cities have serious traffic congestion, making life difficult for local citizens. There are several causes of this problem, but there are also solutions. One cause is overcrowded cities. Another is lack of transportation options. City governments should focus on improving public transportation and encouraging alternative ways of getting around.

Thesis ....

Main idea 1 ....

Main idea 2 ....

Main idea 3 ....

5 Task

> *Zoos are inhumane and should be abolished.*
>
> *To what extent do you agree or disagree with this opinion?*

Give reasons for your answer, and include any relevant examples from your own knowledge or experience.

Introduction

Many people believe that there should be no zoos because they are cruel to animals, and I agree with this opinion. Zoos are like jails for wild animals that should live free, and at the same time they are completely unnecessary because we can see and learn about animals in their natural habitat.

Thesis ....

Main idea 1 ....

Main idea 2 ....

Main idea 3 ....

PRACTICE 9

Write an introduction for each of the tasks in Practice 2 (page 124). Use your thesis statements from Practice 3 (page 127) and the main ideas from the outlines you wrote in Practice 7 (page 133).

1 ....
....
....
....
....
....
....

2 ....
....
....
....
....
....
....

3 ....
....
....
....
....
....
....

4 ....
....
....
....
....
....
....

5 ....

....

....

....

....

....

....

Write the Paragraphs

Once you have written your thesis statement and shown the reader how you plan to develop your essay, you have the basis for writing your body paragraphs. You use the main ideas and supporting details from your outline to write the sentences for each paragraph. Of course, you must use correct grammar and spelling and show variety in your vocabulary and sentence types. (See Chapters 2–4 for practice with these items.)

PRACTICE 10

Look at the following outlines developed from some of the introductions in Practice 8 (page 137). Use each one to write a paragraph. The first one is an example.

1	**Main idea**	Telecommuting is more convenient for the employee.
	Supporting details	No need to commute
		No need for special work clothes
		More time for family responsibilities

Paragraph

Telecommuting makes things more convenient for the employee. For one thing, there is no need to spend time and money commuting between work and home. In addition, the employee can wear casual clothes most days so does not have to spend a lot of time and money shopping for work clothes. Finally, working at home means the employee has more time to devote to family responsibilities such as cooking, cleaning, and child care.

2 **Main idea**   Telecommuting allows the employer to cut costs.

Supporting details   Save on rent with smaller office

Less equipment

Smaller support staff

....

....

....

....

....

....

....

....

....

3 **Main idea**   Telecommuting makes it more difficult to manage workers.

Supporting details   Hard to supervise work

Can't be sure how well employees manage time

Difficult to have staff meetings

....

....

....

....

....

....

....

....

4   **Main idea**   Aging parents get better and less expensive care at home.

      Supporting details   Families love their parents

                                           People feel happiest in their own homes

                                           Homes for the elderly are expensive

5   **Main idea**   Families don't have time or resources.

      Supporting details   Most people have jobs

                                           Young children need time and attention

                                           Not enough space in the house for parents

PRACTICE 11

On a separate sheet of paper, write the body paragraphs for each of the outlines you wrote in Practice 7 (page 133).

Write sentences using structures and grammar that you feel confident about using. Don't write long sentences only in order to impress the examiners. It is better to have shorter, well-structured sentences than long ones filled with errors.

Write the Conclusion

A good conclusion briefly sums up the ideas you developed in your essay. It is a restatement of the thesis and main ideas you laid out in your introduction. Compare the following introduction and conclusion from one essay.

Introduction

The divorce rate is increasing in many places. I believe that the breakdown of the extended family and the stresses of work are the major causes of this situation. Fortunately, although these issues have led to a rise in the divorce rate, there are ways we can solve this problem.

Conclusion

There are a lot of demands in modern life that place stress on a marriage and lead to divorce. However, people can choose to make changes to their lifestyle that can result in a better, stronger marriage.

Discussion

The introduction mentions two causes of divorce: the breakdown of the extended family and the stresses of work. In the conclusion, these two main ideas are summed up as *demands in modern life.* The introduction also states the opinion that there are ways to solve the problem of the rising divorce rate. The conclusion restates this opinion as *people can choose to make changes to their lifestyle that can result in a better, stronger marriage.*

Compare the following introduction and conclusion from another essay.

Introduction

Some people believe that there should be a law against using a cell phone while driving but I do not agree with this point of view. I think that often cell phone use by a driver is necessary and that there are ways to make it safe.

Conclusion

Making cell phone use by drivers illegal would be unfair because many people need to use their phones while in the car. As long as drivers use certain devices, cell phone use is not distracting and not dangerous.

Discussion

The introduction states the writer's opinion: disagreement with laws against cell phone use while driving. This is restated in the conclusion as *Making cell phone use by drivers illegal would be unfair.* The introduction also presents two main ideas: *cell phone use by a driver is necessary* and *there are ways to make it safe.* These ideas are restated in the conclusion as *many people need to use their phones while in the car* and *As long as drivers use certain devices, cell phone use is not distracting and not dangerous.*

144 IELTS WRITING

PRACTICE 12

Write a conclusion for each of the following introductions from Practice 8 (page 137).

1   While telecommuting is becoming increasingly popular, there are both benefits and drawbacks to this way of working. On one hand, it is more convenient for the employee, and it can help the employer cut costs as well. On the other hand, employers often feel it makes it more difficult to manage their workers.

....

....

....

....

....

....

....

....

....

2   Caring for aging parents is an issue many families face today. Some families prefer to keep their parents at home because they will get better and less expensive care that way. Others put their parents in a home for the elderly because they don't have the time or resources to care for them in their own homes. While I understand the reasons for special homes for the elderly, I would prefer to have my own family care for my aging parents.

....

....

....

....

....

....

....

....

....

....

3 Some people believe that things were better in the past before modern technology complicated our lives, but I do not agree with this point of view. I believe that life was worse in a number of ways. The lack of modern machines meant that people worked harder, the lack of modern medicine meant that they died younger, and the lack of modern transportation meant that they had fewer opportunities.

....

....

....

....

....

....

....

....

....

4 Most of the world's major cities have serious traffic congestion, making life difficult for local citizens. There are several causes of this problem, but there are also solutions. One cause is overcrowded cities. Another is lack of transportation options. City governments should focus on improving public transportation and encouraging alternative ways of getting around.

....

....

....

....

....

....

....

....

....

....

5   Many people believe that there should be no zoos because they are cruel
to animals, and I agree with this opinion. Zoos are like jails for wild animals
that should live free, and at the same time they are completely unnecessary
because we can see and learn about animals in their natural habitat.

....

....

....

....

....

....

....

....

....

....

PRACTICE 13

*On a separate sheet of paper, take the introductions you wrote in Practice 9 (page 140) and put
each one together with the corresponding body paragraphs you wrote in Practice 11 (page 143).
Then, complete each essay by writing an appropriate conclusion.*

STEP 3: REVISE

You should allow about 5 minutes to revise your essay after you write.

Use the Revision Checklist

When you revise, you check the content and language of your essay. You need to make sure that the content is well developed and well organized and that you have used correct grammar, spelling, and punctuation. You can use this revision checklist to practice revising.

> ## REVISION CHECKLIST
>
> **Addressing the Task**
> ☐ Thesis Statement
> ☐ Main Ideas
>
> **Coherence**
> ☐ Main Idea—Paragraph
> ☐ Supporting Details
>
> **Cohesion**
> ☐ Introduction—Conclusion
> ☐ Transition Words
>
> **Lexical Resource**
> ☐ Vocabulary Variety
> ☐ Spelling
>
> **Grammatical Range and Accuracy**
> ☐ Sentence Variety
> ☐ Accuracy

Read the following model essay and note how well it follows the items on the checklist.

> *In many parts of the world, people rely on private cars for transportation.*
>
> *In what ways does reliance on private cars affect the way we live?*
>
> *Do the effects tend to be positive or negative?*

Give reasons for your answer, and include any relevant examples from your own knowledge or experience.

In many places, private cars are the most important form of transportation, and this has had a big impact on the way people live. Private cars offer a lot of freedom, but they also cause crowding and pollution, and they encourage isolation. Despite the advantages, I believe they have a negative effect on our lives.

Private cars give us a lot of freedom in our work and personal lives. If you have your own car, you have more job choices because you don't have to worry about how you will get to work. Whether you live close to your job or far away, you can easily commute to work in your car. You also have more freedom to choose where you will live. You don't have to live in a neighborhood close to your job or close to stores or close to a bus route. You can live anywhere you want because your car will take you everywhere you need to go.

When most people have their own car, however, this affects the quality of our roads and air. When there are a lot of private cars, the roads become congested, and there are frequent traffic jams. This makes it difficult to get to places and causes a lot of stress. In addition, cars cause air pollution. This is bad for the natural environment and can also lead to illness.

Another problem with private cars is isolation. When people drive their own cars, they lose opportunities to interact with other people. They don't know their neighbors because they never walk down the street. They don't have the chance to meet people at the bus stop or on the subway.

Private cars have an advantage because they are convenient, but I think the disadvantages outweigh the benefits. I think it is important to support alternative forms of transportation.

Check for Thesis Statement

The thesis is a statement of what the essay is about. The task asks the writer to discuss the effect of cars on our lives and whether they are more positive or negative. In the first paragraph, the writer mentions several effects of cars and then gives an opinion about these effects, which is the thesis statement:

Despite the advantages, I believe they have a negative effect on our lives.

Check for Main Ideas

The main ideas support the thesis. The first paragraph mentions three topics that support the thesis. These will become the main ideas of the paragraphs in the body of the essay.

1 Private cars offer a lot of freedom
2 they also cause crowding and pollution
3 encourage isolation

Check for Supporting Details

The supporting details give information to support the main ideas. In this essay, the body paragraphs each have a main idea and supporting details. Each main idea matches a topic introduced in the first paragraph.

Paragraph 2

Main Idea   Private cars give us a lot of freedom in our work and personal lives.

Supporting Details

- you have more job choices
- You also have more freedom to choose where you will live

Paragraph 3

Main Idea   When most people have their own car, however, this affects the quality of our roads and air.

Supporting Details

- When there are a lot of private cars, the roads become congested, and there are frequent traffic jams.
- cars cause air pollution

Paragraph 4

Main Idea   Another problem with private cars is isolation.

Supporting Details

- When people drive their own cars, they lose opportunities to interact with other people.
- They don't know their neighbors because they never walk down the street.
- They don't have the chance to meet people at the bus stop or on the subway.

Check the Conclusion

The conclusion should sum up the ideas presented in the introduction. In this essay, the introduction mentions some advantages and disadvantages of private cars and states the writer's opinion that cars have a negative effect on our lives. The conclusion sums up the advantages of cars with the word *convenient* and restates the opinion—*but I think the disadvantages outweigh the benefits*—and adds to it by suggesting a solution (*alternative forms of transportation*).

Check for Transition Words

Transition words connect ideas. See Chapter 2 (page 166) for more information on transition words. This essay uses appropriate transition words.

Paragraph	Transition Word	Purpose
Paragraph 1	*but*	Shows contrast
Paragraph 2	*also*	Adds information
Paragraph 3	*however*	Shows contrast
Paragraph 3	*In addition*	Adds information
Paragraph 4	*Another*	Adds information
Paragraph 5	*but*	Shows contrast

Check for Grammar and Spelling

Correct grammar and spelling help keep your ideas clear to the reader. See Chapter 4 for guidance on grammar and Chapter 3 (page 189) for guidance on spelling. There are no grammar or spelling errors in this essay.

Check for Sentence Variety

Using a variety of sentence types in your essay can help you express your ideas more clearly, and it makes your essay more interesting to read. It also shows the range of your writing ability. See Chapter 4 (page 215) for a discussion of different sentence types.

This essay uses a variety of sentence types. Here are some examples.

Paragraph	Sentence Type	Example
Paragraph 1	Compound Sentence	In many places, private cars are the most important form of transportation, and this has had a big impact on the way people live.
Paragraph 2	Complex Sentence	You can live anywhere you want because your car will take you everywhere you need to go.
Paragraph 3	Simple Sentence	In addition, cars cause air pollution.

PRACTICE 14

Read the following model essays. Answer the questions that follow each essay. Use the Revision Checklist to help you answer the questions.

A

> *Using a cell phone while driving is dangerous because it causes the driver to become distracted. Therefore, cell phone use by drivers should be made illegal.*
>
> *To what extent do you agree or disagree?*

Give reasons for your answer, and include any relevant examples from your own knowledge or experience.

Some people believe that there should be a law against using a cell phone while driving, but I do not agree with this point of view. I think that often cell phone use by a driver is necessary and that there are ways to make it safe.

People have cell phones because they need them, and often they need to use them when they are traveling by car. Some people, for example, use their cars on company business. They may need to talk to their boss or to a client while they are on the road. Another example is parents, who need to be in communication with their children. A child may have a schedule change and need a ride home. Parents may need to let their child know that they will arrive home a little bit late.

These are just some examples of reasons why people may need to use phones while driving. They are all important.

Using a cell phone while driving does not have to be dangerous. Most cars have technology that makes it unnecessary to hold or look at your phone while using it. Some people say that just talking on the phone distracts the driver's attention from the road. However, I disagree. I think that a phone conversation is no more distracting than a conversation with a passenger in the car.

In conclusion, I believe that making cell phone use by drivers illegal would be unfair because many people need to use their phones while in the car. As long as drivers use the available technology so that they can keep their eyes on the road while talking on the phone, cell phone use is not distracting and not dangerous.

REVISION CHECKLIST

Addressing the Task
- ☐ Thesis Statement
- ☐ Main Ideas

Coherence
- ☐ Main Idea—Paragraph
- ☐ Supporting Details

Cohesion
- ☐ Introduction—Conclusion
- ☐ Transition Words

Lexical Resource
- ☐ Vocabulary Variety
- ☐ Spelling

Grammatical Range and Accuracy
- ☐ Sentence Variety
- ☐ Accuracy

Questions for A

1   The task asks the writer to agree or disagree with an opinion. Look at the first paragraph of the essay. Find the thesis statement, which states agreement or disagreement with an opinion, and underline it.

2   In the first paragraph, find the topics that support the thesis. Number them. They will become the main ideas of the body of the essay.

3   Put a check (✔) next to the main idea of the second paragraph. Mark each supporting detail with the letter: A, B, C, etc.

4 Put a check (✔) next to the main idea of the third paragraph. Mark each supporting detail with the letter: A, B, C, etc.

5 Underline the transition words in the second and third paragraphs.

6 Check grammar and spelling. Correct any errors.

7 Find and mark one complex sentence (cx/s), one simple sentence (ss), and one adjective clause (adj.c.) in Paragraph 2.

B

> *Obesity is an increasing public health problem in some parts of the world.*
>
> *Explain some possible reasons for this problem and suggest some solutions.*

Give reasons for your answer, and include any relevant examples from your own knowledge or experience.

Obesity has become a major public health issue in a number of countries. Poor diet and lack of exercise are the major reasons behind this. While obesity is a serious problem for these reasons, there are solutions.

The biggest cause of the obesity problem, in my opinion, is poor diet. Fast food restaurants have become widespread, and people like to eat at them because they are cheap and convenient. Unfortunately, the meals they sell are high in calories and low in nutrition. Snack foods, especially chips and sodas, are also very popular. Like fast food meals, these foods provide a lot of calories but little nutrition.

Another major cause of obesity is lack of exercise. People drive everywhere, so they have little opportunity to walk. People also work long hours and don't have much time to go to the gym or play sports. Children seem to prefer sitting in front of the computer to playing active games outside with their friends.

Fortunately, there are solutions to this problem. Education is very important. Public campaigns to explain the importance of good diet and regular exercise could get people to think about changing their habits. In addition, making healthy food more available would encourage people to eat better. Schools, for example, could provide lunches with lots of fresh fruits and vegetables.

Obesity is a problem because it can lead to some serious health conditions. If people are encouraged to eat better and exercise more, however, the situation could be greatly improved.

REVISION CHECKLIST

Addressing the Task
- ☐ Thesis Statement
- ☐ Main Ideas

Coherence
- ☐ Main Idea—Paragraph
- ☐ Supporting Details

Cohesion
- ☐ Introduction—Conclusion
- ☐ Transition Words

Lexical Resource
- ☐ Vocabulary Variety
- ☐ Spelling

Grammatical Range and Accuracy
- ☐ Sentence Variety
- ☐ Accuracy

Questions for B

1 The task asks the writer to explain the reasons for a problem and suggest some solutions. Look at the first paragraph of the essay. Find the thesis statement, which addresses the task, and underline it.

2 In the first paragraph, find the topics that support the thesis. Number them. They will become the main ideas of the body of the essay.

3 Put a check (✔) next to the main idea of the second paragraph. Mark each supporting detail with the letter: A, B, C, etc.

4 Put a check (✔) next to the main idea of the third paragraph. Mark each supporting detail with the letter: A, B, C, etc.

5 Put a check (✔) next to the main idea of the fourth paragraph. Mark each supporting detail with the letter: A, B, C, etc.

6 Underline the transition words in the second and third paragraphs.

7 Check grammar and spelling. Correct any errors.

8 Find and mark one compound sentence (cm/s), one simple sentence (ss), and one compound-complex sentence (cm-cx/s).

C *A growing number of people rely on restaurants and convenience food (frozen food and packaged meals) rather than home-cooked food to supply most of their meals.*

What are the advantages and disadvantages of eating this way?

Give reasons for your answer, and include any relevant examples from your own knowledge or experience.

These days, many people prefer not to prepare their own meals at home, choosing instead to eat at restaurants or buy convenience foods. This popular way of eating has both advantages and disadvantages. For busy people, it is a convenient way to eat, but it is expensive and not very healthful.

The biggest advantage of eating restaurant meals and convenience foods is that it makes mealtime much simpler. Many people are busy with their jobs and taking care of their children. It is hard for them to find time to plan meals, shop, cook, and then clean up after each meal. If all they have to do at dinnertime is choose a restaurant or put something in the microwave oven, then dinner is a much easier event. It becomes a relaxing and pleasant time to be with the family.

Although eating restaurant meals and convenience foods is simpler than cooking at home, it can be quite expensive. Restaurant meals cost a great deal more than meals cooked at home. Convenience foods cost less than restaurant meals, but they are still expensive. It is hard for many families to afford to eat restaurant meals and convenience foods on a regular basis.

Another disadvantage of restaurant meals and convenience foods is that they are not very healthful. They are often high in fat, salt, and sugar. In addition, restaurant portions tend to be big, which makes them higher in calories. Convenience foods may contain vegetables, but they are not fresh. Therefore, they are not a good source of vitamins. Home-cooked meals, on the other hand, can be as nutritious as you want to make them.

Mealtime is easy when you choose restaurant meals or convenience foods, but if you are concerned about costs and health, home-cooked meals are a better option.

REVISION CHECKLIST

Addressing the Task
☐   Thesis Statement
☐   Main Ideas

Coherence
☐   Main Idea—Paragraph
☐   Supporting Details

Cohesion
☐   Introduction—Conclusion
☐   Transition Words

Lexical Resource
☐   Vocabulary Variety
☐   Spelling

Grammatical Range and Accuracy
☐   Sentence Variety
☐   Accuracy

Questions for C

1   The task asks the writer to explain the advantages and disadvantages of a situation. Look at the first paragraph of the essay. Find the thesis statement, which addresses the task, and underline it.

2   In the first paragraph, find the topics that support the thesis. Number them. They will become the main ideas of the body of the essay.

3   Put a check (✔) next to the main idea of the second paragraph. Mark each supporting detail with the letter: A, B, C, etc.

4   Put a check (✔) next to the main idea of the third paragraph. Mark each supporting detail with the letter: A, B, C, etc.

5   Put a check (✔) next to the main idea of the fourth paragraph. Mark each supporting detail with the letter: A, B, C, etc.

6   Underline the transition words in the fourth paragraph.

7   Check grammar and spelling. Correct any errors.

8   Find and mark one compound sentence (cm/s), one simple sentence (ss), and one complex sentence (cx/s).

D

> *Some people say that physical education classes are an important part of a child's education. Others believe that it is more important to focus on academics during school time.*
>
> *Discuss both these views and give your opinion.*

Give reasons for your answer, and include any relevant examples from your own knowledge or experience.

The majority of schools devote most of the school day to academic classes but also set aside time for physical education and other nonacademic classes. However, not everyone agrees with this way of dividing up the school day. While there are people who think that school should only be about academics, others believe that physical education is also important, and I agree with this point of view.

Some people feel that school should be all about academics. According to this point of view, children need to spend their entire school day learning math, science, literature, and history. Devoting time to these subjects is the best way to prepare children for their future university education and careers. If children enjoy playing sports, they should do it outside of school time.

Other people, however, feel that physical education is an important part of a child's education. According to this point of view, physical education teaches children important skills such as teamwork, leadership, and how to win and lose gracefully. In addition, physical education classes are the best way to ensure that children get the regular physical exercise that they need to stay healthy. Finally, if children spend a little time each day being physically active, it helps them concentrate better on their academic work.

I agree that devoting some school time to physical education is necessary. If schools don't give importance to physical education, children will not learn that physical activity is important. They won't get the exercise that they need to grow up healthy. It is not enough to say they can play games and sports in their free time. They won't choose to do these things if no one teaches them that they are important.

Academics are important, but physical education is important, too. Schools need to prepare children for all aspects of life, including taking care of their physical health.

REVISION CHECKLIST

Addressing the Task
- ☐ Thesis Statement
- ☐ Main Ideas

Coherence
- ☐ Main Idea—Paragraph
- ☐ Supporting Details

Cohesion
- ☐ Introduction—Conclusion
- ☐ Transition Words

Lexical Resource
- ☐ Vocabulary Variety
- ☐ Spelling

Grammatical Range and Accuracy
- ☐ Sentence Variety
- ☐ Accuracy

Questions for D

1 The task asks the writer to explain two points of view and give an opinion. Look at the first paragraph of the essay. Find the thesis statement, which addresses the task, and underline it.

2 In the first paragraph, find the topics that support the thesis. Number them. They will become the main ideas of the body of the essay.

3 Put a check (✔) next to the main idea of the second paragraph. Mark each supporting detail with the letter: A, B, C, etc.

4 Put a check (✔) next to the main idea of the third paragraph. Mark each supporting detail with the letter: A, B, C, etc.

5 Put a check (✔) next to the main idea of the fourth paragraph. Mark each supporting detail with the letter: A, B, C, etc.

6 Underline the transition words in the third paragraph.

7 Check grammar and spelling. Correct any errors.

8 Find and mark one compound sentence (cm/s), one sentence with an adjective clause (adj.c.), and one complex sentence (cx/s).

PRACTICE 15

Use the Revision Checklist to revise the essays you wrote in Practice 13 (page 147).

PRACTICE 16

Write an essay in response to each of the following tasks. Remember to allow 40 minutes for each essay, dividing the time as follows:

(STEP 1)	**Plan**	10 minutes
(STEP 2)	**Write**	25 minutes
(STEP 3)	**Revise**	5 minutes

A
> *Some people believe that children learn better when they are placed in classes with children of similar academic abilities. Others believe that children learn better when they are in classes with children representing a diverse range of academic abilities.*
>
> *Discuss both these views and give your opinion.*

Give reasons for your answer, and include any relevant examples from your own knowledge or experience.

Write at least 250 words.

....

....

....

....

....

....

....

....

....

....

....

....

....

....

....

....

....

....

....

B

> *Some people feel that the government should pay the costs of running universities so that a university education will be free for anyone who wants it.*
>
> *To what extent do you agree or disagree with this opinion?*

Give reasons for your answer, and include any relevant examples from your own knowledge or experience.

Write at least 250 words.

....

....

....

....

....

....

....

....

....

....

....

....

....

....

....

....

....

....

....

EXTRA PRACTICE

See the More Writing Practice section (page 223) in the Appendix for more Academic/General Training Task 2 topics that you can use for further writing practice.

Coherence and Cohesion 2

IELTS examiners score your writing on its coherence and cohesion. *Coherence* refers to how easily a reader can understand and follow your ideas. *Cohesion* refers to how well you connect your ideas in your writing.

PARAGRAPHING

A well-organized piece of writing has coherence. If you follow the steps for writing your essays as outlined in the first section of this book, your essay will be coherent. Your essay will have a clearly stated thesis supported by main ideas. A reader can easily understand and follow your ideas.

In a well-organized essay, the main ideas that support the thesis are developed in the body paragraphs. Each paragraph is about one idea. This idea—the main idea—is supported by supporting details. The supporting details explain the main idea with reasons or examples.

This paragraph is coherent. The ideas are easy to follow.

> Telecommuting makes things more convenient for the employee. For one thing, there is no need to spend time and money commuting between work and home. In addition, the employee can wear casual clothes most days so does not have to spend a lot of time and money shopping for work clothes. Finally, working at home means the employee has more time to devote to family responsibilities such as cooking, cleaning, and child care.

The first sentence clearly states the main idea—that telecommuting is convenient for employees. Each of the following sentences, the supporting statements, provides an example of how telecommuting is convenient. It is easy for the reader to follow the writer's ideas.

This paragraph is also coherent. The ideas are easy to follow.

> The staff at your hotel provided us with excellent service. The front desk clerk greeted us cheerfully and patiently answered all our questions. When we realized that our room was too small, we were moved to a larger one at no extra charge. And when we asked for more towels, they were brought to our room right away.

The first sentence clearly states the main idea—that the hotel staff provided excellent service. Each of the following sentences, the supporting statements, provides an example of that excellent service. It is easy for the reader to follow the writer's ideas.

PRACTICE 1

Read the following paragraphs. Underline the main idea in each paragraph. Cross out the sentence that does not support the main idea.

1 Far from being a sort of cruel jail for wild animals, zoos actually play an important role in animal conservation. Modern zoos keep their animals in large enclosures that resemble the natural habitat. Zoos give people the opportunity to see animals up close and learn about their habits and needs. This helps people feel a connection with animals and helps them understand the importance of preserving wild habitat. It makes people more interested in supporting conservation efforts.

2 The most important reason why I chose to move to this neighborhood is its convenient location. It is close to my job, so I can walk to work when the weather is nice. There are two small grocery stores nearby, and the mall is just a short subway ride away. Most of the houses are affordable, although a few are a bit expensive. There is a gym one block from my house, which makes it very easy to get my daily exercise.

3 Spending too much time on the Internet can have a bad effect on children's health. Children need a lot of physical exercise to stay healthy. When they spend a lot of time online, however, they don't get physical exercise. Parents should encourage their children to turn off the computer and spend time outside playing physically active games. Children can easily find information on the Internet that is not suitable for their young minds.

4 I can recommend several interesting things for you to do during your visit to this city. This city is famous for its pleasant climate. You won't want to miss a visit to the shopping district since our city is so famous for its stores. City Park is near there, has a beautiful garden, and is a nice place for a walk on a sunny day. I think you would also enjoy the history museum as it explains a lot of interesting facts about the city and region.

5 The price of corn dropped steadily from 2012 to 2015. It fell from just over $4.00 in 2012 to exactly $4.00 a bushel in 2013. In 2014 there was another slight drop, to around $3.50, and it dropped again, to around $3.00 a bushel in 2015. The price of wheat rose slightly in 2012.

PRACTICE 2

Choose the best main idea to complete each paragraph.

1 .... First, you have to plan your meals. Then, you have to shop for the ingredients and cook. This takes time and effort. When you eat at a restaurant, on the other hand, all you have to do is choose your restaurant and then go there.

A Many people feel that cooking at home is inconvenient.
B There are a lot of people who don't know how to cook.
C Many families these days eat most of their meals at restaurants.
D Restaurants have become very popular places to eat for several reasons.

2 .... First, there were no batteries even though the box clearly stated, "Batteries included." Also, the surface was scratched in several places. On top of that, there was a large dent on the side.

A I saw that a number of items were missing when I opened the package.

B The product is not the same size or color as the one that I ordered.

C When I removed the product from the box, I discovered several problems.

D I will not buy any products from your company in the future.

3 .... More people would be able to live closer to the center of their activities. More people would be able to walk or use public transportation to get to work, go shopping, or go out for an evening with friends. Then, fewer people would need to drive cars on a regular basis and the streets would be emptier.

A Many city residents find that life without a car is not only inexpensive but also convenient.

B The construction of more apartments in downtown areas would do a lot to relieve traffic congestion.

C Modern people have busy lives filled with a variety of work and leisure activities.

D Residential neighborhoods in downtown areas are popular places to live despite their high cost.

4 .... We don't need a large house as it will just be my wife and myself. We would, however, like to be as close to the beach as possible. Also, we like to cook, so we would want a place with a nice kitchen. We would also like to be in a quiet neighborhood if possible. We would need the house for two weeks in August.

A The last time I took a vacation was almost two years ago.

B We always spend our summer vacation at the beach.

C I am looking to buy a house close to where I work.

D I hope you can help us find a suitable house to rent for our vacation.

5 .... The driver of a car needs to keep all his attention on the road, but a phone conversation distracts him from this. Even if he is using a hands-free device, the conversation itself distracts the driver's attention from the road and the traffic around him. This endangers not only the driver and his passengers but other people on the road as well.

A These days, many people are accustomed to using a cell phone while driving.

B Traffic accidents are a growing problem on our busy highways.

C It is a very dangerous habit to use a cell phone while driving.

D Some people find it convenient to use a cell phone while driving.

PRONOUNS

Pronouns help you achieve cohesion in your writing. Using pronouns in place of nouns links ideas and avoids repeating the noun.

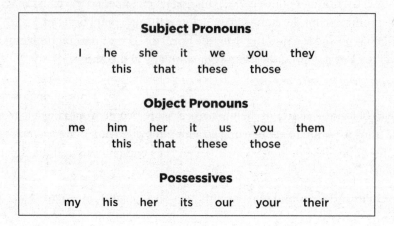

Look at these examples.

> Patricia moved to Brasilia because she got a job there.

In this sentence, the pronoun *she* is used to avoid repeating the name *Patricia*. *She* means *Patricia*.

The noun that a pronoun replaces is called the antecedent. In the above example, *Patricia* is the antecedent for the pronoun *she*.

> Patricia loves her new job. It allows her to meet a lot of new people.

In this sentence, *job* is the antecedent for *it*.

PRACTICE 3

Read the following paragraphs. Draw an arrow from each of the underlined pronouns to its antecedent.

Zoos provide scientists with many important opportunities for research. For example, **1** they give scientists the chance to closely observe animal behavior. While it is true that an animal's behavior in the zoo is not exactly the same as **2** it is in the wild, there is still a lot scientists can learn. **3** They can find out, for example, about an animal's eating habits and nesting habits. **4** They can learn about how an animal responds to stressful situations. These are just a few examples of some things scientists can learn from zoo animals.

The most important public service any city can offer **5** its citizens is a public library. **6** It is a place that serves everybody's interests and needs. At a library, people can find entertaining books to read. **7** They can do research for school or look for a job. **8** They can find interesting movies to watch. No matter how old a person is or what **9** his interests are, **10** he can always find something interesting and useful at a public library. **11** Its doors are open to everyone.

Although I enjoy my new job, I miss some things about my old office. **12** <u>It</u> was a very friendly place to work. My colleagues were always kind and helpful, and I really miss **13** <u>them</u> now. **14** <u>They</u> gave me a farewell party on my last day of work. **15** <u>It</u> was a lot of fun. I hope the people at my new office will be friendly, too.

PRACTICE 4

Read the following paragraphs. Replace each underlined word with an appropriate pronoun.

Restaurant meals have several disadvantages. In the first place, **1** <u>restaurant meals</u> are more expensive than home-cooked meals. In addition, restaurant portions tend to be big, which makes **2** <u>restaurant portions</u> higher in calories. Restaurant chefs often use rich sauces in their cooking. These sauces may be delicious, but **3** <u>the sauces</u> are also often high in calories and fat.

There are several reasons why I have decided to sell my car. For one thing, **4** <u>my car</u> is old and frequently needs repairs. In addition, **5** <u>my car's</u> tires need to be replaced. But the main reason is that I don't use **6** <u>my car</u> very much anymore because I take the bus to work most of the time.

Some parents choose to send **7** <u>some parents'</u> children to school when **8** <u>the children</u> are as young as three or four years old. Other parents feel that **9** <u>other parents'</u> children aren't ready for school at such an early age. The fact is that not all children are the same. Different children have different needs.

I would like to invite you to come see my new house. I know you will really like **10** <u>my new house</u>. I have decorated **11** <u>my new house</u> very nicely with new furniture and paint. There is also a big garden filled with beautiful flowers and I know you will enjoy seeing **12** <u>the flowers</u>.

If it is not clear what the antecedent is, then you should not use a pronoun even if it means repeating words.

Look at this example.

> I rode my bike into a car but, fortunately, it wasn't damaged.

What was damaged? The bike or the car? It isn't clear which one the pronoun *it* refers to. The sentence would be clearer without a pronoun.

> I rode my bike into a car but, fortunately, the bike wasn't damaged.

Look at this example.

> Tom told John that he had been chosen to receive a scholarship.

Who was chosen to receive a scholarship? Tom or John? It isn't clear which person the pronoun *he* refers to. This sentence would also be clearer without a pronoun.

> Tom told John that John had been chosen to receive a scholarship.

PRACTICE 5

Choose the best words to complete the following paragraph.

Librarians are trained to offer their patrons a variety of services. **1** They/Patrons may come to the library looking for print materials such as books or magazines, or **2** they/patrons may need to use the Internet for research. **3** They/Patrons might want to borrow a movie or listen to a recorded book. **4** They/Librarians know that even though information is available on the Internet, many of **5** them/their patrons are also interested in reading books and magazines. **6** They/Patrons will let the librarian know what type of material **7** they/patrons are looking for, and the librarian will offer suggestions and advice.

TRANSITION WORDS AND PHRASES

Transition words and phrases achieve cohesion by linking ideas within and between sentences and paragraphs. Transition words and phrases show relationships between ideas such as sequence, cause and effect, comparison and contrast, added information, and examples.

Sequence

Some transition words and phrases show time sequence.

first	after	finally
second	prior to	in the meantime
next	previously	at the same time
then	while	
before	meanwhile	

These words and phrases are usually used at the beginning of a sentence or clause.

First, you should figure out how much you can afford to pay for rent.

Next, you should look at real estate ads to find apartments in your price range.

You should find out some things about the neighborhood before you sign a lease.

You can ask the landlord questions while he is showing you the apartment.

PRACTICE 6

Complete the paragraphs with the transition words and phrases provided. Use capital letters where appropriate.

We had an excellent experience at your restaurant last night. **1** ...., the waiter seated us at a very comfortable table. **2** ...., he brought us our menus right away. **3** .... we ordered, we didn't have to wait long for our meal. We left a large tip for the waiter **4** .... we went home.

before	after	first	then

Here are some tips for your first day at a new job. **5** ...., you should make sure you arrive on time or even a little bit early. **6** ...., look for your supervisor to let him or her know you are there. **7** .... you start your duties, it is a good idea to introduce yourself to everyone in the office. Remember, it may take you a little while to learn the office routines. Don't worry, after a few days, everything will become familiar, but **8** ...., you should ask your colleagues to explain things to you.

first	in the meantime	next	before

PRACTICE 7

Complete the paragraph with your own ideas. Use sequence transition words and phrases to link your ideas. Write at least four sentences.

I had a very interesting day yesterday. ....

....

....

....

....

....

....

....

Cause and Effect

Some transition words and phrases show a cause and effect relationship between ideas. In a cause and effect relationship, one action (the cause) makes another action happen (the effect).

These words and phrases introduce the **cause**.

since	because	because of	due to	as

I always eat at restaurants <u>because</u> I dislike cooking.
    effect   *cause*

<u>Since</u> the weather was so bad, we cancelled our plans.
       cause   *effect*

These words and phrases introduce the **effect**.

so   thus   therefore   consequently
for this reason   as a consequence

I dislike cooking, <u>so</u> I always eat at restaurants.
    cause   *effect*

The weather was bad. <u>For this reason</u>, we canceled our plans.
    cause   *effect*

Most of these words and phrases are used at the beginning of a sentence or clause.

Drivers should not use cell phones <u>because</u> they are distracting.

It is dangerous to talk on the phone while driving. <u>Therefore</u>, it should be illegal to use a cell phone while driving.

<u>Since</u> restaurant meals are expensive, it is better for the family budget to eat at home.

Many people are too busy to care for their elderly relatives at home. <u>Consequently</u>, there is a growing need for nursing homes.

Because of and *due to* are followed by a noun or gerund.

People usually gain weight <u>because of</u> lack of exercise.

Some people don't have time to exercise <u>because of</u> working long hours.

<u>Due to</u> the increase in prices, sales went down.

PRACTICE 8

Rewrite each pair of sentences, linking the ideas with the transition word or phrase provided.

1   **Effect:**   It is easy to stay informed about current events.
    Cause: The Internet provides us with instant access to news.

    (since)

    ....

    ....

2   **Cause:**   The Grand Hotel has comfortable rooms at reasonable rates.
    Effect: I always stay there when I'm in town.

    (so)

    ....

    ....

3   **Cause:**   Many websites contain information that isn't suitable for children.
    Effect: Parents should control how their children use the Internet.

    (therefore)

    ....

    ....

4   **Effect:**   Many farmers lost their crops.
    Cause: There was a severe drought in that region.

    (because)

    ....

    ....

5   **Cause:**   The rents in this district are very high.
    Effect: Many people can't afford to live here.

    (for this reason)

    ....

    ....

PRACTICE 9

In each pair of sentences, identify which is the cause and which is the effect. Rewrite the sentences, linking the ideas with a transition word or phrase. Then, rewrite the sentences again using a different transition word. Use pronouns as appropriate.

Example

A major blizzard struck the region yesterday. (cause)
There were numerous accidents on the highway. (effect)

A major blizzard struck the region yesterday. As a result, there were
numerous accidents on the highway.

The numerous accidents on the highway yesterday were due to the major
blizzard that struck the region.

1   **A** Smoking is popular among teenagers.
     B Teenagers don't understand the health consequences of smoking.

     ....
     ....

     ....
     ....

2   **A** In most modern families, both parents work full time.
     B Parents don't have enough opportunities to spend quality time with their children.

     ....
     ....

     ....
     ....

3 **A** I recently inherited a large amount of money.
    B I have decided to take a trip around the world.

....

....

....

....

4 **A** Many people think the zoos are cruel places.
    B Zoo animals are kept locked up in cages.

....

....

....

....

5 **A** I would like to find a new job as soon as possible.
    B My current job is boring, and the salary is low.

....

....

....

....

Comparison and Contrast

Some transition words and phrases compare or contrast ideas. When you compare ideas, you show how they are similar. When you contrast ideas, you show how they are different.

These words and phrases **compare** ideas.

likewise	like	similarly	in the same way
	just as	too	also

These words and phrases **contrast** ideas.

unlike	however	but	on the other hand
while	yet	although	even though
conversely	nevertheless	in contrast to	

Most of these words and phrases are used at the beginning of a sentence or clause.

Dogs need to be walked and played with daily. <u>Likewise</u>, pet parrots need frequent attention from their owners.

Greece is a popular winter vacation spot for Europeans. <u>Similarly</u>, many Americans spend their winter vacations in the Caribbean.

<u>While</u> some people don't like the cold winter weather, other people thoroughly enjoy it.

Cars are expensive and cause pollution, <u>yet</u> many people drive them.

However and *on the other hand* can follow the subject. In this case, they are set off by commas.

Big cities are crowded and noisy. Small towns, <u>on the other hand</u>, are peaceful and quiet.

Like and *unlike* are followed by a noun or a gerund.

<u>Like</u> overeating, lack of exercise can lead to weight gain.

<u>Like</u> most people, I enjoy relaxing at home on weekends.

<u>Unlike buses</u>, subways are not affected by traffic jams.

PRACTICE 10

Choose the correct word to complete each sentence.

1   Buses can carry many passengers at one time, ... cars can only
                                                                    (also/while)
    carry a few.

2   Taking a walk every day can help you stay strong and healthy. ....,
                                                                        (Likewise/Nevertheless)
    bike riding is a good way to get exercise.

3   .... cities, small towns generally offer limited job opportunities.
       (Like/Unlike)

4   Many people find small towns boring. ...., others enjoy a small town's
                                               (Similarly/However)
    slow pace of life.

5   .... beach resorts, lakeside resorts offer families the opportunity to
       (Like/Unlike)
    enjoy all kinds of water sports.

PRACTICE 11

Look at the following pairs of sentences. Decide if the relationship between the ideas is one of comparison or contrast. Rewrite the sentences, linking the ideas with a transition word or phrase. Then, rewrite the sentences again using a different transition word.

1   Exercise is important for maintaining health.
    Many people don't exercise regularly.

    ....

    ....

    ....

    ....

2   Some people feel that it is cruel to keep animals in zoos.
Other people believe that zoos provide important opportunities for research and education.

....

....

....

....

3   The price of milk rose sharply in 2020.
There was a significant increase in the price of bread in 2020.

....

....

....

....

4   Many adults struggle with weight gain.
Obesity is a problem for many children.

....

....

....

....

5   Children in small families get a lot of adult attention.
Children in large families may not get all the adult attention they need.

....

....

....

....

Adding Information

Some transition words and phrases connect ideas by adding information.

in addition	additionally	moreover	furthermore	too
also	as well	what's more	besides	

Most of these words and phrases are used at the beginning of a sentence or a clause.

> Country life is more quiet and peaceful than city life. <u>In addition</u>, it is better for your health.

> The Internet makes it easy to stay in touch with friends and relatives. <u>Furthermore</u>, it provides instant access to news and information.

Also can be used at either the beginning or end of a sentence or clause, or it can precede the verb. *Too* and *as well* are generally used at the end of the clause.

> The best way to manage weight is to exercise regularly. You should pay attention to your diet <u>as well</u>.

> The best way to manage weight is to exercise regularly. You should <u>also</u> pay attention to your diet.

PRACTICE 12

Rewrite each pair of sentences, linking the ideas with the transition word or phrase provided.

1   Telecommuting is very convenient for employees.
    It has advantages for employers.

    (as well)

    ....

    ....

2   That store has a really nice selection of merchandise.
    The staff is very helpful and courteous.

    (furthermore)

    ....

    ....

3   Meals cooked at home are less expensive than restaurant meals.
They are usually more nutritious.

(also)

....

....

4   Electric cars don't cause air pollution.
They are easy and inexpensive to maintain.

(in addition)

....

....

5   This neighborhood has many houses that are affordably priced.
It is conveniently located close to stores and public transportation.

(moreover)

....

....

PRACTICE 13

Rewrite the following pairs of sentences, linking the ideas with a transition word or phrase. Then, rewrite the sentences again using a different transition word. Use pronouns as appropriate.

1   Too many private cars on the roads lead to frequent traffic jams.
Too many private cars on the roads create high levels of air pollution.

....

....

....

....

2   City life is stressful because of the crowds and noise.
High levels of crime make cities very dangerous.

....

....

....

....

3   Zoos provide scientists with many opportunities for research.
Zoos allow the general public to learn about the habits of wild animals.

....

....

....

....

4   If you wait until you are 30 to get married, you will have a better idea of the type of person you want to marry.
You will have had more time to establish yourself in your profession.

....

....

....

....

5   Telecommuting means that people don't have to spend time and money traveling between work and home.
Telecommuting gives people more time to devote to family responsibilities such as cooking, cleaning, and child care.

....

....

....

....

Examples

Some transition words and phrases introduce examples of ideas.

for example	for instance	for one thing	specifically
such as	including	to illustrate	namely

Most of these words and phrases are used at the beginning of a sentence or clause.

> Life in the country is better for children. <u>For one thing</u>, the air and water are cleaner.

> Parents send their children to preschool for a variety of reasons. <u>For instance</u>, they may want their children to learn to socialize with others.

> There are many benefits to having a pet. <u>For example</u>, a pet provides constant companionship.

Such as and *including* may follow the word they explain.

> Young people often want to go into high-paying professions <u>such as</u> doctor, lawyer, or business executive.

> City life has many advantages <u>including</u> access to the best educational opportunities.

PRACTICE 14

Match each sentence or phrase in column A with a sentence or phrase in Column B. Add capital letters and periods as appropriate. You will not use all the choices.

A	B
1 There are several advantages to living in this neighborhood	including lack of public transportation and poorly designed roads
2 Zoos provide the public with important educational opportunities	such as high-speed trains and long-distance buses
3 Traffic problems in cities are due to a number of factors	for one thing, it is close to two bus routes
4 Visitors to a zoo can enjoy a variety of fun activities	such as seeing the animals, talking with scientists, and visiting the gift shop
5 People avoid using public transportation for a variety of reasons	for example, they can teach people about the importance of preserving native habitat
	for instance, they feed the animals a special diet
	for one thing, they may feel that train and bus schedules are not convenient

PRACTICE 15

Complete the following sentences with your own ideas.

1 Life in the city is much more interesting than life in the country. For one

   thing, ...

   ....

2 There are many advantages to country life. For example, ...

   ....

3 I am looking for a new place to live because there are too many problems

   with my current apartment. For instance, ...

   ....

4 I would like to spend my vacation at a resort that offers a variety of

   interesting activities such as ....

   ....

5 There are a number of reasons why people use public transportation,

   including ....

   ....

Lexical Resource

3

Lexical resource refers to the vocabulary you use in your writing. IELTS examiners want you to use a range of vocabulary and use it correctly. They also expect you to spell the words correctly.

WORD FAMILIES

Word families are groups of words that are related to each other by meaning. Each word in a word family corresponds to a certain part of speech.

Noun	Verb	Adjective	Adverb
difference	differ	different	differently

When you learn a new word, you learn the other words in its word family, too. When you write, use the correct part of speech.

Examples

The <u>difference</u> between our opinions is not so great. (noun as subject)

I explained the <u>difference</u> between your opinion and mine. (noun as object of the verb)

Our opinions <u>differ</u>. (verb)

Our opinions seem <u>different</u>. (adjective after a linking verb)

We have <u>different</u> opinions on this subject. (adjective before a noun)

We think <u>differently</u> on this subject. (adverb)

Parts of Speech

A **noun** may be used as the subject of a sentence or clause, or as the object of a verb or preposition.

A **verb** shows an action.

An **adjective** describes a noun. It comes before the noun it describes or after a linking verb.

An **adverb** describes a verb or an adjective. An adverb of manner (ends with *-ly*) describes how an action is performed.

A word family may have more than one word per part of speech.

Noun	Noun	Verb	Adjective	Adverb
instruction	instructor	instruct	instructive	instructively

PRACTICE 1

Write the part of speech under the underlined words.

1   We cannot deny the importance of physical education.

2   Enrollment at the academy increased significantly last semester.

3   Most people recognize that smoking is dangerous to the health.

4   I plan to organize a formal party so that we can celebrate the event.

5   Foreign language study should be a requirement in primary schools because young children learn languages easily.

The members of a word family all have the same root word. The suffix determines the part of speech.

Common Suffixes

NOUNS

Suffix	Examples
-age	shortage, shrinkage
-al	referral, approval
-ance/-ence	significance, difference
-ant/-ent	applicant, resident
-acy/-cy	privacy, bankruptcy
-dom	freedom, boredom
-er/-or	teacher, actor
-hood	adulthood, neighborhood
-ism	idealism, journalism
-ity/-ty	ability, safety
-ment	treatment, investment
-ness	darkness, kindness
-ship	hardship, leadership
-tion/-sion/-cion	attention, suspension, suspicion

VERBS

Suffix	Examples
-ate	regulate, dominate
-en	sweeten, straighten
-ify/-fy	notify, satisfy
-ize	apologize, organize

ADJECTIVES

Suffix	Examples
-able/-ible	reasonable, accessible
-al	traditional, special
-ant/-ent	resistant, excellent
-ful	colorful, powerful
-ic	public, scientific
-ive	active, creative
-less	fearless, careless
-ory	satisfactory, contradictory
-ous	numerous, cautious
-y	healthy, cloudy

ADVERBS

An adverb of manner is formed by adding -ly to an adjective.

Adjective	Adverb
endless	endlessly
helpful	helpfully
patient	patiently
punctual	punctually
continuous	continuously
creative	creatively
expectant	expectantly

PRACTICE 2

Choose the correct word to complete each sentence.

Noun	Verb	Adjective	Adverb
competition	compete	competitive	competitively

1   In physical education classes, children learn to .... in a healthy way.

2   Team sports are very ....

3   .... in the job market can make it difficult for people to find employment even if they are highly qualified.

4   These products sold quickly because they were .... priced.

Noun	Verb	Adjective	Adverb
selection	select	selective	selectively

5   Some private schools are quite .... about the students they admit.

6   University students can .... which courses they want to take each semester.

7   I like shopping at this store because they have a wide .... of merchandise.

8   Eat desserts .... if you want to avoid weight problems.

Noun	Verb	Adjective	Adverb
decision	decide	decisive	decisively

9   Some parents make the .... to send their children to school at an early age.

10   Many families .... to care for their elderly parents at home.

11   Once you have a plan, act .... to carry it out.

12   A .... person does not hesitate to act.

Noun	Verb	Adjective	Adverb
persistence	persist	persistent	persistently

13   .... people often achieve their goals.

14   .... got me the job I wanted.

15   I finally got a refund after I .... complained to the manager.

16   A child's learning problems will .... if they are not dealt with early on.

Noun	Adjective	Adverb
reluctance	reluctant	reluctantly

17 Some people give up smoking ....

18 I was .... to complain about the poor service.

19 The .... to follow a regular exercise plan can make weight loss very difficult.

Noun	Verb	Adjective	Adverb
beauty	beautify	beautiful	beautifully

20 We will .... the city by planting trees along the street.

21 The entire cast performed the play ....

22 I know that the .... of this place will impress you.

23 We had a .... view from our room.

Noun	Verb	Adjective	Adverb
authority	authorize	authoritative	authoritatively

24 I can write .... about this issue since I have studied it in depth.

25 Dr. Smith is a leading .... on this subject.

26 This tour book is the .... guide to this region of the country.

27 Your professor will have to .... your absence from class on exam day.

Noun	Adjective	Adverb
efficiency	efficient	efficiently

28 I appreciate the .... of the hotel staff.

29 Spending on heating fuel has gone down because of more .... heating systems.

30 Nursing homes can care for patients more ....

PRACTICE 3

Complete the word families. Use a dictionary as needed.

Noun	Verb	Adjective	Adverb
	demonstrate		
			popularly
intensity			
	███████	able	
	recognize		
	depend		
emotion	███████		
		wide	

PRACTICE 4

Choose a word from each of the word families in Practice 3 above and use it in a sentence.

1 ....
....

2 ....
....

3 ....
....

4 ....
....

5 ....
....

6 ....
....

7 ....

....

8 ....

....

SYNONYMS

Synonyms are words with the same or similar meanings. When you write, use synonyms to avoid repetition. Synonyms may be single words or phrases.

Word	Synonyms
car	automobile, vehicle, form of transportation
house	residence, home, place to live, shelter

TIP

Synonyms don't always have the exact same meaning. Some may be more specific and others more general in meaning.

PRACTICE 5

Choose the synonyms for each word from the list below and write them on the lines. There is more than one synonym for each word. Use a dictionary as needed.

Word

1	choose	....
2	cold	....
3	concentrate	....
4	delicious	....
5	eat	....
6	fall	....
7	fast	....
8	get	....
9	good	....
10	neat	....
11	quiet	....
12	rise	....
13	tell	....

Synonyms

acquire	have a meal
breakfast	increase
calm	inform
chilly	obtain
clean	pay attention to
climb	peaceful
decent	pick
decrease	quick
delectable	rapid
dine	scrumptious
drop	select
excellent	speedy
explain	tasty
focus on	tidy
frosty	wintry
go down	wonderful
go up	

PRACTICE 6

Rewrite the paragraphs by replacing the underlined words with synonyms.

A   The weather in Springfield was very cold last winter. Temperatures fell in December, and they **1** <u>fell</u> again in January. Because of the **2** <u>cold</u> weather, schools were closed for three days. Temperatures rose slightly in February and March. In April they continued to **3** <u>rise</u>.

....

....

....

....

....

....

....

B   I recommend that you eat at the Three Feathers Restaurant during your stay in the city. I always have a good experience when I **4** <u>eat</u> there. It is a very good restaurant. The food is **5** <u>good,</u> and the service is **6** <u>good</u>. The menu is long and there are many delicious dishes to choose from. Sometimes it is hard to know what to **7** <u>choose</u> because everything looks so **8** <u>delicious</u>.

....

....

....

....

....

....

....

C Different people need different kinds of study conditions. For example, I study best in a quiet environment. Noise really bothers me, and I can't study well unless I am in a **9** <u>quiet</u> place. Neatness is also important to me because a messy room distracts me. I really need to study in a **10** <u>neat</u> place in order to be able to concentrate on my work.

....

....

....

....

....

....

....

....

SPELLING

There is no easy way to learn English spelling. You just have to become familiar with the way words are spelled.

There are some things you can do to improve your spelling. You should know and follow spelling rules for adding endings to words. You can also study lists of commonly confused and commonly misspelled words.

Adding Word Endings

Add -s to nouns to make them plural and to present tense verbs to form the third person singular.

book—books	street—streets
work—works	read—reads

NOTE: When a word ends in -s, -z, -ch, -x, or -sh, add -es.

crash—crashes	fix—fixes
buzz—buzzes	catch—catches

Add -ed to regular verbs to form the past tense.

talk—talked	explain—explained

NOTE: When a word ends in -e, add -d only.

recognize—recognized	believe—believed

Add -er and -est to form comparative and superlative adjectives.

old—older—oldest	clean—cleaner—cleanest

NOTE: When a word ends in -e, add -r or -st only.

wide—wider—widest	nice—nicer—nicest

TIP

The best way to become a good speller is to read a lot. The more you see words on the page, the more you will become familiar with how they look.

Words that end in a consonant + *y*. Change the *y* to *ie* before adding the ending. This rule does not apply to words that end in a vowel + *y*.

city—cities		boy—boys
hurry—hurries	BUT	stay—stays
carry—carries		annoy—annoys
tasty—tastier		gray—grayer
starry—starriest		coy—coyest

Words that end consonant-vowel-consonant. Double the final consonant before adding *-ed*, *-er*, or *-est*.

This rule does not apply to words where the final syllable is not stressed or to words ending in *-x*.

cram—crammed		order—ordered
omit—omitted	BUT	box—boxed
thin—thinner		fasten—fastened

PRACTICE 7

Add endings to the following words. Follow the spelling rules.

Add -*s*		Add -*ed*		Add -*er* and -*est*	
1	expect........	13	discuss........	25	strong........
2	match........	14	increase........	26	clean........
3	buzz........	15	admit........	27	dim........
4	dismiss........	16	harden........	28	wealthy........
5	decision........	17	rely........	29	cheap........
6	suffix........	18	refer........	30	hot........
7	animal........	19	help........	31	muddy........
8	entry........	20	apologize........	32	lucky........
9	essay........	21	stray........	33	big........
10	cash........	22	notify........	34	high........
11	satisfy........	23	insist........	35	dirty........
12	delay........	24	offer........	36	short........

Adverbs of Manner

Add *-ly* to adjectives to form adverbs of manner.

      rapid—rapidly   sharp—sharply

For words that end in *-y*, change the *-y* to *i*, and then add *-ly*.

      easy—easily   sleepy—sleepily

For words that end in *-le*, change the *-e* to *-y*.

      gentle—gently   simple—simply

For words that end in *-ic*, add *-ally*.

      public—publically   electronic—electronically

PRACTICE 8

Form adverbs of manner by adding -ly *to the following adjectives. Follow the spelling rules.*

1   powerful........

2   lucky........

3   terrible........

4   safe........

5   energetic........

6   reasonable........

7   traditional........

8   cautious........

9   fantastic........

10   responsible........

11   satisfactory........

TIP

Not all words that end in *-ly* are adverbs. Many are adjectives (examples: lovely, friendly, chilly), nouns (examples: monopoly, assembly), or verbs (examples: apply, comply).

Commonly Confused Words

Some words have the same or similar sound as another word, but the spelling and meaning are different. Look at these pairs of commonly confused words.

affect (verb) *to influence or touch the feelings of someone*
effect (noun) *result*

accept (verb) *to receive something*
except (prep.) *but*

ascent (noun) *rising, going up*
assent (noun) *agreement*, (verb) *to agree*

advice (noun) *guidance or recommendations*
advise (verb) *to give guidance or recommendations*

aid (noun) *assistance*, (verb) *to assist*
aide (noun) *an assistant*

desert (noun) *a dry area*
dessert (noun) *a sweet dish served at the end of a meal*

later (adj.) *the comparative form of "late"*
latter (ad.) *refers to the second of two people or things previously mentioned*

passed (verb) *past tense form of "pass"*
past (noun) *a previous time*, (adj.) *gone by in time*, (prep.) *on the far side*

sight (noun) *something seen; the ability to see*
site (noun) *location*

than (conj.) *used when making comparisons*
then (adv.) *at that time; next*

PRACTICE 9

Choose the correct word to complete each sentence.

affect	effect	accept	except

1   Sad movies always .... me.

2   The waiter was happy to .... our generous tip.

3   The bad weather has had a serious .... on agriculture.

4   There was over 75 percent enrollment during every month ....
    December.

ascent	assent	advise	advice

5 Everyone at the meeting indicated their .... to the plan.

6 He followed his doctor's .... to get more exercise.

7 The teacher might .... the parents to get extra help for their child.

8 The .... of the mountain took over six hours.

aid	aide	desert	dessert

9 Her .... answers her phone calls and takes messages.

10 We were interested to see the variety of cactus growing in the ....

11 I would like your .... in choosing a new apartment.

12 A small dish of fruit is a more healthful .... than a large slice of cake.

later	latter	passed	past

13 More tourists visited the area .... in the year.

14 She owns both a car and a bicycle. The .... is her preferred form of transportation.

15 I have vacationed in the area several times in the ....

16 He studied hard and .... all his exams.

sight	site	than	then

17 Driving a car is more convenient .... riding a bicycle.

18 They chose this .... for their new office building.

19 We ate at a restaurant, and .... we went to the movies.

20 Sunset over the ocean is a beautiful ....

TIP

Make your own
list of words that
are difficult for
you, and practice
spelling them.
Writing the
words frequently
will help you
remember how to
spell them.

Commonly Misspelled Words

Common spelling problems include words with silent letters and words with double letters.

WORDS WITH SILENT LETTERS

There are certain common consonant pairs where one of the consonants in the pair is silent.

gn (silent *n*)	assignment, campaign, design, resign
mn (silent *n*)	autumn, column, solemn
nm (silent *n*)	environment, government
sc (silent *c*)	ascend, descend, fascinate, muscle, scene, science
xc (silent *c*)	excellent, excess, excite
st (silent *t*)	castle, fasten, listen, whistle

WORDS WITH DOUBLE CONSONANTS

Words with double consonants may cause spelling problems. Here are some examples of commonly misspelled words with double consonants.

committee
common
different
disappoint
necessary
occasion
occur
opportunity
possession
possible
recommend
successful

OTHER COMMONLY MISSPELLED WORDS

Study this list of words that are commonly misspelled by test takers.

achievement	percentage
believe	receive
conference	society
definitely	temperature
familiar	their
modern	therefore
nowadays	until
opinion	

PRACTICE 10

Find and correct the spelling mistakes in the following paragraphs. Do not look at the above word list.

A   The charts show the percentag of homes that were heated with solar power in two diffrent years, as well as the reasons why people chose this method of heating there homes. Most people reported that they chose solar power because they are concerned about protecting the enviroment. Some people chose solar power because they recieved money from the goverment to help pay for the installation.

B   I am writing to tell you that I will be visiting Springfield next month. I know you are familar with that city as you have been there several times. Therefor, I hope you can reccomend some interesting things to see and do during my visit. You know I am very interested in modren art, so I would like to take the oppotunity to visit some art galleries. And I would definitly like to do some shopping, so I hope you can give me the names of some of the best stores. I would also like to know about the weather so I can decide what clothes to pack. Are the temparitures high or low at this time of year? I won't finalize my plans untill I hear from you, so please answer as soon as posible.

C   People have different ideas of what sucess is. Some beleive that it means making a lot of money. Others feel that it means the achievment of something important. In my opinon, it means finding happiness. Nowdays, people feel that they have to work long hours to make a lot of money. This makes them look successful in the eyes of soceity. However, I don't think that it is necassary to make a lot of money. Of course, money is nice, but there are other things that are more important.

D   The only way to acheive success in anything is to work hard. Natural ability isn't enough. The most talented musician has to practice a lot in order to become an exellent performer. The smartest student has to complete all assinements well and answer all test questions correctly. Even smart and talented people may fail to reach thier goals sometimes and feel disapointment. But if they keep working hard, they can become successfull. So you should lisen to your parents and teachers when they tell you to work hard. You won't regret it.

Grammatical Range and Accuracy

4

IELTS examiners want you to use a variety of grammatical forms and structures. You should use them correctly.

ARTICLES

A singular noun is usually preceded by an article. A plural or noncount noun may also be preceded by an article.

Articles		
a	an	the

Indefinite Articles: *a/an*

A and *an* precede singular nouns only. Use *a* with nouns that begin with a consonant sound. Use *an* with nouns that begin with a vowel sound.

Vowels				
a	e	i	o	u

TIP

Sometimes a word begins with a vowel but not with a vowel sound.

example: *university—I studied at a university in England.*

When the first letter of a word is a silent consonant, the word begins with a vowel sound.

example: *honor—It is an honor to meet you.*

Indefinite means that the noun does not refer to any specific thing. Look at these examples.

Example	Explanation
A cell phone is useful in emergencies.	No specific cell phone. Any cell phone is useful in emergencies.
I need an egg to make this cake.	No specific egg. Any egg will do to make the cake.

Definite Article: *the*

The can precede singular, plural, and noncount nouns. *The* is used when the noun refers to something specific. Look at these examples.

Example	Explanation
The moon was bright last night.	Only one in existence.
The park is closed after dark.	Both speaker and audience know the reference.
The prices <u>in this store</u> are very high.	A phrase in the sentence defines the noun.
<u>A machine</u> squeezes juice from oranges. <u>The machine</u> can process 100 pounds of fruit an hour.	The second mention of something in the text.

No Article

When a plural or noncount noun is indefinite, an article is not required.

Example	Explanation
Cities are often crowded.	No specific cities. Many cities are crowded.
Money is hard to get and hard to keep.	No specific money. Money in general could be described this way.

PRACTICE 1

Complete the paragraph with a, an, the *or* Ø *(to indicate no article is needed). Remember, the first mention of an item in the text is considered indefinite.*

1 .... oranges make delicious 2 .... juice. After harvesting, 3 ....

oranges are placed in 4 .... washer. 5 .... washer uses 6 .... water and

7 .... soap to clean 8 .... oranges. 9 .... soap is special food-grade

soap. Next, 10 .... oranges go to 11 .... extractor, and 12 .... extractor

squeezes 13 .... fruit.

PRACTICE 2

Write a paragraph describing the steps for washing dishes. Use as many words as you can from the lists below. Write four or five sentences. Use articles correctly.

Nouns	Verbs	Adjectives
sink	fill	warm
water	add	hot
soap	put	cold
dishes	soak	clean
sponge	scrub	dirty
rack	rinse	
towel	dry	

....

....

....

....

....

....

....

....

SUBJECT-VERB AGREEMENT

The main verb must agree with the subject of the sentence or clause. If the subject is singular, the verb must be singular. If the subject is plural, the verb must be plural.

The <u>chart</u> <u>shows</u> enrollment in different classes.
(singular subject, singular verb)

The <u>charts</u> <u>show</u> enrollment in different classes.
(plural subject, plural verb)

It is not always easy to tell whether a subject is singular or plural.

Noncount noun subjects take a singular verb.

<u>Milk</u> <u>contains</u> important nutrients.

<u>Education</u> <u>opens</u> doors to new opportunities.

<u>Money</u> <u>doesn't buy</u> happiness.

A gerund used as the subject of a sentence or clause takes a singular verb.

Smoking is bad for the health.

Sleeping provides both your body and your mind with needed rest.

Eating sweets leads to weight gain.

It is not always easy to tell what the subject is. Sometimes there is a phrase or clause between the subject and the verb.

The prices at that store are quite low.
(plural subject, plural verb)

The man who owns these houses doesn't live near here.
(singular subject, singular verb)

Tourists from all over the world visit here every year.
(plural subject, plural verb)

Some nouns look plural but are actually singular.

- Nouns that end with –ics are often singular, especially when they refer to a field of study (*physics, economics, mathematics*).
- The names of diseases are singular (*measles, rickets*).
- The noun *news* is singular.

Physics is a subject I hope to study some day.
(singular subject, singular verb)

Rickets is caused by a lack of minerals in the diet.
(singular subject, singular verb)

News travels fast.
(singular subject, singular verb)

The names of companies are singular, even if they include plural words.

National Tires has increased its prices.
(singular subject, singular verb)

Affordable Books sells used textbooks to students.
(singular subject, singular verb)

Downtown Properties manages several of the apartment buildings in this neighborhood.
(singular subject, singular verb)

Sums of money take singular verbs.

Five hundred dollars is a lot to pay for a hotel room.
(singular subject, singular verb)

Twenty dollars covers the cost of a movie ticket and a snack.
(singular subject, singular verb)

Two dollars and fifty cents pays for a bus ride across the city.
(singular subject, singular verb)

Words that begin with *every* and *no* (*everybody, everything, nobody, nothing*) take singular verbs.

> **Nobody knows** what happened.
> (singular subject, singular verb)

> **Everyone has agreed** to the proposal.
> (singular subject, singular verb)

> **Nothing stays** the same forever.
> (singular subject, singular verb)

PRACTICE 3

Choose the correct verb to complete each sentence.

1   Speedy Talk Systems (manufacture/manufactures) cell phones.

2   Most of the stores on the first floor of the mall (sell/sells) clothing.

3   I thought that two hundred dollars (was/were) a low price for these shoes.

4   All the animals at City Zoo (have/has) been well cared for.

5   Everybody (enjoy/enjoys) working at this place.

6   Bad news always (spread/spreads) quickly.

7   The view from these windows (are/is) spectacular.

8   Prices always (rise/rises) during the tourist season.

9   Eating at restaurants (cost/costs) more than eating at home.

10   Pink sand (cover/covers) the beaches of the island.

11   All of the people in this class (are/is) first-year students.

12   Chocolate (come/comes) from cacao beans.

13   Everything (seem/seems) to happen at once.

14   Nobody (were/was) at the office last Saturday.

15   Ten dollars (don't/doesn't) buy much these days.

16   Regular exercise (help/helps) you stay healthy.

17   Measles (are/is) an infectious disease.

18   The rents in this city (have/has) risen a lot in the past year.

19   Ice cream (were/was) my favorite dessert when I was young.

20   Collecting stamps (are/is) a hobby of mine.

REAL FUTURE CONDITIONALS

A conditional sentence describes an action or situation that is necessary (the condition) in order for another action or situation to occur (the result).

A conditional sentence is made up of two clauses—an *if* clause, or condition, and a main clause, or result.

If smoking is banned in public places, the air will be cleaner .
              condition   result

The order of the clauses can be reversed without changing the meaning of the sentence. When the main clause is first, no comma is used between the clauses.

The air will be cleaner if smoking is banned in public places.
           result   condition

A conditional can be either real or unreal. Real conditionals are about things that are really true or that can really happen. Real future conditionals are about things that can really happen in the future.

In a real future conditional sentence

- The verb in the main clause is in the future tense.
- The verb in the *if* clause is in the present tense.

Sam will have a lot of expenses if he buys a new house.
    future verb   present verb

The sentence above is a real future conditional. It is really possible that Sam will buy a new house in the future. If he does, the result will be that he will have a lot of expenses.

If Sam doesn't get the job, he won't buy a new house.
     present verb   future verb

The sentence above is also a real future conditional. It is really possible that Sam won't get the job. If he doesn't get the job, the result will be that he won't buy a house.

PRACTICE 4

Complete the paragraphs with the correct form of the verb in parentheses.

A   In my opinion, talking on a cell phone while driving is dangerous. Therefore, it should be illegal for drivers to use cell phones. If it **1** .... (be) illegal, then people **2** .... (have) to stop this dangerous habit. If some people **3** .... (continue) to use cell phones while driving, they **4** .... (have) to pay a fine. Nobody likes to pay a fine. I also think there should be education about the risks of this habit. People **5** .... (stop) using cell phones while driving if they **6** .... (understand) how dangerous it is.

B   I think parents should send their children to preschool. There are many advantages to

it. If a child **7** .... (start) school young, she **8** .... (learn)

to socialize with other children. She **9** .... (not have) this opportunity

if she **10** .... (stay) at home all day. Also, she **11** ....

(learn) many important skills if she **12** .... (go) to preschool. She will

listen to stories, draw pictures, and have fun with blocks and other toys. These activities

aren't just games. They help the child's brain develop. If a child **13** ....

(do) these things in school every day, it **14** .... (help) her later when it's

time to learn to read and write.

UNREAL CONDITIONALS

Unreal conditionals are about things that aren't real or can't really happen.

If Mary had a better job, she would earn more money.
     condition   result

The sentence above is a present unreal conditional. The truth is that Mary doesn't have a
better job and she doesn't earn more money.

Mary would have more job opportunities if she lived in the city.
          result   condition

The sentence above is also a present unreal conditional. The truth is that Mary doesn't live
in the city and she doesn't have more job opportunities.

A **present unreal conditional** is about something that is not true in the present.

- The verb in the *if* clause is in the past tense.
- The verb in the main clause uses *would* + base form.

If Mary earned more money, she would buy a bigger car.
     past tense verb   would + base form

In a present unreal conditional sentence, the correct form of the verb *be* is always *were*, no
matter what the subject is.

If Mary were rich, she would buy many things.

PRACTICE 5

Complete the paragraph with the correct form of the verb in parentheses.

I live in a small town. If I **1** .... (live) in a city, I **2** .... (have)

many more opportunities. For example, cities have museums. If I **3** .... (be)

able to go to museums frequently, I **4** .... (learn) a lot about history, science,

and art. I also **5** .... (have) the chance to meet a wider variety of people if I

6 .... (live) in a city. In general, my life **7** .... (be) a lot more

interesting if I **8** .... (have) a home in the city.

A **past unreal conditional** is about something that wasn't true in the past.

- The verb in the *if* clause is in the past perfect tense.
- The verb in the main clause uses *would* + *have* + past participle.

If Mary <u>had gotten</u> up early this morning, she <u>would have gotten</u> here on time.

      past perfect   would + have +

         verb   past participle

The sentence above is a past unreal conditional. The truth is that Mary didn't get up early this morning and didn't get here on time.

Mary <u>would have passed</u> the test if she <u>had studied</u> more last weekend.

      would + have +   past perfect

      past participle   verb

The sentence above is also a past unreal conditional. The truth is that Mary didn't study enough last weekend and didn't pass the test.

PRACTICE 6

Complete the paragraph with the correct form of the verb in parentheses.

I didn't make my hotel reservation early. If I **1** .... (make) my reservation early, they **2** .... (give) me a better room. As it was, the room they gave me was small, and the bed was lumpy. If the bed **3** .... (be) more comfortable, I **4** .... (sleep) better. Since I didn't sleep well, I got up late. I **5** .... (have) time for breakfast if I **6** .... (get) up early. But, I didn't have time for breakfast, and I was hungry all morning. Next time, I will make my hotel reservation early.

PRACTICE 7

Complete the real and unreal conditionals with your own ideas.

1   If you smoke, ...

2   More people will use public transportation if ....

3   There would be fewer traffic problems in cities if ....

4   If I lived in a bigger apartment, ...

5   I would have paid the rent on time if ....

6   If I had grown up in a city/small town, ...

ADJECTIVE CLAUSES WITH SUBJECT RELATIVE PRONOUNS

An adjective clause describes or identifies a noun in the main clause.

People <u>who work at home</u> don't have to spend time commuting.
        adjective clause

The sentence above is made up of a main clause (*People don't have to spend time commuting*) and an adjective clause (*who work at home*). The adjective clause identifies the noun *people*. It tells us which people we are talking about.

An adjective clause immediately follows the **antecedent**. The antecedent is the noun that the clause describes.

<u>Restaurants</u> <u>that serve breakfast</u> open early.
antecedent   *adjective*
                clause

An adjective clause can be **restrictive** or **nonrestrictive**.

A restrictive clause provides information that is necessary to identify the noun. All of the above examples are restrictive clauses.

A nonrestrictive clause provides extra information that is not necessary to identify the noun.

<u>Dr. Jones,</u> <u>who is the director of the zoo,</u> is committed to caring for the animals.
antecedent   *adjective*
                clause

You could remove a nonrestrictive clause from a sentence and the identity of the noun would still be clear. Nonrestrictive clauses are set off with commas.

An adjective clause begins with a **relative pronoun** such as *who, whom, whose, that,* or *which.*

Children <u>who</u> go to preschool learn to socialize with other children.
     relative
     pronoun

The relative pronoun can be the subject or object of the clause. In all the examples above, the relative pronoun is the subject of the adjective clause.

The correct relative pronoun to use depends on whether the antecedent is a person, a thing, or something that possesses, and whether the clause is restrictive or nonrestrictive. In some cases, you have more than one choice.

Relative Pronouns—Subject

	Restrictive	Nonrestrictive
People	who that	who
Things	which that	which
Possessives	whose	whose

PRACTICE 8

Underline the adjective clause and circle the relative pronoun in each sentence. Identify each clause as restrictive or nonrestrictive.

1   The waiter who served us was very polite.

....

2   Houses that are well insulated burn less heating fuel.

....

3   My apartment, which is on the top floor, gets a lot of sunlight.

....

4   School is fun for children whose teachers provide them with interesting activities.

....

5   The front desk clerk, who was very busy at the time, forgot to give me my room key.

....

6   Public transportation is convenient for commuters who travel during rush hour.

....

7   You should avoid eating snacks that are high in fat and sugar.

....

8   The local zoo, which is open 365 days a year, is always crowded on holidays.

....

PRACTICE 9

Choose the correct relative pronouns to complete the paragraph.

People 1 .... (who/whose) elderly parents are unable to care for themselves have a difficult choice to make. Will they care for their parents at home? Or will they put their parents in the hands of nursing home workers 2 .... (who/which) can provide them with care 24 hours a day? People 3 .... (who/which) have full-time jobs often don't have the time or energy to provide the needed care. On the other hand, nursing homes can be quite expensive, and nursing homes 4 .... (who/which) charge less may not provide excellent care. It is a difficult decision 5 .... (whose/that) requires a lot of thought and discussion. If a family decides to use a nursing home, they should choose a home 6 .... (that/ whose) is pleasant, comfortable, and convenient to visit. And they should visit frequently. Nursing home residents 7 .... (which/whose) families visit them often live longer, happier lives.

ADJECTIVE CLAUSES WITH OBJECT RELATIVE PRONOUNS

An adjective clause begins with a relative pronoun. The relative pronoun can be the subject or the object of the clause. In the following example, the relative pronoun is the object of the clause.

The <u>house</u>   <u>that we bought</u> is in a nice neighborhood.
antecedent   adjective clause

In the sentence above, *we* is the subject of the clause, and *bought* is the main verb. The relative pronoun *that*, with the antecedent *house*, is the object of the verb.

The <u>nursing home</u>   <u>that you choose</u> should have a professionally trained staff.
        antecedent   adjective clause

In the sentence above, *you* is the subject of the clause, and *choose* is the main verb. The relative pronoun *that*, with the antecedent *nursing home*, is the object of the verb.

An adjective clause can be restrictive or nonrestrictive. The adjective clauses in both the sentences above are **restrictive**. They are necessary to identify the antecedent. In restrictive clauses, it is possible to omit the relative pronoun (except *whose*) when it is the object of the clause.

The <u>house</u>   <u>we bought</u> is in a nice neighborhood.
antecedent   adjective clause

The <u>nursing home</u> <u>you choose</u> should have a professionally trained staff.
        antecedent   adjective clause

Nonrestrictive clauses provide extra information that is not necessary to identify the antecedent.

My <u>supervisor,</u> <u>who you met at the office party,</u> was just promoted.
antecedent   adjective clause

My <u>garden,</u>   <u>which many people admire,</u> was severely damaged by the drought.
antecedent   adjective clause

Whom rather than *who* is considered the correct form for an object relative pronoun in formal, written English. In spoken English, however, and often in written English as well, *who* is often used as an object pronoun.

Relative Pronouns—Object

	Restrictive	Nonrestrictive
People	who whom that nothing	who whom
Things	which that nothing	which
Possessives	whose	whose

PRACTICE 10

Underline the adjective clause and circle the relative pronoun in each sentence. Identify each clause as restrictive or nonrestrictive.

1   We really enjoyed the meal that you prepared for us last night.

     ....

2   Our house, which we bought just three years ago, is too small for our growing family.

     ....

3   I don't have a phone number for the woman whose purse I found.

     ....

4   The sales manager, whom I spoke with about my problem, was very helpful.

     ....

5   This is not the bus that I usually ride to work.

     ....

6   I have not yet met the staff members who we hired last week.

     ....

7   Our city's subway system, which transports thousands of commuters daily, should be expanded.

     ....

8   The man whose ideas we heard last night is an experienced city planner.

     ....

PRACTICE 11

Choose the correct relative pronouns to complete the paragraph.

Acme Fashions, **1** .... (that/which) many people name as their favorite store, has some of the most stylish clothes in town. Unfortunately, the quality is not very high. The dress **2** .... (that/who) I bought there yesterday had a hole in the back and a stain near the hem. When I tried to return the dress to the store, the man **3** .... (who/whose) I asked to assist me was very rude. He said I had damaged the dress myself. In my opinion, it is not good policy to treat your customers, **4** .... (who/that) you rely on to keep your business going, in this way. I cannot wear the damaged dress and I expect the store to return the money **5**................................... (whom/that) I spent on it. Otherwise, I will have to do my shopping somewhere else.

ACTIVE AND PASSIVE VOICE

A sentence can be in either active or passive voice. Most sentences use active voice, but passive voice is used in certain situations. Passive voice is often used in describing process diagrams.

In an active voice sentence, the subject performs the action expressed by the main verb.

<u>Telecommuters</u> <u>work</u> at home.
   subject   verb

The sentence above is in active voice. The subject, *telecommuters*, performs the action, *work*.

In a passive voice sentence, the subject receives the action.

<u>The apartment</u> <u>was painted</u> by the tenant.
   subject   verb

The sentence above is in passive voice. The subject, *apartment*, did not perform the action, *paint*. The apartment didn't paint. The tenant painted the apartment.

Use passive voice when the agent (the one that performs the action) is unknown or unimportant. You don't have to mention the agent in a passive voice sentence, but you can. If you mention the agent, use the preposition *by*, as in the example above.

- Passive voice is formed with the verb be and the past participle form of the main verb.
- Passive voice can be used in any verb tense by changing the tense of the verb be.
- Passive voice sentences can be made negative by adding not to the verb be.

Simple present

The roads <u>are repaired</u> once a year.
The roads <u>aren't repaired</u> in the winter.

Present continuous

The cars <u>are being parked</u> right now.
The cars <u>aren't being parked</u> on the street.

Present perfect

That problem <u>has already been</u> studied.
That problem <u>hasn't been studied</u> yet.

Simple past

The accident <u>was reported</u> an hour ago.
The accident <u>wasn't reported</u> right away.

Future

The book <u>will be published</u> next month.
The book <u>is going to be published</u> next month.
The book <u>won't be published</u> this month.

Modals

The rent <u>must be paid</u> at the beginning of the month.
The rent <u>shouldn't be paid</u> late.

PRACTICE 12

Identify the following sentences as active or passive.

1 .... Many accidents are caused by drivers with cell phones.

2 .... More than half the first-year students enrolled in science classes.

3 .... Several new houses were washed away by the flood.

4 .... All kinds of clothes can be made from cotton.

5 .... Since the flood, people have built new houses farther away from the river.

6 .... As part of the renovation plans, the old fountain will be removed.

7 .... Now all the houses on this street are being heated with solar energy.

8 .... My friend kindly lent me his bicycle last week.

PRACTICE 13

Complete the paragraph with the passive form of the verbs in parentheses. Use the correct verb tense.

Autumn is a busy time in an apple orchard. It is finally time to harvest the apples. The farmer worked hard all year to take care of the apple crop. In the winter, the trees **1** .... (prune) to remove any dead or dying branches. In the summer, the trees **2** .... (spray) to keep pests away. Now the fruit is ready. The apples **3** .... (harvest) as soon as they are ripe. They **4**........................ (pack) in large wooden bins, then they **5** .... (take) to the cider mill. At the cider mill, the fruit **6** .... (crush) until the juice runs out. The juice **7** .... (collect) in large containers. Nothing tastes better than fresh apple cider!

PARALLEL STRUCTURE

The items in a list or series must all follow the same grammatical form. This is called parallel structure.

> When the weather is bad, you should drive <u>slowly</u> and <u>cautiously</u>.

Slowly and *cautiously* are both adverbs. This sentence has parallel structure.

> Most young children like to <u>hear</u> stories, <u>sing</u> songs, and <u>play</u> games.

Hear, sing, and *play* are all present tense verbs. This sentence has parallel structure.

Subjects

Subjects not parallel

> <u>Smoke</u> and <u>overeating</u> are both bad for your health.

Overeating is a gerund; *smoke* is not. The subjects are not parallel.

Subjects parallel

> <u>Smoking</u> and <u>overeating</u> are both bad for your health.

Smoking and *overeating* are both gerunds. The subjects are parallel.

Verbs

Verbs not parallel

> Children at preschool <u>play</u> with toys, <u>are singing</u> songs, and <u>learn</u> social skills.

The first and third verbs are in the present tense, while the second verb is in the present continuous. The verbs are not parallel.

Verbs parallel

> Children at preschool <u>play</u> with toys, <u>sing</u> songs, and <u>learn</u> social skills.

All three verbs are in the present tense. The verbs are parallel.

Adverbs

Adverbs not parallel

> Everyone should drive <u>attentively</u>, <u>slowly</u>, and <u>be safe</u>.

The first two items on the list are adverbs. The third item is a verb + adjective. The items are not parallel.

Adverbs parallel

> Everyone should drive <u>attentively</u>, <u>slowly</u>, and <u>safely</u>.

All three items on the list are adverbs. They are parallel.

Phrases

Phrases not parallel

> Teachers ask parents <u>to bring their children to school</u> on time and <u>for occasional help</u> in the classroom.

The first item on the list is a verb phrase. The second item is a prepositional phrase. The phrases are not parallel.

Phrases parallel

> Teachers ask parents <u>to bring their children to school</u> on time and <u>to give occasional help</u> in the classroom.

Both items are verb phrases. They are parallel.

Voice

Voice not parallel

> When you travel, you <u>see</u> new places and new friendships <u>are formed</u>.

The first verb on the list is active voice; the second one is passive voice. They are not parallel.

Voice parallel

> When you travel, you <u>see</u> new places and <u>form</u> new friendships.

Both verbs are active. They are parallel.

An auxiliary verb and the "to" of an infinitive verb do not have to be repeated in order to have parallel structure. All of the following examples have parallel structure.

> Drivers <u>should turn</u> off their cell phones and <u>concentrate</u> on their driving.

> I want <u>to find</u> a new job, <u>get</u> a new apartment, and <u>take</u> a long vacation.

> They <u>are cleaning</u> and <u>painting</u> the hallways this week.

> I <u>haven't found</u> a job, <u>gotten</u> an apartment, or <u>taken</u> a vacation yet.

> Convenience food <u>is cooked</u> and <u>frozen</u> at a processing plant.

PRACTICE 14

Rewrite the sentences to make them parallel.

1   Work and playing are both important things to include in your life.

    ....

    ....

2   I like traveling, writing, and to meet new people.

....

....

3   Children learn foreign languages quickly and with ease.

....

....

4   The teacher told the students to study hard, rest well before a test, and that they should come to class on time.

....

....

5   At the zoo, they feed the animals once a day, and they are bathed once a week.

....

....

6   A subway carries many passengers, is traveling rapidly, and costs little to ride.

....

....

7   At my company, telecommuters are asked to check in with their boss daily and for a report at the end of the week.

....

....

8   The last time I took my car to the mechanic, the oil was changed, and they checked the brakes.

....

....

PRACTICE 15

Write one sentence on each of the following topics. Use parallel structure.

1   Things you enjoy doing in your spare time

   ....

   ....

2   Reasons why people shouldn't smoke

   ....

   ....

3   Reasons why people should use public transportation

   ....

   ....

4   Reasons why some people don't use public transportation

   ....

   ....

5   Advantages of zoos

   ....

   ....

6   Disadvantages of zoos

   ....

   ....

7   Things teachers ask their students to do

   ....

   ....

8   Reasons why you like your job or school

   ....

   ....

SENTENCE TYPES

IELTS examiners want you to vary the sentence types you use. There are four types of sentences: simple, compound, complex, and compound-complex.

Simple Sentence

A simple sentence has one subject and one verb.

<u>Children</u> <u>develop</u> important skills at preschool.
subject   verb

<u>Smoking</u>   <u>is</u> bad for your health.
subject   verb

<u>Zoos</u>   <u>provide</u> many opportunities for research.
subject   verb

Compound Sentence

A compound sentence is made up of two or more independent clauses linked by a coordinating conjunction. An independent clause is a clause that can stand alone as a sentence.

<u>Many employees want to telecommute</u>, but <u>their bosses won't allow it.</u>
     independent clause   conjunction   independent clause

<u>The streets are congested during rush hour,</u> so <u>many commuters ride the train.</u>
     independent clause   conjunction   independent clause

<u>We can take a bus to the museum,</u> or <u>we can walk there.</u>
     independent clause   conjunction   independent clause

Coordinating Conjunctions

Conjunction	Use	Example
and	adds information	Cars are convenient, and people like to drive them.
but	shows a contradiction or contrast	Cars are expensive, but many people own them.
or	shows a choice	You can drive your car, or you can take a bus.
yet	shows a contradiction or contrast	Sam is a vocal supporter of public transportation, yet he never rides the subway.
so	shows a result	Cars are expensive, so I don't own one.
for	shows a cause	We decided not to sell the car, for no buyers could be found.

Complex Sentence

A complex sentence is made up of an independent clause and one or more subordinate clauses.

There will be less traffic congestion when the city extends the subway lines.
independent clause ____ *subordinate clause*

Since I work at home most days, rush hour traffic is not a problem for me.
subordinate clause ____ *independent clause*

I walked to work yesterday even though it was raining.
independent clause ____ *subordinate clause*

Subordinating Conjunctions

Conjunction	Use	Example
because, as, since	show cause	I use public transportation because I don't like driving.
although, even though, though, while	show a contradiction or contrast	Sam bought an expensive car even though he doesn't have much money.
after, as, before, since, until, when, while	show time or sequence	When I got on the bus, I paid the fare.
if, unless	show condition	I will catch the early bus if I leave the house on time.

See the section on transition words in Chapter 2 (page 166) for more information on subordinating conjunctions.

Compound-Complex Sentence

A compound-complex sentence has two or more independent clauses and one or more subordinate clauses.

Many people have quit smoking, but others continue the habit
independent clause ____ *independent clause*

even though the dangers are well known.
subordinate clause

I bought a house in the country, and I will move there soon
independent clause ____ *independent clause*

because I am tired of city life.
subordinate clause

PRACTICE 16

Identify the sentence type of each sentence.

1   ....   There are good preschools everywhere, but many families don't take advantage of them because they prefer to keep their children at home.

2   ....   Telecommuting has become more common in recent years.

3   ....   I learned to drive when I was 16, and I have been driving ever since then.

4   ....   Modern technology has improved our lives in many ways.

5   ....   Some companies encourage telecommuting since it saves the company money.

6   ....   The waiter was very polite and efficient, so we gave him a large tip.

7   ....   Seventy percent of the students enrolled in science classes, but only 30 percent enrolled in language classes.

8   ....   Children learn to speak foreign languages fluently when they study them in primary school.

PRACTICE 17

Combine each set of sentences into one sentence using the conjunctions provided.

Compound sentences

1   Some neighborhoods are noisy and crowded.
    Others are quiet and clean.

    (but)

    ....

    ....

2   I enjoy water sports.
    I always spend my vacation at the beach.

    (so)

    ....

    ....

3   You can have dinner alone.
I can cook for you.

(or)

....

....

Complex sentences

4   I will move to a new apartment.
I can find one closer to my job.

(if)

....

....

5   This neighborhood was quiet and peaceful.
They built a large shopping mall nearby.

(before)

....

....

6   I usually eat at restaurants.
I don't like to cook.

(because)

....

....

Compound-complex sentences

7   People like living in this city.
Rents are high.
Crime is a growing problem.

(even though, and)

....

....

8   Life in a small town is peaceful and quiet.
Many young people move away.
They can't find jobs.

(but, because)

....

....

PRACTICE 18

Write four sentences about each of the following topics. Use each of the four sentence types—simple, compound, complex, and compound-complex—once per topic.

1   Zoos

....

....

....

....

....

2   The importance of physical education

....

....

....

....

....

3   Life in a city/life in a small town

....

....

....

....

....

PUNCTUATION

IELTS examiners expect you to use correct punctuation.

Beginning and Ending Sentences

Begin every sentence with a capital letter. End every sentence with a period or question mark.

> Eating at restaurants is more expensive than eating at home.
> Are home-cooked meals really more nutritious?

Commas

Use a comma between items in a list of three or more things.

> Most children don't learn to read, write, or do math until they start primary school.
> Our waiter was polite, friendly, and efficient.

Use a comma before a coordinating conjunction.

> I like eating at restaurants, but they are expensive.
> We can repair the item for you, or you can return it to the store for a refund.

Use a comma after a subordinating clause at the beginning of a sentence.

> After the subway system is constructed, there will be fewer traffic jams.
> If more people used public transportation, there would be fewer traffic jams.

Use a comma after an introductory word or phrase.

> Furthermore, there would be less air pollution.
> After dessert, we paid the bill and went home.

Use a comma to separate nonessential information—a phrase or clause that can be removed from the sentence without changing the meaning of the sentence.

> Tomatoes, which were originally cultivated in Mexico, are used in recipes around the world.
> The Grand Hotel, one of the most expensive in the city, is right across the street from the park.

Apostrophes

Apostrophes take the place of the omitted letter in a contraction.

> do not = don't
> we are = we're
> I am = I'm
> she is = she's
> Lee is = Lee's
> it is = it's
> who is = who's
> he has not = he hasn't
> they have = they've
> let us = let's

> **TIP**
>
> Be careful not to confuse *it's* and *its*.
> *It's* is a contraction for *it is*.
>
> *It's raining right now.*
>
> *Its* is a possessive adjective or pronoun.
>
> *The car has a dent in its side.*

An apostrophe is used to show possession.

Add *'s* to the end of singular nouns and irregular plural nouns.

> **Susan's car**
> **The manager's responsibility**
> **My uncle's house**
> **The children's books**

Add *'* only to the end of regular plural nouns.

> **The animals' cages**
> **The teachers' meeting**

PRACTICE 19

Add the correct punctuation to each sentence.

1 telecommuting which has become an increasingly popular way to work is not favored by many supervisors

2 when children start school at an early age do they learn better

3 some people feel that physical education isnt as important as academics

4 childrens interests change as they grow up

5 after I got home I noticed the stains on the jacket

6 clearly peoples ideas are influenced by things they see on TV and the Internet

7 some houses were heated with solar power and others were heated with oil or gas

8 what is the best age to begin foreign language study

9 we had to go along with our parents decision even though we didnt agree with it

10 when I was a child I wanted either a dog a cat or a parrot as a pet but my parents wouldnt let me have one

11 london one of the biggest cities in the world is a fascinating place to visit

12 in the evening you can visit one of our citys famous theaters

Appendix

MORE WRITING PRACTICE

This section contains a selection of model essays written in response to IELTS writing tasks. Use these tasks for writing practice; then study the models as ways to respond to the tasks.

First, choose a task. Cover up the provided model essay, and read the task. Write your own response; then uncover the model and compare it with your writing.

Remember, there is no one correct way to respond to any of the tasks. The models show just one possible way of responding to particular questions. They are models of essays that are well organized and that address the task.

For an **Academic Task 1** essay, notice how the information in the graph or diagram is summarized and compared in the model essay and in your own. You won't use the exact same words, but your essay should contain the same information and comparisons.

For a **General Training Task 1** essay, you use your own ideas so the content of your essay will be different from the model essay. However, the structure should be similar. Notice how the model responds to each of the three points presented in the task. Make sure your essay also responds to each of the three points.

For an **Academic/General Training Task 2** essay, you also use your own ideas. The content of your essay will be different from the model essay, but the structure should be similar. Notice how the model essay develops a theme with main ideas and supporting details. Check your essay to make sure it follows the same type of structure.

ACADEMIC WRITING TASK 1

1   You should spend about 20 minutes on this task.

> *The graph below shows the annual number of rides taken on two forms of public transportation in the city of Williamsville.*
>
> *Summarize the information by selecting and reporting the main features, and make comparisons where relevant.*

Write at least 150 words.

Annual Ridership, Williamsville: 2016–2020

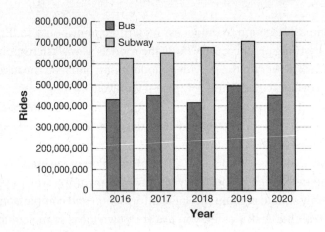

The bar graph shows the total number of rides taken by bus and by subway in Williamsville for each year from 2016 to 2020. The size of the annual ridership varied in different ways for each of the two forms of transportation.

The annual number of bus rides went up and down during the time period shown on the graph. In 2016, annual bus ridership was a little over 400,000,000. This number rose slightly to around 450,000,000 in 2017. It dropped a little in 2018, rose to almost 500,000,000 in 2019, and then dropped again in 2020 to about 450,000,000.

Annual subway ridership, on the other hand, rose steadily during the same time period. In 2016, a little over 600,000,000 rides were taken by subway. This number rose to around 650,000,000 in 2017 and continued to climb steadily until it reached around 750,000,000 in 2020.

In every year shown on the graph, subway ridership was significantly higher than bus ridership. In addition, bus ridership went up and down in this time period, while subway ridership rose consistently.

2   You should spend about 20 minutes on this task.

> *The table below shows the average weekly salaries of men and of women working in different occupations.*
>
> *Summarize the information by selecting and reporting the main features, and make comparisons where relevant.*

Write at least 150 words.

Average Weekly Salary by Occupation 2020

	Men	Women
Technicians	$1400	$900
Service Workers	$1300	$950
Professionals	$2000	$1900
Administrative/Clerical Workers	$1350	$1000
Manual Laborers	$1100	$850

The table shows how much men and women earned on average each week in different types of jobs during 2020. For each type of job, men earned more than women.

Men's average salaries varied according to occupation. Professionals earned the highest salary, an average of $2000 a week. The next highest earning group was technicians, with an average weekly salary of $1400. Manual laborers earned the least—$1100 a week on average.

Women's average salaries also varied by occupation, but in each case they were lower than men's salaries. Like men, women professionals earned the highest salary—$1900 a week on average. This is $1000 less than professional men's salaries. The second highest earners were administrative/clerical workers, earning $1000 a week—$350 less than male administrative/clerical workers, and $400 less than the second highest earning group for men (technicians). As with men, women manual laborers earned the least. Their average weekly salary was just $850, $250 less than men's.

Both men and women earned different amounts depending on their job, but women consistently earned less than men in similar occupations.

3   You should spend about 20 minutes on this task.

> *The diagram below shows the process of maple syrup production.*
>
> *Summarize the information by selecting and reporting the main features, and make comparisons where relevant.*

Write at least 150 words.

Maple Syrup Production

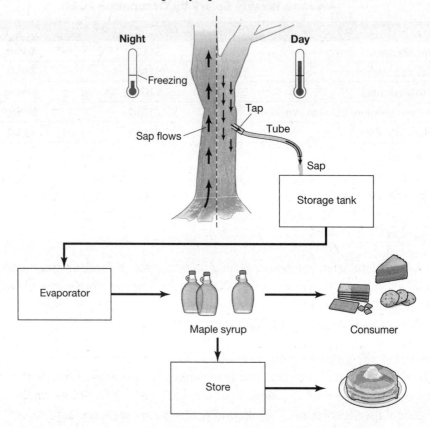

The diagram presents the steps for making syrup from the sap of the maple tree. It takes several steps to go from the sap in a tree to syrup we can eat at home or use for making other products.

The process begins when nighttime temperatures are below freezing and daytime temperatures are above freezing. This is when the sap flows. A tap is put into a tree, and a tube is connected to it. The sap moves through the tube to a storage tank. From there, it goes to an evaporator where it is boiled until it becomes syrup. It takes 40 gallons of sap to make one gallon of syrup. The syrup is packaged in bottles and cans. Some of it is shipped to stores. People buy it and enjoy eating at home. Some of the syrup is used to make candy or as an ingredient in cakes and other foods.

4 You should spend about 20 minutes on this task.

> *The diagram below shows a neighborhood before and after a mall was constructed.*
>
> *Summarize the information by selecting and reporting the main features, and make comparisons where relevant.*

Write at least 150 words.

Neighborhood Changes

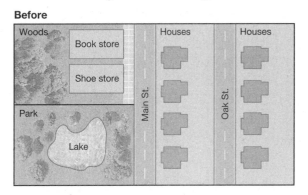

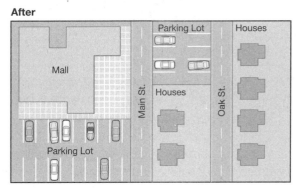

The diagrams illustrate changes that happened in a neighborhood after a mall was built. The new mall took up space where previously there had been other things.

Before the mall was built, there were two stores on Main Street—a bookstore and a shoe store. Behind the stores, there was an area of woods. Next to the woods, there was a park with a lake in the middle. Across the street from the stores and the park, there were houses along Main Street. Behind those houses were more houses along Oak Street.

After the mall was built, things along Main Street looked quite different. The mall was built where the two stores, the woods, and part of the park had been before. The rest of the park was turned into a parking lot, and the lake was removed. Across the street from the mall, another parking lot was built in a place where houses had been before. The rest of the houses on Main Street and all the houses on Oak Street did not change.

5   You should spend about 20 minutes on this task.

> *The graph below shows fast food consumption among men and women in 2020.*
>
> *Summarize the information by selecting and reporting the main features, and make comparisons where relevant.*

Write at least 150 words.

Average Percentage of Daily Calories from Fast Food: 2020

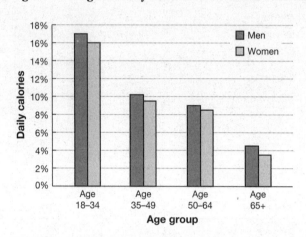

The bar graph shows how much fast food men and women of different age groups consumed every day in 2020. In both groups, the percentage of daily calories from fast food decreased as age increased.

According to the graph, men consumed less fast food as they got older. The 18–34 age group had the highest rate, getting around 17% of daily calories from fast food. There was a significant drop, to just over 10%, between this group and the next, age 35–49. Then, there was a smaller drop, to around 9%, in the 50–64 age group. The oldest age group, age 65 and over, had a much lower consumption rate, with just over 4% of daily calories coming from fast food.

Among women, there was a similar decrease in fast food consumption with age increase. Women age 18–34 got 16% of their daily calories from fast food. Like men, there was a significant drop between this and the next age group, to a little under 10%, and then a smaller drop to the next age group. The oldest age group consumed far less, under 4%, than the other age groups.

There was a similar decrease in fast food consumption with age increase for both men and women, although women tended to consume slightly less than men across all age groups.

6   You should spend about 20 minutes on this task.

> The graph below shows home heating fuel choice according to the year the house was built.
>
> Summarize the information by selecting and reporting the main features, and make comparisons where relevant.

Write at least 150 words.

Heating Fuel Choice

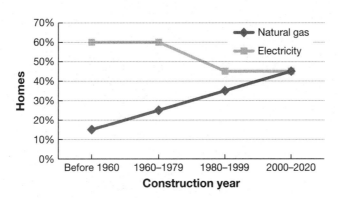

The line graph shows the percentage of houses using two different types of heating fuel according to the year of construction of the houses. The information shows that electricity is more commonly used in older homes, while newer homes use natural gas at a similar rate as electricity.

Many more older homes are heated with electricity than with natural gas. Sixty percent of homes built before 1960, as well as an equal percentage of homes built between 1960 and 1979, use electricity for heat. The percentage falls significantly, to around 45%, for homes built between 1980 and 1999. This figure stays the same for houses built between 2000 and 2020.

Many fewer older homes are heated with natural gas. Just 15% of homes built before 1960 are heated with this type of fuel. The figure rises steadily, until we see that 45% of homes built between 2000 and 2020 use natural gas for heat.

While electricity is the most common source of heat in older homes, equal percentages of the newest homes shown on the graph use electricity and natural gas.

7 You should spend about 20 minutes on this task.

> *The diagram below shows the sorting process in single-stream recycling.*
>
> *Summarize the information by selecting and reporting the main features, and make comparisons where relevant.*

Write at least 150 words.

Single Stream Recycling

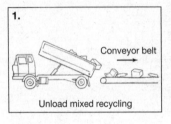
1. Unload mixed recycling

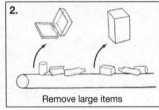
2. Remove large items

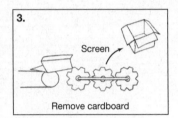
3. Remove cardboard

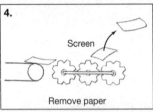
4. Remove paper

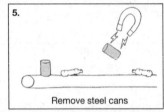
5. Remove steel cans

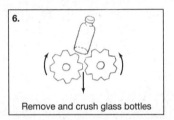
6. Remove and crush glass bottles

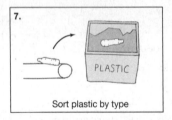
7. Sort plastic by type

> The diagram shows how recycled items are sorted in the single-stream recycling system. When the items are delivered to the recycling plant, they arrive all mixed together, and then they are sorted by machines.
>
> First, a truck puts the items onto a conveyor belt. As everything moves down the belt, people remove the large items. Next, the items are sent to a screen. Pieces of cardboard move over the screen and are dumped into a container. The rest of the items fall through the screen. These items continue on the conveyor belt to another screen. This screen removes paper, while the rest of the items fall through it. After this, a magnet takes out the steel cans, while glass bottles are removed from the belt and crushed. Now the only items left on the belt are plastic bottles. In the final step, these bottles move through an optical sorter, which sorts the plastic by type.

8 You should spend about 20 minutes on this task.

> *The diagram below shows the Petersburg Art Museum before and after renovations.*
>
> *Summarize the information by selecting and reporting the main features, and make comparisons where relevant.*

Write at least 150 words.

Petersburg Art Museum

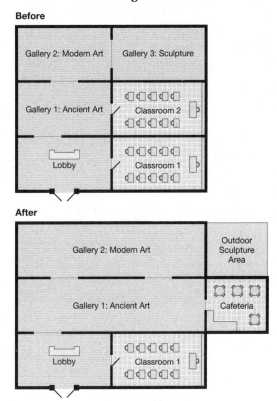

The diagrams illustrate the changes that were made to the Petersburg Art Museum during renovations. Some areas of the museum were enlarged, and new additions were made in the process.

Before the renovations, the museum had six rooms of equal size. The entrance was through the lobby. Behind that area was Gallery 1, which contained ancient art. Behind Gallery 1 was Gallery 2, with modern art. Next to Gallery 2 was Gallery 3, which held sculpture. There were two classrooms next to the lobby and Gallery 1.

After the renovations, the museum was larger and looked very different. The only things that stayed the same were the lobby and Classroom 1. Gallery 1 was expanded into the area where Classroom 2 had been. Gallery 2 was expanded into the area where Gallery 3 had been. The sculptures were moved outdoors to a garden. A cafeteria was added next to the expanded Gallery 1.

9   You should spend about 20 minutes on this task.

> The graph below shows the number of visitors to two different tourist attractions in the city of Grenby during one particular week.
>
> Summarize the information by selecting and reporting the main features, and make comparisons where relevant.

Write at least 150 words.

Daily Visitors

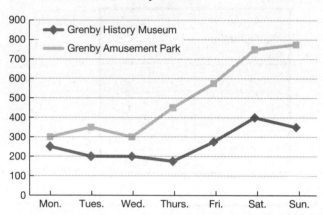

The line graph shows how many people visited the Grenby History Museum and the Grenby Amusement Park each day for a week. For both places, the number of visitors was higher on the weekend than it was during the week.

The number of visitors to the Grenby History Museum was low early in the week but picked up on the weekend. On Monday, there were around 250 visitors. This number dropped slightly on Tuesday and Wednesday, and dipped again on Thursday, to just below 200 visitors. The number rose on Friday, then soared to 400 on Saturday, the busiest day of the week, and then fell slightly on Sunday.

The Grenby Amusement Park also received fewer visitors during the week than on the weekend. On Monday there were 300 visitors. This number rose slightly on Tuesday and then fell back to 300 on Wednesday. The number climbed for the rest of the week until it reached over 700 on both Saturday and Sunday.

Both places were busier on the weekend than during the week, although the amusement park received more visitors every day than the museum did.

10 You should spend about 20 minutes on this task.

> *The charts below show how the average household budget was spent in two different years.*
>
> *Summarize the information by selecting and reporting the main features, and make comparisons where relevant.*

Write at least 150 words.

Household Spending

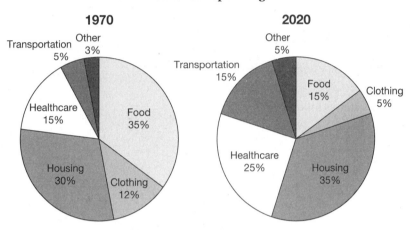

The pie charts show average household expenses in 1970 and 2020. The way the budget was divided up was very different in each of those years.

In 1970, the largest part of the budget was spent on food and housing. Thirty-five percent of the total was spent on food and 30% on housing. This accounted for well over half the budget. Healthcare (15%) and clothing (12%) together took up over one fourth of the budget, while the smallest amounts were for transportation (5%) and other expenses (3%).

In 2020, household spending was somewhat different. In that year, housing and healthcare accounted for the largest part of the budget. Together they made up a little over half of total spending. In the meantime, transportation had risen from 5% to 15% of the budget, while food had dropped from 35% to 15%. Spending on clothing had dropped to 5% of the total, and other expenses had risen slightly to 5%.

In both years, spending on housing made up one of the larger parts of the budget, while the division of the rest of the budget changed significantly.

GENERAL TRAINING WRITING TASK 1

11 You should spend about 20 minutes on this task.

> *You would like to take some time off of work to attend a training course.*
>
> *Write a letter to your supervisor asking for permission to attend the course. In your letter*
>
> - *describe the training course.*
> - *say how it will help improve your job performance.*
> - *explain how much time you need off and ask for permission.*

Write at least 150 words.

You do **NOT** need to write any addresses.

Begin your letter as follows:

Dear _____,

Dear Mr. Chan,

I would like to ask your permission for a few days off from work. I hope to attend a software training course that will help me with my job. The course lasts one week.

A special course on using publications software will be given next month. Participants in this course will learn how to use the software to design and publish newsletters, brochures, and other materials.

As you know, I have recently taken on responsibility for producing our company newsletter. I have some ideas for improving the appearance of the newsletter, but I lack the technical knowledge. This course would help me produce a really great-looking newsletter for our clients to read.

The course begins on the first of next month and goes from Monday until Friday. Therefore, I would have to be away from work for the whole week. However, I feel the skills I will gain will be well worth it. I hope you will let me take this time off for the course.

Please let me know what you think.

Sincerely,

Gina Barduhn

---

12   You should spend about 20 minutes on this task.

> *A friend has invited you to a birthday party, but you will be unable to attend.*
>
> *Write a letter to your friend. In your letter*
>
> - *thank your friend for the invitation.*
> - *explain why you won't be able to attend.*
> - *suggest another time to see your friend.*

Write at least 150 words.

You do **NOT** need to write any addresses.

Begin your letter as follows:

Dear _____ ,

Dear Rosa,

I just received the invitation to your birthday party. I'm very sorry to tell you that I won't be able to attend because I have another event on that same night. However, I hope we'll have another chance to get together soon.

First I want to thank you for the invitation. Turning 30 is an important milestone in life, and I feel honored that you want me to celebrate the occasion with you.

Unfortunately, I have an important family event to attend on the same night as your party. My cousin will be graduating from college, and his parents have planned a special party to celebrate. Of course, I'm very proud of my cousin but sorry his party is on the same night as yours.

However, I'd still like to celebrate with you. Are you free for dinner some evening next week? I'd like to take you to the restaurant of your choice. Just let me know which evening is best for you.

I'm so sorry I can't be at your party, but I send you many wishes for a very happy birthday.

Your friend,

Robin

13   You should spend about 20 minutes on this task.

> *You live in a small apartment building. You are frequently bothered by noise from your upstairs neighbor's apartment.*
>
> *Write a letter to your neighbor. In your letter*
>
> - *describe the situation.*
> - *explain why it is a problem for you.*
> - *suggest a solution.*

Write at least 150 words.

You do **NOT** need to write any addresses.

Begin your letter as follows:

> *Dear _____,*

Dear Mr. Robertson,

I am writing to let you know about a difficulty I am having with noise from your apartment. Your dog barks all the time. This is a problem for me since I am home all day, but I have a suggestion that I think could improve things.

Your dog, Fifi, barks all morning and all afternoon until you return from work. Since she quiets down when you get home, I am sure that you are unaware of this situation.

Because I work at home, I must listen to this noise all day long. It makes it very difficult for me to concentrate on my work, and I am sure that Fifi is not happy, either.

My suggestion is that you hire a dog walker. This person could come to your apartment once or twice during the day, take Fifi for a walk, and feed her. This way, Fifi would have some company and some activity, and she might feel less anxious about being alone.

I hope you like my suggestion.

Your neighbor,

Priscilla Montgomery

14   You should spend about 20 minutes on this task.

> *You borrowed an item from a friend. While it was in your possession, it got damaged.*
>
> *Write a letter to your friend. In your letter*
>
> - *thank your friend for lending the item to you.*
> - *explain how it got damaged.*
> - *tell your friend what you plan to do about it.*

Write at least 150 words.

You do **NOT** need to write any addresses.

Begin your letter as follows:

   Dear _____,

Dear Samantha,

I am very sorry that I have bad news about your bicycle. I am so grateful to you for lending it to me. Unfortunately, I had a small accident with it, but, don't worry, I can fix it.

First, I want to thank you for lending me your bicycle. I know it is an important possession of yours. It really helped me out to have it during the week that my car was at the mechanic's.

Last Friday on the way home from work, I ran into a tree while trying to avoid a large puddle. Fortunately, I was not injured, but the front wheel of the bike was bent.

The good news is that it won't be hard to fix. I will buy a new wheel tomorrow and put it on the bike myself. I have done this sort of repair before, and I guarantee you that I know how to do it right.

Please accept my apologies for the damage, and thanks again for letting me use your bike.

Your friend,

Evelyn

15 You should spend about 20 minutes on this task.

You are planning to take a vacation.

Write a letter to a friend. In your letter

- ■ *describe the vacation spot you have chosen.*
- ■ *explain how you plan to spend your time there.*
- ■ *invite your friend to join you on your vacation.*

Write at least 150 words.

You do **NOT** need to write any addresses.

Begin your letter as follows:

Dear _____,

Dear Lee,

I want to tell you about a vacation I am planning. I am going to a mountain resort that has lots of opportunities for outdoor activities, and I hope you can go with me.

I plan to go to Rocky Ridge Retreat in the Ridgeback Mountains. This resort is in a beautiful mountain location with spectacular views in all directions. In addition to a hotel, there are several restaurants, some tennis courts, and a small lake.

There are lots of fun activities available in the area. I look forward to hiking and rock climbing. I might also rent a horse for some trail rides since there is a stable nearby. And, of course, I plan to swim and boat in the lake.

I would like to invite you to go to the resort with me. I think you would really enjoy it since I know you love the mountains. I am planning my vacation for the second half of August, and I know you will be free then.

Let me know if this plan sounds good to you.

Your friend,

Jamie

16   You should spend about 20 minutes on this task.

You are applying for a new job.

Write a letter to a former supervisor asking for a reference. In your letter

- *describe the job you are applying for*
- *say why you are qualified for the job*
- *explain why you want a reference from this person*

Write at least 150 words.

You do **NOT** need to write any addresses.

Begin your letter as follows:

> *Dear _____,*

Dear Ms. Kim,

I am writing to ask if you will write a job reference letter for me. I am applying for a position as office manager, a job for which I feel well qualified. I am asking you for a reference because you know my skills well.

The Acme Supply Company is looking for a new office manager. This job requires keeping track of customer orders, scheduling appointments, and managing office supplies and equipment.

I think this is the perfect job for me. I am very good at organizing things, which is the most important part of the job. I also enjoy interacting with customers and providing them with excellent service.

Since I worked in your office as an administrative assistant for five years, you know my skills and my personality well. You know that I had many opportunities to learn about running an office, and you had the chance to observe my organizational skills. I feel confident that you will write me a good reference.

Please let me know if you can do this favor for me.

Sincerely,

Stephen Calder

17   You should spend about 20 minutes on this task.

> *You are planning to travel and would like someone to take care of your apartment while you are away.*
>
> *Write a letter to a friend. In your letter*
>
> - *explain why you will be away.*
> - *ask your friend to take care of your apartment.*
> - *describe the tasks you want your friend to do.*

Write at least 150 words.

You do **NOT** need to write any addresses.

Begin your letter as follows:

Dear _____ ,

Dear Amina,

I thought you should know about my latest plans. I am going away on a long business trip, and I need someone to look after my apartment. There are just a few simple things that need to be done.

My company is sending me to South America. I will visit our branch offices in several different countries and will be traveling for a month. I think it will be an exciting trip.

I need someone to look after things at home while I am away. I hope that you can help me with this. You live nearby so I don't think it will be inconvenient for you.

I would like you to visit my apartment two or three times a week. You can water the plants and check to make sure there aren't any problems. Also, you can pick up the mail and leave it on the kitchen table for me.

I hope you will be able to help me with this. Let me know as soon as you can.

Your friend,

Mo

18   You should spend about 20 minutes on this task.

> *You recently purchased an item from a local store, but you are not satisfied with your purchase.*
>
> *Write a letter to the manager of the store. In your letter*
>
> - *describe the item you bought and why you need it.*
> - *explain why you are not happy with it.*
> - *say what you would like the manager to do.*

Write at least 150 words.

You do **NOT** need to write any addresses.

Begin your letter as follows:

> *Dear Sir or Madam,*

Dear Sir or Madam,

I am writing about a purchase I made recently at your store. Last week I bought a desk, but now I realize that it doesn't suit my needs. I would like you to do something about this.

I bought a five-drawer desk for use in my home office. The salesclerk assured me that the desktop was large enough for both my computer and printer. She also said that one of the drawers could be locked.

When I got the desk home, I realized that it was not large enough. Both my computer and printer fit on it, but then there is not enough room left for me to work. Also, none of the drawers can be locked, so I have nowhere to keep valuable documents.

I bought the desk on sale, so it is not returnable. However, since the salesclerk didn't give me correct information, I think you should let me return it. I will take store credit if you have another desk I can use. If not, I would like a full refund.

I hope you agree with my solution.

Sincerely,

Ricard Florian

19   You should spend about 20 minutes on this task.

A friend from overseas is planning to visit you soon.

Write a letter to your friend. In your letter

- *explain why you are looking forward to the visit.*
- *describe the accommodations you have available for your friend.*
- *suggest some things to do during the visit.*

Write at least 150 words.

You do **NOT** need to write any addresses.

Begin your letter as follows:

Dear _____,

Dear Ivan,

I hope you're well. I'm excited about your upcoming visit. I have everything ready for you at my apartment and lots of ideas for things we can do while you're here.

I'm so happy that you've decided to spend your vacation here. It's been a long time since we've seen each other, and you've never been to my city. I look forward to showing you around. I know you'll love it here.

I hope you'll be comfortable at my apartment. It's small but very nice. I'm sorry I don't have an extra bedroom, so you'll have to sleep in the living room. However, I think the sofa is very comfortable.

There will be lots of interesting things going on in the city during the week of your visit. There will be a special exhibit at the art museum, which I think you'll enjoy. Since it's summer time, there will be some concerts and plays in the park. We could also go to a baseball game. We have a great team here.

I'm really looking forward to your visit. See you soon.

Your friend,

Boris

---

20 You should spend about 20 minutes on this task.

> *You recently enjoyed a meal at an expensive restaurant, and you were impressed with the good service you received.*
>
> *Write a letter to the restaurant manager. In your letter*
>
> - *explain the circumstances of your visit to the restaurant.*
> - *describe the service you received.*
> - *say what you would like the manager to do.*

Write at least 150 words.

You do **NOT** need to write any addresses.

Begin your letter as follows:

> *Dear Sir or Madam,*

Dear Sir or Madam,

I thought you should know about my recent experience at your restaurant. When I ate there last weekend, I received excellent service from the waiter. I think he should be rewarded.

Last Saturday, my husband and I had dinner at your restaurant along with some friends of ours. We were there to celebrate my birthday. The restaurant was very busy that evening.

From the moment we arrived, we were treated courteously by the staff. Even though the restaurant was crowded, we were seated right away. When we noticed that our steak was overdone, the waiter immediately took it back to the kitchen. He brought us another steak and didn't charge us for it. In addition, he brought me a free piece of cake for dessert because it was my birthday.

I was very impressed by your staff. They were very busy but acted politely and respectfully at all times. Our waiter, especially, did an excellent job, and I think he should be recognized for it. We left a large tip, but I think you could consider giving him a bonus.

I hope you will consider my suggestion.

Sincerely,

June Cho

ACADEMIC/GENERAL TRAINING WRITING TASK 2

21   You should spend about 40 minutes on this task.

> *People should never eat meat because raising animals for human consumption is cruel.*
>
> *To what extent do you agree or disagree with this opinion?*

Give reasons for your answer, and include any relevant examples from your own knowledge or experience.

Write at least 250 words.

There are people who believe that we should not eat meat because it involves cruelty to animals, but I completely disagree with this point of view. Meat is important for good nutrition, people like it, and most farmers do not treat their animals cruelly.

Meat is important for a balanced diet because it is a major source of protein. It is possible to get some protein from other foods such as whole grains, eggs, and milk. Even eggs and milk, however, come from farm animals, and plant sources of protein are not as good as meat. Growing children, especially, need to eat meat in order to stay healthy and strong.

In addition, people like to eat meat. Most people are accustomed to having it at least once a day and may feel like they haven't eaten well if they don't have it. Meat also tastes good. There are so many ways to prepare it, and some recipes are an important part of a family or cultural tradition.

Even though some people say that farm animals are treated cruelly, that is not a reason for everyone to give up eating meat. In the first place, it is simply not true that farm animals are not treated well, in most cases. It is in the farmer's best interest to keep the animals healthy and happy because it is the only way to get a good product that people will buy. And while there may be cases of animals being treated cruelly, I am sure that it is not common.

Meat tastes good, and it is good for us. Raising animals for meat is not cruel. It is a necessity for our health and well-being.

22 You should spend about 40 minutes on this task.

> *In some educational systems, children are required to study one or more foreign languages. In others, foreign language study is not a requirement.*
>
> *What are the potential benefits of foreign language study?*
>
> *Do you think the foreign language study is an important part of education?*

Give reasons for your answer, and include any relevant examples from your own knowledge or experience.

Write at least 250 words.

Foreign language study has many benefits. It improves children's minds as well as their understanding of the world, and I believe it should be a requirement in all schools.

Foreign language study has enormous benefits for children's intellectual development. Some people think that learning more than one language confuses children, but this is not true. Many studies have shown that children who speak two languages develop intellectual skills at an earlier age than other children. Researchers have also found that learning foreign languages helps children develop greater critical thinking skills, creativity, and flexibility of mind.

Foreign language study broadens children's understanding of the world. Speaking a foreign language helps children understand other ways of thinking about the world. It also exposes them to the customs and cultures of other countries. When children study a foreign language at a young age, they learn to appreciate different ways of life rather than to fear them or be ignorant of them.

I strongly feel that all children should be required to study a foreign language. That way, they can receive the intellectual and cultural benefits from an early age. In addition, it is a well-known fact that it is easier for young children to learn a foreign language. Therefore, starting foreign language study earlier rather than later is more likely to result in a successful experience.

There are many advantages to foreign language study for children. In fact, I find it difficult to understand why it is not required in all schools everywhere. I definitely think it should be.

23   You should spend about 40 minutes on this task.

> *A growing number of people work by telecommuting, that is, the employee works from home, using a computer and the Internet to connect with the office.*
>
> *What are the advantages and disadvantages of working this way?*

Give reasons for your answer, and include any relevant examples from your own knowledge or experience.

Write at least 250 words.

While telecommuting is becoming increasingly popular, there are both benefits and drawbacks to this way of working. Telecommuting has many conveniences for the employee, and it can help the employer cut costs as well. On the other hand, employers often feel it makes it more difficult to manage their workers.

Telecommuting makes things more convenient for the employee. For one thing, there is no need to spend time and money commuting between work and home. In addition, the employee can wear casual clothes most days and so does not have to spend a lot of time and money shopping for work clothes. Finally, working at home means the employee has more time to devote to family responsibilities such as cooking, cleaning, and child care.

Telecommuting is also beneficial to the employer because it helps cut costs. With fewer employees in the office, the employer can save on rent by having a smaller office. The employer will also need less office equipment. Moreover, the employer will be able to get by with a smaller support staff.

There are, however, some disadvantages for the employer because telecommuting makes staff management more difficult. It isn't easy to supervise workers when they aren't in the office and, without good systems in place, it is hard to know how well employees are managing their time. It is also less convenient to organize staff meetings when most of the staff spend most of the time away from the office.

Telecommuting can make some things easier for employers and employees, but it can make other things more difficult. Employees and their bosses have to decide together whether or not telecommuting works for them.

24   You should spend about 40 minutes on this task.

> *Traffic congestion is a growing problem in many of the world's major cities.*
>
> *Explain some possible reasons for this problem, and suggest some solutions.*

Give reasons for your answer, and include any relevant examples from your own knowledge or experience.

Write at least 250 words.

Most of the world's major cities have serious traffic congestion, making life difficult for local citizens. There are several causes of this problem, but there are also solutions. One cause is overcrowded cities. Another is lack of transportation options. City governments should focus on improving public transportation and encouraging alternative ways of getting around.

Cities are crowded places. People want to live in cities because they want to be close to their jobs and to stores. But when you have a lot of people living close together, you have traffic problems. The streets are filled with cars, taxis, and buses taking people to the places they need to go. Even when people move to the suburbs, they still have to travel to the city to get to their jobs.

Transportation is a big problem in some cities. Where there isn't a good bus or subway system, people will often choose to travel by private car. This is what leads to traffic congestion. People may not enjoy sitting in their car in the middle of a traffic jam, but they may find it more convenient than waiting for a crowded bus that runs on an infrequent schedule.

The way to get private cars off the streets is to improve public transportation and to make alternative forms of transportation easier. People will use public transportation more if it is convenient. This means that buses have to run frequently and go to the places that people want to go. It might also mean building a subway system, which is unaffected by crowded streets because it runs underground. Some cities have also had success with building bike lanes, making it easier for people to use bicycles as their main means of transportation.

Many people live in overcrowded cities with few choices for transportation. Investment in public transportation and alternative transportation would do much to alleviate the traffic problems that result. Traffic congestion is a serious problem, but it can be solved.

25 You should spend about 40 minutes on this task.

> *Some people believe that studying abroad is important because it expands a person's knowledge and understanding of the world. Others feel that it is better to study at home because that is the best way to prepare for a career in the student's own country.*
>
> *Discuss both these views, and give your opinion.*

Give reasons for your answer, and include any relevant examples from your own knowledge or experience.

Write at least 250 words.

Some students like to spend time studying in a foreign country so that they can learn more about the world. Others prefer to complete all their studies in their own country so they will be ready for a career there. In my opinion, studying abroad can contribute a lot to anyone's education, and it can even help students be better prepared for any career they choose.

Students who choose to study abroad are interested in learning more about the world. Studying abroad gives them the opportunity to gain knowledge beyond what they learn in the classroom. By spending time in a foreign country, they learn about other ways of thinking and living. They learn to get along with different kinds of people and to appreciate different ways of doing things.

Students who choose to study at home are concerned about being prepared for a professional career. They may feel that spending a semester or a year abroad will distract them from their studies. They may feel that the education they get in their own country is the best preparation they can get for work in their own country.

I understand that students want to be well prepared for their careers, but I don't believe that a classroom is the only place to get that preparation. We have a global economy, so it is important to understand how things are done in other countries. The best way to learn about that is by spending time in other countries. Additionally, living in another country, studying there, and making friends there helps open a student's mind to new things and new ideas. In my opinion, that is the best kind of preparation anyone can get for a professional career.

We can learn a lot both inside and outside the classroom, especially if that classroom is in a foreign country.

26 You should spend about 40 minutes on this task.

> *These days' children are surrounded by electronic devices such as personal computers, tablet computers, and smart phones, and they learn to use them at a very early age.*
>
> *What are the advantages and disadvantages of this situation?*

Give reasons for your answer, and include any relevant examples from your own knowledge or experience.

Write at least 250 words.

Almost everything we do involves a computer in one way or another, so of course children are exposed to electronic devices from the day they are born. People tend to think of this situation as a great advantage, but there are also drawbacks.

Most families have at least one desktop or laptop computer at home, and they often have tablet computers and smart phones as well. This means that even babies are accustomed to seeing these devices and watching how they are used. Because of their natural curiosity, small children like to explore these devices, and often they end up understanding how to use them even better than their parents do. Since we live in a world of electronics, we can consider this an important part of children's learning. They need good computer skills for their future success.

On the other hand, there are disadvantages when children have too much exposure to electronic devices. For one thing, using a computer may exercise the brain, but it does nothing to exercise the body. If children spend most of the time doing things with a computer, then they don't play outside or get any kind of physical exercise. In addition, computers can also be bad for children's intellectual and creative development. If children depend on computers to provide entertainment, then they don't learn to rely on themselves. They don't have the opportunity to invent their own games or find their own solutions to problems.

We all rely on computers, and it is important for children to know how to use them. It is also important, however, for children to learn how to do other things and to have other kinds of experiences as well. Parents need to make sure that their children have a balance of different kinds of activities in their lives.

27   You should spend about 40 minutes on this task.

> *Some people believe that people should be required to retire from their careers at a certain age. Others believe that people should be allowed to work as long as they like.*
>
> *Discuss both these views, and give your opinion.*

Give reasons for your answer, and include any relevant examples from your own knowledge or experience.

Write at least 250 words.

Some people think there should be a mandatory retirement age, while others think that there should be no limits to how long a person is allowed to work. I agree with the second point of view.

Some people believe that workers should have to retire at a specific age, usually 62 or 65. The reason may be that after a certain age people can't perform their jobs as well because they lose some of the physical and intellectual abilities they had when they were younger. Another reason is that people feel that employment opportunities should go to younger people. Older people have had their chance, and they should make room for younger people to advance in their careers and support their families.

On the other hand, there are people who think that everyone should be able to work as long as they choose. For some people, continuing to work is a necessity because they need money. Other people want to work because they enjoy it and it gives meaning to their lives. In addition, older people have a lot of knowledge that comes from years of experience. Therefore, they can make important contributions to their professions that younger people cannot.

I am against a mandatory retirement age. There can't be one retirement age for all because every person's circumstances are different. A 70-year-old person may be full of energy and in excellent health, while a 50-year-old person could be sick all the time. One person may want to rest after years of work while another gets meaning and inspiration from continuing at her job. Finally, people who need money should not be prevented from earning a salary.

There are some good reasons for having a mandatory retirement age, but I think it is more important to realize that each individual situation is different. People should be allowed to plan their retirement for the time that suits them best.

28   You should spend about 40 minutes on this task.

> *In some places, money earned from tourism has become an important part of the economy.*
>
> *What are the advantages and disadvantages of relying on tourism as a major source of revenue?*

Give reasons for your answer, and include any relevant examples from your own knowledge or experience.

Write at least 250 words.

Many places in the world depend on tourism to bring money to their area. There are both benefits and drawbacks to this situation.

Many people greet tourism with open arms because of the boost it gives to the local economy. Tourism means that restaurants and hotels, stores and roads will be built. There will be new opportunities for business owners and new jobs in construction and service for the local population.

Money flowing into an area may look like a good thing, but there is another side to the story. Many places have a tourist season. That means there are a lot of jobs for part of the year and then nothing for the rest of the year. So, employment is only for part of the time. People may earn a lot during the tourist season, but since this money has to last them for the rest of the year, it really isn't very much.

In addition, all the new businesses and structures that are created in a tourist area do not necessarily benefit the local residents. Prices are almost always higher in a tourist area. Tourists may be able to shop in the stores and eat at the restaurants, but most of the local residents probably can't afford it. Tourists enjoy leisure activities such as golf, tennis, or horseback riding, while local residents work hard to earn as much money as they can during the tourist season.

Tourism brings in money, but it is not always as good as it looks. Not everybody benefits from it.

29   You should spend about 40 minutes on this task.

> *Zoos are inhumane and should be abolished.*
>
> *To what extent do you agree or disagree with this opinion?*

Give reasons for your answer, and include any relevant examples from your own knowledge or experience.

Write at least 250 words.

Many people believe that there should be no zoos because they are cruel to animals, and I agree with this opinion. Zoos are like jails for wild animals that should live free, and at the same time they are completely unnecessary because we can see and learn about animals in their natural habitat.

Wild animals are born to live freely in the wild. Each different kind of animal is adapted to live in its specific habitat. It has the skills it needs to survive and live happily in the place where it was born. If you take a wild animal from its natural habitat and put it in a zoo, it is like putting it in jail. Zoos try to make areas for their animals that are similar to their natural habitats, but they are only imitations. In addition, the animals are not free to move beyond the walls of their cages. A zoo is nothing like an animal's wild home, and living in a zoo must be very depressing for the animals.

People say that zoos are important for research, but I don't believe this is true. It may be easier for researchers to observe animals when they are in a zoo. However, since a zoo is not an animal's natural home, you cannot assume that a zoo animal's behavior is natural. The only way to see how animals really behave is to study them in the wild. Therefore, research is not a reason to have zoos.

In my opinion, all zoos should be shut down. It is cruel to keep animals locked up in cages. Zoos are also not the best places to do research on animals. I can see no good reason for the existence of zoos.

30   You should spend about 40 minutes on this task.

> *Many stores sell organic fruits and vegetables (produced without the use of chemical fertilizers, pesticides, and herbicides) even though they often cost more than conventional fruits and vegetables.*
>
> *Why do some people prefer to eat organic food?*
>
> *Do you think organic food is worth the extra cost?*

Give reasons for your answer, and include any relevant examples from your own knowledge or experience.

Write at least 250 words.

In many places, you can buy organic fruits and vegetables that have been grown without chemicals. People like this kind of food because it is better for their health than conventional food. It also costs more, but I believe it is worth the higher price.

People choose organic fruits and vegetables for many reasons, but I believe the main reason is health. Conventional fruits and vegetables are grown with chemicals that are used to fertilize the soil and kill weeds and insects. These fruits look big and clean when they are in the store. However, they are also filled with chemicals. You may not be able to see the chemicals, but they are there. People who are concerned about eating these chemicals buy organic fruits and vegetables. They are worried about getting cancer and other diseases from eating conventional food. Many parents, especially, feel it is important for their growing children to eat clean fruits and vegetables that are chemical free.

Organic fruits and vegetables are expensive, but they are worth what they cost. Buying conventional food is cheaper, but it isn't cheap to be sick, especially with a major disease like cancer. It is important to stay healthy to have a happy, productive life. People who buy organic fruits and vegetables are investing money in their own health and in a healthy future for their children.

If somebody served you a plate of chemicals, you wouldn't eat them. But that's what you are eating when you eat conventional fruits and vegetables. Spend the extra money, buy organic, and stay healthy.

ACADEMIC WRITING TASK 1: CHARTS, GRAPHS, TABLES

PRACTICE 1 (PAGE 6)

1	B		**3**	A		**5**	D
2	E		**4**	C			

PRACTICE 2 (PAGE 11)

Graphic A

Graphic type: line graph
Title: New Residential Construction
What: number of single-family houses built
When: 2014–2020
Where: regions of the United States
Topic: the number of single-family houses built in different regions of the United States between 2014 and 2020

Graphic B

Graphic type: bar graph
Title: Number of Tourists by Season
What: number of tourists
When: the four seasons of the year
Where: two cities, Dover and Troy
Topic: the number of tourists who visited the cities of Dover and Troy in each of the four seasons of 2014

Graphic C

Graphic type: pie charts
Title: Clydesdale University Enrollment
Who: men and women
What: enrollment in fields of study
Where: Clydesdale University
Topic: The enrollment of men and women in different fields of study at Clydesdale University.

Graphic D

Graphic type: table
Title: Hours per Week Spent on the Internet, by Age
Who: people of different ages
What: work/study and leisure activities
When: hours per week
Topic: number of hours per week people of different ages spend in work/study and leisure activities on the Internet.

Graphic E

Graphic type: pie charts
Title: Rockingham, Transportation
Who: workers
What: transportation to work
When: 2010 and 2020
Topic: How workers in the city of Rockingham normally traveled to work in 2010 and 2020

PRACTICE 3 (PAGE 14)

Graphic A

Comparisons

1   the number of houses built in each region
2   the number of houses built in different years

Graphic B

Comparisons

1   tourist visits to Dover in different seasons
2   tourist visits to Troy in different seasons

Graphic C

Comparisons

1   men's preferred fields of study
2   women's preferred fields of study

Graphic D

Comparisons

1   work/study time on Internet for people of various ages
2   leisure activities time on Internet for people of various ages

Graphic E

Comparisons

1   how people traveled to work in 2010
2   how people traveled to work in 2020

PRACTICE 4 (PAGE 16)

Graphic A

Comparison

1   the number of houses built in each region

Details

A   most houses built in the South
B   900,000 in 2014 (highest year), 300,000 in 2018 (lowest year)

C fewest houses built in the Northeast

D under 200,000 in 2014, under 100,000 in 2018

Comparison

2 the number of houses built in different years

Details

A most houses built in 2014 in all regions

B fewest houses built in 2018 in all regions

C after 2018, numbers rose in most regions

D after 2018, numbers still fell in Northeast

Graphic B

Comparison

1 tourist visits to Dover in different seasons

Details

A most tourists in the winter—25,000

B fewest tourists in the spring—5,000

C steady rise spring to fall, biggest increase from fall to winter

Comparison

2 tourist visits to Troy in different seasons

Details

A most tourists in the summer—22,000

B fall similar to summer—20,000

C fewest tourists in the spring—just under 5,000

D winter similar to fall—5,000

Graphic C

Comparison

1 men's preferred fields of study

Details

A most popular—engineering, 45%

B second most popular—social sciences, 25%

C least popular—humanities, 10%

Comparison

2 women's preferred fields of study

Details

A most popular—education, 35%

B second most popular—humanities, 30%

C least popular—social science, 15%

Graphic D

Comparison

1   work/study time on Internet for people of various ages

Details

A   people in their 20s spend the most time on this

B   also high for people in their 30s, 40s, and 50s

C   lowest for teens and people in their 60s

Comparison

2   leisure activities time on Internet for people of various ages

Details

A   highest for people in their teens

B   lowest for people in their 40s and 50s

C   goes up again for people in their 60s

Graphic E

Comparison

1   how people traveled to work in 2010

Details

A   highest percentage of people drove alone—50%

B   second highest percentage of people used a carpool or bus—15% each

C   lowest percentage walked or biked—5% each

Comparison

2   how people traveled to work in 2020

Details

A   highest percentage of people drove alone—35%

B   second highest percentage of people used a carpool—20%

C   more people biked than in 2010—10%

D   lowest percentage walked—5%

PRACTICE 5 (PAGE 21)

1	G	4	H	7	F	10	C
2	J	5	A	8	E		
3	B	6	I	9	D		

PRACTICE 6 (PAGE 21)

1   The graph shows <u>how many</u> schools were <u>built</u> in each <u>area</u> of the country in 2020.

2   The graph shows <u>how many</u> people <u>spent time in the</u> Palm Island Resort in each of the years from 2015 to 2020.

3 The charts show the percentages of <u>male and female</u> shoppers who shopped at Mayfield's Clothing Store at <u>various</u> times of the day.

4 The table shows the <u>various kinds</u> of career interests reported by students at Bingham University.

5 The graph shows the number of people <u>who ride the bus</u> in the city <u>during the week</u>.

PRACTICE 7 (PAGE 23)

1 A   **2** C   **3** C

PRACTICE 8 (PAGE 24)

Sample answers. Wording may vary.

Graphic A

The graph shows how many single-family houses were built in different areas of the United States in each of the years from 2014 and 2020. There was a significant difference in the number of houses built in each region, and these numbers all dropped between 2014 and 2018.

Graphic B

The graph shows how many tourists spent time in the cities of Dover and Troy in each of the four seasons of the year. Each city was busier with tourists at a different time of year.

Graphic C

The pie charts show the percentages of male and female students enrolled in various fields of study at Clydesdale University. The charts show that men and women differ greatly in terms of which fields of study they tend to prefer.

Graphic D

The table shows how much time per week people of various ages spend on two different kinds of activities on the Internet. People divide their time differently between work/study and leisure activities, depending on their age.

Graphic E

The pie charts show how workers in the city of Rockingham normally traveled to work in 2010 and 2020. In 2010, half the workers drove alone, while this number had dropped in favor of other means of transportation by 2020.

PRACTICE 9 (PAGE 27)

Paragraph 1—C
Paragraph 2—B

PRACTICE 10 (PAGE 28)

Graphic I

Paragraph 2

The sales numbers for each food item were different in the summer from what they were in the ~~winter.~~ *Iced coffee sales rose significantly, to an average of 40 servings sold daily. The item with the second highest number of sales was ice cream, with an average of 35 servings sold daily.* ~~Sales of ice cream go up in the summer when the weather is hot.~~ *Hot coffee fell to daily sales of just 30 servings. Soup and salad had the lowest number of sales, with 25 servings sold daily on average.*

Graphic II

Paragraph 1

The number of male cell phone subscribers rose significantly between 2000 and 2020. In 2000, a little over 500 men subscribed to cell phone service. ~~Women also subscribed to the service at that time.~~ *The number increased considerably over the next few years until it reached 2500 in the year 2010. There was no change in the number of subscribers between 2010 and 2015, but then it rose slightly between 2015 and 2020, when there were about 2750 male subscribers.*

Paragraph 2

The number of women subscribing to cell phone service rose in most years between 2000 and 2020. ~~Before 2000, cell phone use was not very common.~~ *In 2000, 500 women subscribed to cell phone service. By 2010, the number of female subscribers had increased to 2500. There was a slight drop between 2010 and 2015, to about 2250 subscribers, and that number stayed steady between 2015 and 2020.*

PRACTICE 11 (PAGE 30)

The number of medical degrees rose almost every year between 2017 and 2020. It **1** rose/ climbed/increased slightly between 2017 and 2018 from 40 degrees granted to 45. Then, in 2019, the number of degrees granted rose **2** sharply/significantly to 70. There was a slight **3** drop/fall/decrease in 2020, when about 65 medical degrees were granted at Clifford University. The number of engineering degrees, on the other hand, dropped steadily from 2017 to 2020. It **4** dropped/fell/decreased from about 45 degrees granted in 2017 to 40 in 2018. In 2019 there was another **5** slight drop, when just 35 engineering degrees were granted. The number **6** dropped/fell/decreased again, to 30 degrees granted 2020.

PRACTICE 12 (PAGE 31)

Sample answers. Wording will vary.

Graphic A

The number of houses built in each region differed significantly. In each of the years shown on the graph, the most houses were built in the South. About 900,000 new houses were built there in 2014. This number dropped to just 300,000 in 2018, the year with the least construction, but it was still the highest number of all the regions. The region with the lowest number of houses built in each of the years was the Northeast. Under 200,000 new houses were built there in 2014, and fewer than 100,000 were built in 2018.

In all the regions shown on the graph, 2014 was the year with the most construction, and the numbers decreased steadily until 2018. In three of the regions, the numbers rose slightly or stayed steady from 2018 to 2020. In the Northeast, the numbers continued to drop.

Graphic B

The busiest tourist season for Dover was winter. During that season, 25,000 tourists visited the city. The least busy time of year was spring, with only 5,000 tourists visiting. The number of tourist visits rose by 5,000 between spring and summer and then again between summer and fall. The biggest increase was between fall and winter, when the number of visits rose from 15,000 to 25,000.

The busiest tourist season for Troy, on the other hand, was summer, with about 22,000 visits. Fall was also a busy season, with 20,000 visits from tourists. The least busy season was spring, with just under 5,000 tourist visits. Winter was almost equally quiet, with 5,000 tourist visits.

Graphic C

According to the charts, the most popular field of study for men at Clydesdale University is engineering, with 45% of male students enrolled in this field. The second most popular field is social sciences, with 25% enrollment. The least popular field of study is humanities. Only 10% of men choose this field of study.

The charts show that women's popular fields of study are quite different from men's. The most popular field of study for women at Clydesdale is education, with 35% choosing to study this field. The second most popular is humanities, with 30% of women enrolled. This five percentage point difference between the top two popular fields is much smaller than the difference between the men's top two popular fields of study. The least popular field of study for women is social sciences, with 15% enrollment.

Graphic D

According to the table, people in their 20s spend the most time studying or working on the Internet, at an average of 50 hours a week. The hours are also high for people in their 30s, 40s, and 50s. The people who spend the least amount of time studying or working on the Internet are teens, with an average of 15 hours a week, and people in their 60s and older, with an average of 17 hours.

The people who spend the most time on the Internet on leisure activities are teens, with an average of 22 hours per week. The numbers go down after the teen years, until they reach their lowest for people in their 50s. These people spend just 11 hours a week on leisure activities. The number goes up to 20 hours a week for people over age 60.

Graphic E

In 2010, driving alone in a car was the most common way to get to work, with 50% of workers choosing this method. The next most common means of transportation were carpools and bus. Each of these methods was chosen by 15% of workers. The least popular methods were walking and biking, each one used by just 5% of workers.

In 2020, driving alone in a car was still the most common way to get to work, but it was used by just 35% of workers. The percentage of workers using carpools had risen slightly to 20%. The percentage of people biking to work had also risen, from 5% to 10%. Walking was still the least popular form of transportation, with 5% of workers choosing this method, the same as in 2010.

PRACTICE 13 (PAGE 32)

Sample answers. Answers will vary.

Graphic A

The graph shows how many single-family houses were built in different areas of the United States in each of the years from 2014 and 2020. There was a significant difference in the number of houses built in each region, and these numbers all dropped between 2014 and 2018.

The number of houses built in each region differed significantly. In each of the years shown on the graph, the most houses were built in the South. About 900,000 new houses were built there in 2014. This number dropped to just 300,000 in 2018, the year with the least construction. However, it was still the highest number of all the regions. The region with the lowest number of houses built in each of the years was the Northeast. Under 200,000 new houses were built there in 2014 and fewer than 100,000 were built in 2018.

In all the regions shown on the graph, 2014 was the year with the most construction, and the numbers decreased steadily until 2018. In three of the regions, the numbers rose slightly or stayed steady from 2018 to 2020. In the Northeast, the numbers continued to drop.

In general, there were big differences in the number of houses built in the various regions of the country, but most of the regions seem to follow the same rising and falling trends.

Graphic B

The graph shows how many tourists spent time in the cities of Dover and Troy in each of the four seasons of the year. Each city was busier with tourists at a different time of year.

The busiest tourist season for Dover was winter. During that season, 25,000 tourists visited the city. The least busy time of year was spring, with only 5,000 tourists visiting. The number of tourist visits rose by 5,000 between spring and summer and then again between summer and fall. The biggest increase was between fall and winter, when the number of visits rose from 15,000 to 25,000.

The busiest tourist season for Troy, on the other hand, was summer, with about 22,000 visits. Fall was also a busy season, with 20,000 visits from tourists. The least busy season was spring, with just under 5,000 tourist visits. Winter was almost equally quiet, with 5,000 tourist visits.

In general, Dover had a steadily rising number of tourist visitors throughout the year, while Troy had two very busy tourist seasons and two very quiet ones.

Graphic C

The pie charts show the percentages of male and female students enrolled in various fields of study at Clydesdale University. The charts show that men and women differ greatly in terms of which fields of study they tend to prefer. According to the charts, the most popular field of study for men at Clydesdale University is engineering, with 45% of male students enrolled in this field. The second most popular field is social sciences, with 25% enrollment. The least popular field of study is humanities. Only 10% of men choose this field of study.

The charts show that women's popular fields of study are quite different from men's. The most popular field of study for women at Clydesdale is education, with 35% choosing to study this field. The second most popular is humanities, with 30% of women enrolled. This five percentage point difference between the top two popular fields is much smaller than the difference between the men's top two popular fields of study. The least popular field of study for women is social sciences, with 15% enrollment.

Overall, there is a significant difference between men and women at Clydesdale in terms of their study interests.

Graphic D

The table shows how much time per week people of various ages spend on two different kinds of activities on the Internet. People divide their time differently between work/study and leisure activities, depending on their age.

According to the table, people in their 20s spend the most time studying or working on the Internet, at an average of 50 hours a week. The hours are also high for people in their 30s, 40s, and 50s. The people who spend the least amount of time studying or working on the Internet are teens, with an average of 15 hours a week. The numbers are also low for people in their 60s and older, with an average of 17 hours a week.

The people who spend the most time on the Internet on leisure activities are teens, with an average of 22 hours per week. The numbers go down after the teen years, until they reach their lowest for people in their 50s. These people spend just 11 hours a week on leisure activities. The number goes up to 20 hours a week for people over age 60.

In general, people of working age spend more time studying or working on the Internet, while younger and older people spend more time on leisure activities.

Graphic E

The pie charts show how workers in the city of Rockingham normally traveled to work in 2010 and 2020. In 2010, half the workers drove alone, while this number had dropped in favor of other means of transportation by 2020.

In 2010, driving alone in a car was the most common way to get to work, with 50% of workers choosing this method. The next most common means of transportation were carpools and bus. Each of these methods was chosen by 15% of workers. The least popular methods were walking and biking, each one used by just 5% of workers.

In 2020, driving alone in a car was still the most common way to get to work, but it was used by just 35% of workers. The percentage of workers using carpools had risen slightly to 20%. The percentage of people biking to work had also risen, from 5% to 10%. Walking was still the least popular form of transportation, with 5% of workers choosing this method, the same as in 2010.

Overall, the biggest change between 2010 and 2020 was the drop in the number of workers driving to work alone, while the use of some of the other methods of transportation rose slightly or stayed the same.

PRACTICE 14 (PAGE 36)

A

1   **Thesis statement:** *The graph shows how many men and women in Marysville paid for cell phone service from 2000 to 2020.*

2   **Comparison/main idea:** *number of subscribers of each gender*

3   **Main idea of paragraph 2:** *The number of male cell phone subscribers rose significantly between 2000 and 2020.*

Supporting details: (A) *In 2000, a little over 500 men subscribed*
(B) *The number increased considerably over the next few years*
(C) *There was no change in the number of*
(D) *Then, the number rose slightly*

4   **Main idea of paragraph 3:** *Similarly, the number of women subscribing to cell phone service rose in most years between 2000 and 2020.*

   Supporting details: (A) *In 2000, 500 women subscribed*
   (B) *By 2010, the number of female subscribers had increased*
   (C) *There was a slight drop between 2010 and 2015*
   (D) *that number stayed steady between 2015 and 2020*

5   **Transitional words of paragraph 2:**   Then
   Transitional words of Paragraph 3:   Similarly
   Transitional words of Paragraph 4:   Overall

6   There are no grammar or spelling errors.

7   Possible answers:
   ss: *The number of male cell phone subscribers rose significantly between 2000 and 2020.*
   cx/s: *Then, the number rose slightly between 2015 and 2020, when there were about 2750 male subscribers.*
   cm/s: *There was a slight drop to about 2250 subscribers between 2010 and 2015, and that number stayed steady between 2015 and 2020.*

B

1   **Thesis statement:** *The graph shows how many students were registered at Riverside School and Litchfield School in each of the years from 2016 to 2019.*

2   **Comparison/main idea:** *number of students at each school*

3   **Main idea of paragraph 2:** Main idea: *Enrollment at Riverside School rose steadily over the four-year period shown on the graph.*

   Supporting details: (A) *There was a small increase*
   (B) *Then, enrollment started to rise more rapidly*
   (C) *In 2018, there were 1200 students enrolled in Riverside School*
   (D) *in 2019 enrollment was close to 1500*

4   **Main idea of paragraph 3:** *Enrollment in Litchfield School, on the other hand, mostly fell during the same period.*

   Supporting details: (A) *There was a small rise between 2016 and 2017*
   (B) *In 2018, enrollment fell*
   (C) *It also fell in 2019*

5   **Transitional words of paragraph 2:** Then, and
   Transitional words of paragraph 3: on the other hand, also
   Transitional words of paragraph 4: While

6   There are no grammar or spelling errors.

7   Possible answers:
   ss: *Then, enrollment started to rise more rapidly.*
   cm/s: *In 2018, there were 1200 students enrolled in Riverside School, and in 2019 enrollment was close to 1500.*
   cx/s: *While enrollment changed each year at both schools, it increased at Riverside School and fell at Litchfield School.*

C

1   **Thesis statement:** *The table shows how many movie tickets were sold at the Springfield Cinema at different times of the weekend.*

2   **Comparison/main idea:** *Saturday sales, Sunday sales*

3   **Main idea of paragraph 2:** *On Saturday, the most popular times to see a movie were in the evening.*

    Supporting details: (A) *Sales started out relatively low*
                          (B) *After that, sales rose*

4   **Main idea of paragraph 3:** *On Sunday, on the other hand, the most popular time to see a movie was in the afternoon.*

    Supporting details: (A) *Sales started out highest for the 3:00 show*
                          (B) *Then, sales dropped steadily*

5   **Transitional words of paragraph 2:** After that
    Transitional words of paragraph 3: on the other hand, Then
    Transitional words of paragraph 4: In general

6   There are no grammar or spelling errors.

7   Possible answers:
    ss: *The table shows how many movie tickets were sold at the Springfield Cinema at different times of the weekend.*
    cm/s: *On Saturday sales were highest in the evening, and on Sunday sales were highest in the afternoon.*
    cm-cx/s: *Then, sales dropped steadily, and they reached their lowest for the 9:00 show, when just 50 tickets were sold.*

D

1   **Thesis statement:** *The charts show the top levels of education reached by adults in two countries.*

2   **Comparison/main idea:** *The levels of education . . . for each country.*

3   **Main idea of paragraph 2:** *In Country A, most adults had at least some schooling.*

    Supporting details: (A) *Only five percent of the adult population had not gone to school at all*
                          (B) *fifteen percent stopped studying after primary school*
                          (C) *Forty-five percent of the population ended their studies after secondary school*
                          (D) *while thirty percent completed vocational/technical school.*
                          (E) *five percent, got university degrees.*

4   **Main idea of paragraph 3:** *In Country B, more of the adult population reached higher levels of education than in Country A.*

   Supporting details: (A) *Five percent had no schooling.*
   (B) *Another five percent did not go beyond primary school.*
   (C) *Thirty-five percent of the adult population . . . stopped studying after secondary school.*
   (D) *Thirty percent studied at vocational/technical school*
   (E) *twenty-five percent got university degrees.*

5   **Transitional words of paragraph 3:** Another, on the other hand

6   There are no grammar or spelling errors.

7   Possible answers:
   ss: *In Country A, most adults had at least some schooling.*
   cm/s: *Only five percent of the adult population had not gone to school at all, and just fifteen percent stopped studying after primary school.*
   cx/s: *Forty-five percent of the population ended their studies after secondary school, while thirty percent completed vocational/technical school.*

PRACTICE 15 (PAGE 43)

Answers will vary.

PRACTICE 16 (PAGE 43)

Sample answers. Answers will vary.

A

The pie charts show the different agricultural products raised in the Western Region and the Eastern Region of a country. Each region concentrates on different products.

The Eastern Region has a slightly more even distribution among the different products than the Western Region does. In the Eastern Region, the top two products are meat, making up 35% of total agricultural production, and dairy, making up 30% of the total. Vegetables account for 20% and grain for 15% of agricultural production in that region.

In the Western Region, the top two products—grain and meat—account for 80% of the total agricultural production. Dairy makes up 15% of the total, while vegetables are only 5% of agricultural production in that part of the country.

Each region has a different approach to agricultural production. In the Eastern Region, it is distributed among different products, while in the Western Region, it is concentrated more heavily on two different types of product.

B

The table shows how much rainfall there is in two different cities in each of the twelve months of the year. The amount of rain in each city is very different throughout most of the year.

Woodsville receives much more rain than Blacksboro does. The rainiest months in Woodsville are November, December, and January, with an average rainfall of 6, 5.5, and 5 inches, respectively. After January, the amount of rain decreases steadily. In July, the driest month of the year, Woodsville receives an average of just 0.75 inches of rain. After that, the amount of rainfall increases as the year approaches the rainy season.

Blacksboro is a drier area than Woodsville is. The rainiest months of the year in Blacksboro are January and February, with an average rainfall of 3 and 4 inches, respectively. After that, the amount of rainfall decreases until the driest month, July, when just 0.01 inches of rain fall. Then, the average rainfall increases over the next few months, but it never gets as high as the average in Woodsville. Both Woodsville and Blacksboro experience rainy and dry seasons, but Woodsville receives more rain over the course of the year than Blacksboro does.

ACADEMIC WRITING TASK 1: PROCESS DIAGRAMS

PRACTICE 1 (PAGE 47)

1	B, steps	3	D, changes	5	C, changes
2	E, steps	4	A, steps		

PRACTICE 2 (PAGE 52)

Diagram A

Title: Cotton Cloth Production
Description: the process of producing cloth and clothes from cotton

Diagram B

Title: Dragonfly Life Cycle
Description: stages in the life cycle of a dragonfly

Diagram C

Title: Benfield Neighborhood
Description: a neighborhood before and after construction

Diagram D

Title: Blackstone River
Description: the area around a river before and after a flood

Diagram E

Title: Wind Turbine

Description: process of generating electricity with a wind turbine

PRACTICE 3 (PAGE 54)

Diagram A

1 harvest	5 spinning machine—make yarn
2 gin—remove seeds, pack bales	6 loom—weave cloth
3 blower—loosen bales	7 dye cloth
4 carding machine—comb cotton	8 make clothes

Diagram B

1 lay eggs	6 molts
2 eggs hatch	7 flies
3 nymph eats	8 hunts and eats
4 grows	9 lives a few weeks or months
5 leaves water	

Diagram C

Before	After
barn	new houses in place of barn, old house, and cornfield
house	new road in place of fence
animals	new houses in place of one part of woods
fence	one part of woods turned into park
cornfield	
woods	

Diagram D

Before	After
oxbow	oxbow cut off from river
houses on both sides of river	river straight
trees by riverbank	no houses on one side of river
bridge	trees nearest the river gone
	bridge gone

Diagram E

1 wind blows against turbine	5 motor moves turbine to face wind
2 blades and rotor spin	6 electric current moves down tower
3 driveshaft spins generator, makes electric current	7 moves through substation
	8 distributed to homes
4 monitor measures wind speed	9 wind moves past turbine

PRACTICE 4 (PAGE 58)

1	C, E, J	**5**	H
2	G, K	**6**	A
3	D	**7**	F
4	B	**8**	I

PRACTICE 5 (PAGE 58)

1 The diagram shows a housing site prior to and following building.

2 The diagram shows the steps for manufacturing boxes from recycled cardboard.

3 The diagram explains the process for producing juice from apples.

4 The diagram illustrates the growth of a frog from egg to maturity.

5 The diagram shows the steps for making chocolate from cacao beans.

PRACTICE 6 (PAGE 59)

A It takes several steps to go from cotton in the field to clothes you can buy and wear.

B It goes through several stages from an egg in the water to a mature dragonfly in the air.

C The neighborhood changed from a quiet area to a crowded place to live.

D Many things were washed away by the floodwaters.

E The electricity is generated by the turbine and then is distributed to people's homes.

PRACTICE 7 (PAGE 59)

Sample answers. Answers may vary.

Diagram A

The diagram illustrates the steps for manufacturing cloth and clothes from cotton. It takes several steps to go from cotton in the field to clothes you can buy and wear.

Diagram B

The diagram shows the growth of a dragonfly from the beginning to the end of its life cycle. It goes through several stages from an egg in the water to a mature dragonfly in the air.

Diagram C

The diagram shows a neighborhood prior to and following the building of new houses. The neighborhood changed from a quiet area to a busy place to live.

Diagram D

The diagram illustrates a river area prior to and following a flood. Many things were washed away by the floodwaters.

Diagram E

The diagram explains the steps for producing electricity by using a wind turbine. The electricity is generated by the turbine and then is distributed to people's homes.

PRACTICE 8 (PAGE 61)

1	The cotton is packed in bales.	5	The raisins are sorted.
2	The cloth is dyed.	6	A new room was built.
3	The cloth is sold to a factory.	7	The walls were painted.
4	The raisins are dried in the sun.	8	The desk was placed by the window.

PRACTICE 9 (PAGE 62)

The diagram shows the steps for making frozen orange juice concentrate from fresh oranges. First, the fruit **1** is prepared. When the oranges are ripe, they **2** are harvested. Then, they **3** are loaded onto trucks. The trucks carry the oranges to the processing plant. There, they **4** are washed before the juice **5** is made. The washed oranges go through the extractor, which extracts the juice. Next, the juice goes to the evaporator, where it **6** is turned into concentrate. The concentrate **7** is frozen. Then, it **8** is canned in the canner. The cans of juice **9** are distributed to grocery stores. Customers buy the frozen concentrate and enjoy it at home.

PRACTICE 10 (PAGE 64)

The diagram shows the process of recycling plastic bottles to make new products. It takes several steps to go from used bottles to new products made out of the same material. The **1** first step is to send the used bottles to the recycling plant. **2** After someone finishes drinking from a bottle, she puts it in a recycling bin with other used bottles. **3** Then/Next, a truck picks up the bottles and transports them to the recycling plant. **4** Before the bottles can be recycled, they have to go through the washer. **5** Then/Next, they are sent to another machine, where they are shredded into small pieces. **6** Next/Then, the shredded pieces go into the extruder. This machine turns the pieces into pellets. **7** Finally, the pellets are used to make new plastic products such as bottles, cups, and toys.

PRACTICE 11 (PAGE 66)

Sample answers. Answers may vary.

1   The nature center is next to the lake.
2   The parking lot is behind the nature center.

3   There are two cars in the parking lot.

4   There is a picnic area across the road from the nature center.

5   There are trees to the left of the picnic area.

6   Ducks are swimming on the lake.

PRACTICE 12 (PAGE 67)

Sample answers. Answers will vary.

Diagram A

The diagram illustrates the steps for manufacturing cloth and clothes from cotton. It takes several steps to go from cotton in the field to clothes you can buy and wear.

To begin, the cotton is harvested by machine. Then, it goes through a gin, where the seeds are removed and the cotton is packed into bales. Next, the bales go through a blower, which blows and loosens the cotton. Then, the cotton goes through a carding machine. The cotton has to be straightened by this machine before the yarn can be made. After going through the carding machine, a spinning machine makes the cotton into yarn. Then, the yarn is woven into cloth on a loom. The next step is to dye the woven cloth in a dye vat. Then, the cloth is ready to be made into clothes. All kinds of clothes such as dresses, shirts, and pants can be made from cotton.

Diagram B

The diagram shows the growth of a dragonfly from the beginning to the end of its life cycle. It goes through several stages from an egg in the water to a mature dragonfly in the air.

The life cycle of the dragonfly begins in the summer. First, the eggs are laid under the water. After one week, the eggs hatch and nymphs come out. Throughout the fall and winter, the dragonfly nymph lives under the water. It eats and grows during this time. In the spring, the nymph leaves the water by crawling up a plant. Then, it molts. Now it is an adult dragonfly. During the summer, the dragonfly flies in the air. It hunts and eats flying insects. It lives like this for a few weeks or months, and then its life is over. The dragonfly's life cycle takes about one year to complete.

Diagram C

The diagram shows a neighborhood prior to and following the building of new houses. The neighborhood changed from a quiet area to a busy place to live. Before the construction, the neighborhood had a farm. There was a barn with a house next to it, and there were some animals in the yard. A fence divided this area from a cornfield. On the other side of the road there were some woods. There was just one house in the woods.

After construction, there was no farm. New houses were built where the barn, farmhouse, and animals used to be. The fence was taken away and a new road was put in its place. On the other side of the new road, more new houses were built in the former cornfield. On the other side of the old road, even more new houses were built in the woods. One part of the woods was turned into a park. What was once open land became a neighborhood filled with houses.

Diagram D

The diagram illustrates a river area prior to and following a flood. Many things were washed away by the floodwaters.

Before the flood, there was a big bend in the river called an oxbow. Several houses had been built on both sides of the river. Also, many trees were growing by the riverbank. A bridge crossed the river near the houses.

After the flood, things looked very different. The oxbow was cut off from the river and became a lake. The river followed a straight path where the oxbow used to be. Most of the houses were washed away. In fact, on one side of the river there were no houses left. There were also fewer trees by the riverbank. The trees that had been closest to the river were washed away. Finally, the bridge completely disappeared, and there was no way to cross the river at that place.

Diagram E

The diagram explains the steps for producing electricity by using a wind turbine. The electricity is generated by the turbine and then is distributed to people's homes.

First, the wind blows against the turbine, and this causes the blades and the rotor to spin. The moving blades and rotor make the driveshaft spin. The spinning driveshaft causes the gearbox and the generator to spin. The spinning generator creates an electric current. A wind speed monitor on the back of the turbine measures the speed and direction of the wind. Then, the rotating motor can move the turbine so that it faces into the wind.

The electric current moves from the generator down a cable in the turbine tower. From there it goes through a substation and then moves on to people's homes. The wind that blows past the turbine moves with reduced speed and energy.

PRACTICE 13 (PAGE 70)

A

1   **Topic sentence:** *The diagram shows the process of recycling plastic bottles to make new products.*

2   **General statement:** *It takes several steps to go from used bottles to new products made out of the same material.*

3   **Steps:**   *She puts it in a recycling bin.*
The bottles are picked up by truck.
They are transported to the recycling plant.
They have to be washed.
They are sent to another machine, where they are shredded into small pieces.
The shredded pieces go into the extruder … turns the pieces into pellets
The pellets are used to make new plastic products.

4   **Transition words/phrases:** first, after, then, before, after, next, finally

5   There are no grammar or spelling errors.

6   Possible answers:
ss: *This machine turns the pieces into pellets.*
cm/s: *Then, the bottles are picked up by truck, and they are transported to the recycling plant.*
cx/s: *After someone finishes drinking from a bottle, she puts it in a recycling bin.*

B

1   **Topic sentence:** *The diagram illustrates the changes that were made to the Taftsville Public Library.*

2   **General statement:** *The library was larger and had more rooms after the renovations were done.*

3   **Items:**   *desk*
reference area
children's room
two rooms for adults, one nonfiction and the other fiction

4   **Changes:**   *The desk was moved closer to the front door.*
a new reading area
The old children's room was divided into two rooms, one for magazines and one for the new reference area.
a new children's room was built
a new garden was created

5   **Transition words/phrases:** before, additionally, after, also

6   There are no grammar or spelling errors.

7   Possible answers:
ss: *There was a large children's room on the right.*
cx/s: *Although changes were made to the other areas of the library, the two adult rooms remained in the same place.*
cm-cx/s: *The library was larger and it had more rooms after the renovations were done.*

C

1   **Topic sentence:** *The diagram shows how a wood pellet boiler is used to provide heat and hot water for a house.*

2   **General Statement:** *The pellets are burned to produce heat, which is then distributed through the house.*

3   **Steps:**   *a truck delivers wood pellets to the house*
                     they are stored in a large container
                     the pellets move to the boiler
                     they are burned to heat up water
                     Some of it goes to pipes under the floor.
                     Some of it also goes to a radiator.
                     Some of the hot water goes to a hot water tank.
                     it returns as cool water to the boiler
                     it is heated to be used again

4   **Transition words/phrases:** to begin, then, next, also, additionally, after

5   There are no grammar or spelling errors.

6   Possible answers:
      ss: *Next, the hot water moves to several places in the house.*
      cm/s: *To begin, a truck delivers wood pellets to the house, and they are stored in a large container.*
      cx/s: *The pellets are burned to produce heat, which is then distributed through the house.*

D

1   **Topic sentence:** *The diagram explains the process of making frozen orange juice concentrate from fresh oranges.*

2   **General statement:** *It takes several steps to go from oranges on the tree to frozen concentrate that can be mixed and consumed at home.*

3   **Steps:**   *the ripe oranges are harvested.*
                     transported to the processing
                     the oranges go through a fruit washer.
                     they are sent through an extractor, which squeezes out the juice
                     the extracted juice goes through the juice evaporator, which concentrates it
                     the juice concentrate is frozen in the freezer
                     the frozen concentrate is put into cans
                     The cans of frozen concentrate are distributed to grocery stores
                     The customer mixes the frozen concentrate with water
                     enjoys a delicious glass of orange juice

4   **Transition words/phrases:** first, then, after, next, then, then, finally

5   There are no grammar or spelling errors.

6   Possible answers:
      ss: *First, the ripe oranges are harvested.*
      cx/s: *After the trucks are unloaded at the plant, the oranges go through a fruit washer.*
      cm-cx/s: *Then, the extracted juice goes through the juice evaporator, which concentrates it, and then the juice concentrate is frozen in the freezer.*

PRACTICE 14 (PAGE 77)

Answers will vary.

PRACTICE 15 (PAGE 78)

Sample answers. Answers will vary.

A

The diagram presents the steps for preparing coffee beans for consumption. It takes several steps to go from coffee beans on a plant to the coffee that we drink at home.

The process begins when the coffee beans are harvested. After the harvest, the beans go through a depulper, which is a machine that separates the seeds from the flesh of the bean. Then, the beans are put into fermenting tanks. After one to three days in the tanks, the coffee beans are spread out in the sun to dry. This takes eight to ten days. When the beans are dry, they are sorted as they move down a conveyor belt. The sorted beans go into the roaster, where they are roasted. Then, they are ground in a grinder and packed in bags. The bags of coffee are transported to grocery stores for sale. Finally, the customer buys the coffee and brews and drinks it at home.

B

The diagrams illustrate the changes that were made to City Park when a swimming pool was built. Some things were moved, and some areas became smaller in order to make room for the pool.

Before the swimming pool was built, there was a parking lot on either side of Park Road, one larger and one smaller. Past the larger parking lot, there were two basketball courts. Past the smaller parking lot, there was a garden with a fountain in the middle.

After the swimming pool was built, things were rearranged. The larger parking lot remained in the same place, but the original smaller parking lot was gone. A new small parking lot was created in the place of one of the basketball courts, and the swimming pool was built in the place of the original smaller parking lot. The pool area also took some room from the garden. The garden, therefore, became smaller, and the fountain was removed.

GENERAL TRAINING WRITING TASK 1: LETTER

PRACTICE 1 (PAGE 81)

1   describe a problem/suggest a solution
2   make an invitation/ask for advice
3   describe a problem/suggest a solution
4   make an invitation/describe a thing or place
5   describe a problem/ask for help/describe a thing or place

PRACTICE 2 (PAGE 83)

1	E	**3**	C	**5**	A
2	G	**4**	D		

PRACTICE 3 (PAGE 84)

Sample answers. Answers will vary.

1 using a different way to get to work
can't ride because of an injury

2 touring bike
new, expensive bike

3 friend likes bike riding but doesn't have a bike
friend is looking for a way to get more exercise

4 barking dog
piano

5 can't hear TV
can't relax

6 take dog to training school
add insulation

PRACTICE 4 (PAGE 86)

Answers will vary.

PRACTICE 5 (PAGE 90)

Sample answers. Answers will vary.

A

Point 1
noise of guests arriving
loud music
noise lasts until late at night

Point 2
can't sleep until party is over
have to get up early for work
don't get enough hours of sleep

Point 3
Let me know about party plans
sleep somewhere else
change work schedule

B

Point 1
at first—interesting
I was inexperienced
now—boring

Point 2
at a larger firm
wider variety of clients

Point 3
you have contacts
you have experience

PRACTICE 6 (PAGE 91)

Answers will vary.

PRACTICE 7 (PAGE 94)

Sample answers. Answers will vary.

1	A	**3**	B	**5**	A
2	B	**4**	A	**6**	B

PRACTICE 8 (PAGE 96)

Sample answers. Wording may vary.

1   I am writing to let you know about a difficulty I am having with noise from your apartment.

2   I am writing to ask you about a valuable possession that was broken while you were staying at my apartment last week.

3   I wanted to let you know that I have recently moved to a new neighborhood.

4   I thought you should know about a problem in my apartment that needs some repairs.

PRACTICE 9 (PAGE 98)

1	A	**2**	C	**3**	B	**4**	B

PRACTICE 10 (PAGE 99)

Answers will vary.

PRACTICE 11 (PAGE 101)

Possible answers. Wording may vary.

1   Unfortunately, this situation disturbs my sleep. The noise makes it impossible for me to fall asleep until the party is over. Since I have to get up early in the morning, I end up with less sleep than I need.

2   The vase I am talking about is a porcelain vase that was on the coffee table in the living room. It is mostly blue with gold around the rim. It has flowers and butterflies hand painted all over it.

3   I had been looking for some time for a house closer to my job. Before, it took me almost an hour to get to work by bus. Now, I can walk to the office in just 15 minutes. This makes my life easier in many ways.

4   The leak in the kitchen sink is causing a serious problem. The area under the sink is very damp, and the wood is beginning to rot. I believe the cause is a hole in the drainpipe.

PRACTICE 12 (PAGE 103)

Answers will vary.

PRACTICE 13 (PAGE 104)

1 B   2 A   3 C   4 A

PRACTICE 14 (PAGE 106)

1 B   3 A   5 A
2 A   4 B   6 B

PRACTICE 15 (PAGE 107)

Sample answers. Answers will vary.

1   Dear Sir or Madam,

I want to let you know about a very disappointing purchase I made at your store last week. I bought a very nice-looking jacket, but when I got home, I found out that it was damaged. When I tried to return it to the store, I was shocked to learn that returns aren't allowed. I hope you can help me solve this problem.

The jacket looked nice in the store, but when I got it home, I found that it had several problems. When I put it on, I discovered a hole under the left arm. The lining was torn, too. Also, two buttons were missing from the cuffs.

When I took the jacket back to the store, the associate told me that you don't accept merchandise returns. She said that I might have caused the damage after I bought the jacket.

This situation is unacceptable. I did not damage the jacket. I think that the store should give me a complete refund. If this is not possible, I will accept store credit to use for buying a different jacket.

I hope we can quickly agree on a solution to this problem.

Sincerely,
Matthew Davis

2 Dear Julia,

I am getting ready to make a trip to your city next month. This will be a business trip, but I will also have some free time. I hope you can give me some advice about the best places to visit, and I also hope we can get together while I'm there.

My company is sending me to your city to lead a training session. A company there recently bought some of our software, and I will train the staff on how to use it. I will be busy with the training Monday through Thursday. Then, I will have time on Friday and Saturday to enjoy the city.

Could you suggest some places for me to visit during my two free days? You know I like art and would enjoy visiting art museums and galleries. I am also interested in learning about the history of your city and would like to visit any important historical sites.

Additionally, I hope you will be able to join me for dinner on Friday evening. Please suggest a restaurant where we can meet.

Thank you for your advice. I'm looking forward to seeing you.

Your friend,
Lucas

3 Dear Mr. Jones,

I am writing to tell you about the parking problem at our building. I frequently have trouble finding a place to park. Something has to be done about this.

Often when I get home from work, the parking lot is full. There are supposed to be enough spaces in the lot for each tenant to park one car. If the lot is full, that means other people are using our spaces or some tenants have more than one car.

When I can't find space in the parking lot, I have to park on the street. I don't like to do this because I work late and I don't like walking on the street alone at night.

I would like to offer some suggestions for solving this problem. First, you could post some signs in the lot explaining that it is for building tenants only. In addition, you could assign each apartment a space and paint the apartment number on it. That way, each tenant will always have his or her own place to park.

Please let me know what you think of my ideas.

Sincerely,
Irene du Breuil

4   Dear Yolanda,

I want to tell you about the wonderful time at my summer rental house. It's a really nice little cottage. There are a lot of fun things to do here, and I know you would enjoy visiting.

The cottage where I am staying is small but quite comfortable. It has one large room downstairs and two small bedrooms upstairs. The best part is the porch, where I can sit and enjoy a view of the lake. There are pine trees all around. They provide shade, so the house is always cool and comfortable.

Since I am staying right by the lake, I spend a lot of time in the water. I swim every morning before breakfast. After breakfast, I usually explore the lake in my canoe. In the afternoon, I like to lie on the beach and enjoy the sun.

I hope you can come spend a week here and enjoy this beautiful place with me. It is so relaxing.

Let me know when you can come. Any time next month would be fine with me.

Your friend,
Elena

5   Dear Sir or Madam,

I am writing to tell you about a lost item. I left a bag in one of your taxis yesterday. It was a very special bag, and I hope you can help me find it.

When I got home yesterday, I realized my bag was missing. I was returning from a trip to visit my grandmother and rode in one of your taxis from the train station to my home on Maple Avenue. I know I had the bag on the seat beside me during the ride, so I must have left it in the taxi.

The bag is very special to me. It's a beautiful leather bag that belonged to my grandmother, and she gave it to me during my visit. It is brown and has my grandmother's initials—AJR—on the side. It has a gold buckle and a long shoulder strap.

I hope you can help me find the bag. I don't know the number of the taxi, but I think the driver's name was Burt. If you have a lost and found department, my bag might be there.

Please let me know if you can help me. I would really appreciate it.

Sincerely,
Martha Strathmore

PRACTICE 16 (PAGE 111)

A

1 **Thesis/topic statement:** *I thought you'd be interested in a bicycle I am selling.*

2 **Main ideas of paragraph 1:**   (1) *I just don't have time to use it much anymore.*
                                                                 (2) *it's a really great racing bicycle*
                                                                (3) *and I think you would really like it*

3 **Main ideas of paragraph 2:** *I used to enjoy riding my bicycle frequently, but these days I usually don't have time for it.*

    Supporting details: (A) *My new job is very demanding, and I am working many more hours a week than I used to.*
                                                    (B) *we have a gym at the office, and I try to get my regular exercise there*

4 **Main idea of paragraph 3:** *The bicycle is a really nice ten-speed racing bicycle.*

    Supporting details: (A) *It's lightweight and fast*
                                                    (B) *it has a rack for carrying packages*
                                                    (C) *it is a very nice silver color*

5 **Main idea of paragraph 4:** *I think you'd like it because it's a great bicycle for racing*

    Supporting details: (A) *racing is what you like to do*
                                                (B) *silver is your favorite color*
                                             (C) *I can let you have it at a special price*

6 Possible answers.
    Transitional words/phrases:
    Paragraph 1:   However
    Paragraph 2:   Another reason
    Paragraph 3:   Also

7 There are no grammar or spelling errors.

8 Possible answers:
    ss: *The bicycle is a really nice ten-speed racing bicycle.*
    cm/s: *I used to enjoy riding my bicycle frequently, but these days I usually don't have time for it.*
    cm-cx/s: *I think you'd like it because it's a great bicycle for racing, and I know racing is what you like to do.*

B

1 **Thesis statement:** *I wanted to let you know that I have recently moved to a new neighborhood.*

2 **Main ideas of paragraph 1:**   (1) *The reason is that I wanted to be closer to my job.*
                                                                 (2) *It is a quiet and pretty place to live*
                                                                 (3) *I hope you will visit me here soon*

3   **Main idea of paragraph 2:** *I had been looking for some time for a house closer to my job.*

    Supporting details: (A) *Before, it took me almost an hour to get to work by bus*
                                    (B) *Now, I can walk to the office in just 15 minutes*
                                    (C) *This makes my life easier in many ways*

4   **Main idea of paragraph 3:** *My new neighborhood is very nice.*

    Supporting details: (A) *There are many tall trees and lots of gardens, so it is very pretty.*
                                    (B) *It is also quiet because there is very little traffic*

5   **Main idea of paragraph 4:** *I hope you will be able to visit me at my new house*

    Supporting details: (A) *We could have lunch and then take a walk*
                                    (B) *I think you would enjoy seeing the gardens*

6   Possible answers.
    Transition words:
    Paragraph 2:   Before, Now
    Paragraph 3:   also

7   There are no grammar or spelling errors.

8   Possible answers:
    ss: *This makes my life easier in many ways.*
    cm/s: *It is a quiet and pretty place to live, and I hope you will visit me here soon.*
    cx/s: *It is also quiet because there is very little traffic.*

C

1   **Thesis statement:** *I am writing to ask you for advice about my vacation.*

2   **Main ideas of paragraph 1:**   (1) *I will have some time off of work soon*
                                              (2) *I would like to spend most of that time at the beach*
                                              (3) *I hope you have some suggestions for me*

3   **Main idea of paragraph 2:** *I will have the entire month of August off of work.*

    Supporting details: (A) *I haven't had a vacation in a long time*
                                    (B) *I am really looking forward to this*
                                    (C) *we have been very busy at the office*

4   **Main idea of paragraph 3:** *I would like to spend my month off at a nice beach resort.*

    Supporting details: (A) *a hotel next to the beach that provides all meals*
                                    (B) *I prefer a quiet atmosphere*
                                    (C) *I can't spend too much money*

5   **Main idea of paragraph 4:** *I hope you can suggest a good place for my vacation.*

    Supporting details: (A) *I know you travel a lot*
                                    (B) *I prefer a quiet atmosphere*
                                    (C) *If you could let me know the names of some of your favorite ones*

6 Possible answers.

Transition words:

Paragraph 2:	Therefore
Paragraph 2:	Since
Paragraph 3:	Also

7 There are no grammar or spelling errors.

8 Possible answers:

ss: *I will have the entire month of August off of work.*

cm/s: *I can't spend too much money, but I would like a comfortable place to stay.*

cx/s: *If you could let me know the names of some of your favorite ones, I would appreciate it.*

D

1 **Thesis statement:** *I am writing about a problem in my apartment that needs some repairs.*

2 **Main ideas of paragraph 1:** (1) *The kitchen sink has been leaking for some time now*
(2) *I believe the drainpipe should be replaced*
(3) *I think you should take a look at it*

3 **Main idea of paragraph 2:** *The leak in the kitchen sink is causing a serious problem.*

Supporting details: (A) *Because the area under the sink has become very damp, the wood is beginning to rot.*
(B) *the cause of the dampness is a hole in the drainpipe*

4 **Main idea of paragraph 3:** *In my opinion, the drainpipe should be replaced as soon as possible.*

Supporting details: (A) *the problem will only get worse*
(B) *the entire cabinet will have to be replaced*

5 **Main idea of paragraph 4:** *I suggest that you come to my apartment and take a look at the leaky sink*

Supporting details: (A) *I can show you the damaged area*
(B) *we can discuss the best action to take*

6 Possible answers.

Transition words:

Paragraph 2:	Unfortunately
Paragraph 3:	In my opinion
Paragraph 3:	Otherwise

7 There are no grammar or spelling errors.

8 Possible answers:

ss: *The leak in the kitchen sink is causing a serious problem.*

cx/s: *Because the area under the sink has become very damp, the wood is beginning to rot.*

cm/s: *I can show you the damaged area, and we can discuss the best action to take.*

PRACTICE 17 (PAGE 118)

Answers will vary.

PRACTICE 18 (PAGE 119)

Sample answers. Answers will vary.

A Dear Sir or Madam,

I am writing to let you know about a problem I had at your hotel recently. My room was very noisy, but the hotel staff did not move me as I requested. I think you should speak to your staff about this type of problem.

When I arrived at the hotel, I was given a room with a single bed, as I had requested. Unfortunately, the room faced a noisy side street, and I knew I would be unable to get a good night's rest.

I explained the problem to the front desk clerk and asked to be given another room. She said there were no more single rooms available but that I could have a double room at a higher price. When I protested about paying a higher price, the clerk said that she couldn't give me a less expensive room.

I made my reservation a long time ago, and I paid a high price for my room. I think that in a case like this, the customer should be given a better room without having to pay extra. I believe you should explain to your staff that keeping customers happy is a high priority.

I hope you agree with me and will speak to your staff.

Sincerely,
Louis V. Montero

B Dear Miranda,

I want to tell you about a change I am making in my life. I really like your neighborhood and have decided to look for a small apartment to rent there. I hope you can help me with my search.

I have always loved your neighborhood because it is so conveniently located. There are stores and movie theaters nearby, and the neighborhood park is a really nice place to take walks. Most of all, it is close to my job, so I would be able to ride my bike to work.

I would like to find a small one-bedroom apartment. I would prefer to live in a small building where the rents are not too high. If I could live close to the park, that would be great, but it's not a requirement.

I hope you can help me find something. Please let me know if you hear of any available apartments. Also, maybe you could suggest some nice buildings where I could look for vacancies.

Thanks for your advice, and I look forward to being your neighbor!

Your friend,
Ramona

ACADEMIC/GENERAL TRAINING WRITING TASK 2: PERSONAL OPINION

PRACTICE 1 (page 122)

1	D	3	C	5	B
2	A	4	E		

PRACTICE 2 (page 124)

1	B, C	3	A	5	B
2	A, C	4	B, C		

PRACTICE 3 (page 127)

Answers will vary.

PRACTICE 4 (page 130)

1	C	3	A	5	C
2	A	4	B		

PRACTICE 5 (page 130)

1	C	3	C	5	D
2	B	4	A		

PRACTICE 6 (page 131)

1 Develop social skills
2 Learn skills for primary school
3 Safe place for children
4 Disadvantages of preschool
5 People can't smoke in many places
6 Such laws aren't enough
7 People can still smoke some of the time
8 There could be notices on TV, the radio, and the Internet

PRACTICE 7 (page 133)

Answers will vary.

PRACTICE 8 (page 137)

2 **Thesis:** Aging parents can live in a special home, but it is better for them to live with their families.
   Main idea 1: family care means better care and fewer costs
   Main idea 2: some families don't have time or resources to care for parents themselves

3   **Thesis:** Life in the past was worse.
     Main idea 1: lack of modern machines meant harder work
     Main idea 2: lack of modern medicine meant dying young
     Main idea 3: lack of modern transportation meant fewer opportunities

4   **Thesis:** There are several causes of the traffic congestion problem, but there are also solutions.
     Main idea 1: cause: overcrowded cities
     Main idea 2: cause: lack of transportation options
     Main idea 3: solution: improve public transportation

5   **Thesis:** I agree that there should be no zoos because they are cruel.
     Main idea 1: Zoos are like jails for animals
     Main idea 2: Zoos are unnecessary

PRACTICE 9 (PAGE 140)

Answers will vary.

PRACTICE 10 (PAGE 141)

Possible answers. Answers may vary slightly.

2   Telecommuting also allows the employer to cut costs. With fewer employees in the office, the employer can save on rent by having a smaller office. The employer will also need less office equipment. Moreover, the employer will be able to get by with a smaller support staff.

3   On the other hand, some employers feel that telecommuting makes it more difficult for them to manage their workers. It is hard to supervise the work when it is done away from the office. In addition, the employer can never be sure how well the employees are managing their time. It is also difficult to have staff meetings when some or most of the employees are not usually in the office.

4   Some families feel that their aging parents can get better and less expensive care at home. In the first place, families care for their parents with love in a way that no one else can do. Furthermore, their parents feel happiest in their own homes, surrounded by their children and grandchildren. On top of this, homes for the elderly are expensive, and many families cannot afford them.

5   Some families, on the other hand, don't have the time or resources to care for their aging parents at home. Most people have jobs and this means they are away from home for much of the time. In addition, they need to devote time and attention to their children if their children are still young. Finally, many people live in apartments and don't have enough space in their home for their parents.

PRACTICE 11 (PAGE 143)

Answers will vary.

PRACTICE 12 (PAGE 145)

1 Telecommuting can make some things easier for employers and employees, but it can make other things more difficult. Employees and their bosses have to decide together whether or not telecommuting works for them.

2 Families can care for their aging parents themselves or they can send them to special homes. The best choice is to keep parents, or any relative who needs help, at home whenever possible.

3 Life in the past was very difficult. People worked had, died young, and had few opportunities to improve their lives. Modern technology has improved our lives greatly.

4 Many people live in overcrowded cities with few choices for transportation. Investment in public transportation and alternative transportation would do much to alleviate the traffic problems that result. Traffic congestion is a serious problem, but it can be solved.

5 In my opinion, all zoos should be shut down. It is cruel to keep animals locked up in cages. Zoos are also not the best places to do research on animals. I can see no good reason for the existence of zoos.

PRACTICE 13 (PAGE 147)

Answers will vary. See The Revise section of Academic Task 2 (page 148) and the More Writing Practice section (page 223) in the Appendix for sample responses.

PRACTICE 14 (PAGE 151)

A

1 **Thesis statement:** *people believe that there should be a law against using a cell phone while driving, but I do not agree with this point of view.*

2 **Main ideas of paragraph 1:** (1) *cell phone use by a driver is necessary*
(2) *there are ways to make it safe*

3 **Main idea of the second paragraph:** *People have cell phones because they need them, and often they need to use them when they are traveling by car.*

Supporting details: (A) *Some people, for example, use their cars on company business.*
(B) *Another example is parents, who need to be in communication with their children.*

4 **Main idea of paragraph 3:** *There are devices that make cell phone use less distracting.*

Supporting details: (A) *Drivers can use earphones, for example, so that they don't have to hold the phone and can keep both hands on the steering wheel.*
(B) *Devices make holding and looking at the phone unnecessary.*
(C) *Then, talking on a cell phone is no more distracting than talking to a passenger in the car.*

5 **Transition words:**
Paragraph 2:   and, for example, Another
Paragraph 3:   However

6 There are no grammar or spelling errors.

7 Possible answers:
cx/s: *They may need to talk to their boss or to a client while they are on the road.*
ss: *They are all important.*
adj.c.: *who need to be in communication with their children.*

B

1 **Thesis statement:** *While obesity is a serious problem for these reasons, there are solutions.*

2 **Main ideas of paragraph 1:**   (1) *Poor diet*
(2) *lack of exercise*
(3) *there are solutions*

3 **Main idea of paragraph 2:** *The biggest cause of the obesity problem . . . is poor diet.*

Supporting details: (A) *Fast food restaurants have become widespread*
(B) *Snack foods . . . are also popular*

4 **Main idea of paragraph 3:** *The other major cause of obesity is lack of exercise.*

Supporting details: (A) *People drive everywhere.*
(B) *People work long hours.*
(C) *Children prefer to sit in front of the computer.*

5 **Main idea of paragraph 4:** *there are solutions to this problem.*

Supporting details: (A) *Education is very important.*
(B) *making healthy food more available*

6 **Transition word:**
Paragraph 2:   Unfortunately, also, Like
Paragraph 3:   Another, also

7 There are no grammar or spelling errors.

8 Possible answers:
cm/s: *People drive everywhere, so they have little opportunity to walk.*
ss: *Education is very important.*
cm-cx/s: *Fast food restaurants have become widespread, and people like to eat at them because they are cheap and convenient.*

C

1   **Thesis statement:** *This popular way of eating has both advantages and disadvantages.*

2   **Main ideas of paragraph 1:**   (1) *convenient*
                                                     (2) *expensive*
                                                     (3) *not very healthful*

3   **Main idea of paragraph 2:** *The biggest advantage of eating restaurant meals and convenience foods is that it makes mealtime much simpler.*

    Supporting details: (A) *Many people are busy with their jobs and taking care of their children.*
                                      (B) *If all they have to do at dinnertime is choose a restaurant or put something in the microwave oven, then dinner is a much easier event.*

4   **Main idea of paragraph 3:** *it can be quite expensive*

    Supporting details: (A) *Restaurant meals cost a great deal more than meals cooked at home.*
                                      (B) *Convenience foods cost less than restaurant meals, but they are still expensive.*
                                      (C) *It is hard for many families to afford to eat restaurant meals and convenience foods on a regular basis.*

5   **Main idea of paragraph 4:** *they are not very healthful*

    Supporting details: (A) *They are often high in fat, salt, and sugar.*
                                      (B) *restaurant portions tend to be big, which makes them higher in calories.*
                                      (C) *Convenience foods may contain vegetables, but they are not fresh, so they are not a good source of vitamins.*
                                      (D) *Home-cooked meals, on the other hand, can be as nutritious as you want to make them.*

6   **Transition words:**
    Paragraph 4:   Another, In addition, Therefore, on the other hand

7   There are no grammar or spelling errors.

8   Possible answers:
    cm/s: *Convenience foods may contain vegetables, but they are not fresh.*
    ss: *They are often high in fat, salt, and sugar.*
    cx/s: *Although eating restaurant meals and convenience foods is simpler than cooking at home, it can be quite expensive.*

D

1   **Thesis statement:** *While there are people who think that school should only be about academics, others believe that physical education is also important, and I agree with this point of view.*

2   **Main ideas of paragraph 1:**   (1) *people who think that school should only be about academics*
(2) *others believe that physical education is also important*
(3) *I agree with this point of view*

3   **Main idea of paragraph 2:** *Some people feel that school should be all about academics.*

Supporting details: (A) *children need to spend their entire school day learning math, science, literature, and history*
(B) *the best way to prepare children for their future university education and careers*
(C) *If children enjoy playing sports, they should do it outside of school time.*

4   **Main idea of paragraph 3:** *Other people, however, feel that physical education is an important part of a child's education.*

Supporting details: (A) *physical education teaches children important skills*
(B) *physical education classes are the best way to ensure that children get the regular physical exercise that they need*
(C) *if children spend a little time each day being physically active, it helps them concentrate better on their academic work.*

5   **Main idea of paragraph 4:** *I agree that devoting some school time to physical education is necessary.*

Supporting details: (A) *children will not learn that physical activity is important*
(B) *They won't get the exercise they need to grow up healthy.*
(C) *It is not enough to say they can play games and sports in their free time.*

6   **Transition words:**
Paragraph 3:   however, According to, In addition, Finally

7   There are no grammar or spelling errors.

8   Possible answers:
cm/s: *Academics are important, but physical education is important, too.*
adj.c.: *They won't get the exercise that they need to grow up healthy.*
cx/s: *If children enjoy playing sports, they should do it outside of school time.*

PRACTICE 15 (PAGE 158)

Answers will vary.

PRACTICE 16 (PAGE 159)

Sample answers. Answers will vary.

A

There are different ideas about the best way to group children for learning. According to some people, the best way is to group children with others who have similar academic skills. But there are those who feel it is better to place children in groups with mixed abilities. I agree with the second point of view.

Some people believe that children do best when they study with others of similar abilities. They say that this allows children to learn at the right pace. By following this method, faster children will not be held back by slower children, and slower children will not be frustrated by trying to move ahead too fast.

Other people, however, think that children do better when they are in a mixed-level class. For one thing, children who are working at a higher level can serve as models for other children. They show the lower-level children what might be possible for them. Also, higher-level children can help others with their work. This provides them with challenges and reinforces their own learning.

I feel that the best method is to place children in mixed-level classes. A classroom filled with variety opens children's minds in many ways. In addition, no two children are exactly alike. Therefore, it is impossible to have a completely homogenous class, so why try to have one when you can have all the advantages of a mixed-level class?

There may be some advantages to having children study only with others of similar abilities, but I feel that there are many more advantages to studying in a mixed-level group.

B

Some people believe that the government should provide complete financial support to universities in order to make higher education available to all who want it. I completely support this opinion. Everyone benefits when more people are educated, and many deserving people are denied a university education because they cannot afford to pay for it.

Society as a whole benefits when more people are educated. Some people may complain about supporting others' education through the taxes they pay to the government. "Why should I pay my hard-earned money for someone else to go to school?" they may say. But the fact is that it is not only the individual who benefits from the education. A person who studies to become a doctor may save the life of someone you love. A person who studies to become an engineer may design roads and bridges that you use every day. There are endless examples. Educated people contribute important things to society, and we all benefit from it.

There are many smart and talented people who would benefit from a university education but cannot afford it. This is not fair. Higher education should not be available only to those who have enough money to pay for it. Then only a small, exclusive group would be able to become professionals while many other people would waste their talents and dreams on jobs that didn't interest them. Everybody who has the desire, skills, and talents to pursue a university education should be allowed to do so.

A university education should not be something that only wealthy people have the right to attain. Everyone, individuals as well as society as a whole, wins when higher education is made available to all.

COHERENCE AND COHESION

PRACTICE 1 (PAGE 162)

1 <u>Far from being a sort of cruel jail for wild animals, zoos actually play an important role in animal conservation.</u> ~~Modern zoos keep their animals in large enclosures that resemble the natural habitat.~~ Zoos give people the opportunity to see animals up close and learn about their habits and needs. This helps people feel a connection with animals and helps them understand the importance of preserving wild habitat. It makes people more interested in supporting conservation efforts.

2 <u>The most important reason why I chose to move to this neighborhood is its convenient location.</u> It is close to my job, so I can walk to work when the weather is nice. There are two small grocery stores nearby, and the mall is just a short subway ride away. ~~Most of the houses are affordable, although a few are a bit expensive.~~ There is a gym one block from my house, which makes it very easy to get my daily exercise.

3 <u>Spending too much time on the Internet can have a bad effect on children's health.</u> Children need a lot of physical exercise to stay healthy. When they spend a lot of time online, however, they don't get physical exercise. Parents should encourage their children to turn off the computer and spend time outside playing physically active games. ~~Children can easily find information on the Internet that is not suitable for their young minds.~~

4 <u>I can recommend several interesting things for you to do during your visit to this city.</u> ~~This city is famous for its pleasant climate.~~ You won't want to miss a visit to the shopping district since our city is so famous for its stores. City Park is near there, has a beautiful garden, and is a nice place for a walk on a sunny day. I think you would also enjoy the history museum as it explains a lot of interesting facts about the city and region.

5 <u>The price of corn dropped steadily from 2012 to 2015.</u> It fell from just over $4.00 in 2012 to exactly $4.00 a bushel in 2013. In 2014 there was another slight drop, to around $3.50, and it dropped again, to around $3.00 a bushel in 2015. ~~The price of wheat rose slightly in 2012.~~

PRACTICE 2 (PAGE 162)

1	A	3	B	5	C
2	C	4	D		

PRACTICE 3 (PAGE 164)

1	zoos	6	library	11	library
2	behavior	7	people	12	office
3	scientists	8	people	13	colleagues
4	scientists	9	person	14	colleagues
5	city	10	person	15	party

PRACTICE 4 (PAGE 165)

Restaurant meals have several disadvantages. In the first place, **1** <u>they</u> are more expensive than home-cooked meals. In addition, restaurant portions tend to be big, which makes **2** <u>them</u> higher in calories. Restaurant chefs often use rich sauces in their cooking. These sauces may be delicious, but **3** <u>they</u> are also often high in calories and fat.

There are several reasons why I have decided to sell my car. For one thing, **4** <u>it</u> is old and frequently needs repairs. In addition, **5** <u>its</u> tires need to be replaced. But the main reason is that I don't use **6** <u>it</u> very much anymore because I take the bus to work most of the time.

Some parents choose to send **7** <u>their</u> children to school when **8** <u>they</u> are as young as three or four years old. Other parents feel that **9** <u>their</u> children aren't ready for school at such an early age. The fact is that not all children are the same. Different children have different needs.

I would like to invite you to come see my new house. I know you will really like **10** <u>it</u>. I have decorated **11** <u>it</u> very nicely with new furniture and paint. There is also a big garden filled with beautiful flowers and I know you will enjoy seeing **12** <u>them</u>.

PRACTICE 5 (PAGE 166)

Librarians are trained to offer their patrons a variety of services. **1** <u>Patrons</u> may come to the library looking for print materials such as books or magazines, or **2** <u>they</u> may need to use the Internet for research. **3** <u>They</u> might want to borrow a movie or listen to a recorded book. **4** <u>Librarians</u> know that even though information is available on the Internet, many of **5** <u>their</u> patrons are also interested in reading books and magazines. **6** <u>Patrons</u> will let the librarian know what type of material **7** <u>they</u> are looking for, and the librarian will offer suggestions and advice.

PRACTICE 6 (PAGE 167)

We had an excellent experience at your restaurant last night. **1** <u>First</u>, the waiter seated us at a very comfortable table. **2** <u>Then</u>, he brought us our menus right away. **3** <u>After</u> we ordered, we didn't have to wait long for our meal. We left a large tip for the waiter **4** <u>before</u> we went home.

Here are some tips for your first day at a new job. **5** <u>First</u>, you should make sure you arrive on time or even a little bit early. **6** <u>Next</u>, look for your supervisor to let him or her know you are there. **7** <u>Before</u> you start your duties, it is a good idea to introduce yourself to everyone in the office. Remember, it may take you a little while to learn the office routines. Don't worry, after a few days, everything will become familiar, but **8** <u>in the meantime</u>, you should ask your colleagues to explain things to you.

PRACTICE 7 (PAGE 167)

Possible answer. Answer will vary.

I had a very interesting day yesterday. First, I got up very early in the morning. It was still dark outside. After breakfast, I took a long walk on the beach. While I was walking, I watched the sunrise over the ocean. It was spectacular. I stayed on the beach for several hours. Then, I went back to town and had a big lunch at a nice restaurant.

PRACTICE 8 (PAGE 169)

1 It is easy to stay informed about current events since the Internet provides us with instant access to news.

   or

   Since the Internet provides us with instant access to news, it is easy to stay informed about current events.

2 The Grand Hotel has comfortable rooms at reasonable rates, so I always stay there when I'm in town.

3 Many websites contain information that isn't suitable for children. Therefore, parents should control how their children use the Internet.

4 Many farmers lost their crops because there was a severe drought in that region.
   or
   Because there was a severe drought in that region, many farmers lost their crops.

5 The rents in this district are very high. For this reason, many people can't afford to live here.

PRACTICE 9 (PAGE 170)

Possible answers. Answers will vary.

1 **A** effect   **B** cause

   Teenagers don't understand the health consequences of smoking. As a result, smoking is popular among them.

   Smoking is popular among teenagers because they don't understand its health consequences.

2 **A** cause   **B** effect

   In most modern families, both parents work full time. Therefore, they don't have enough opportunities to spend quality time with their children.

   Since in most modern families both parents work full time, they don't have enough opportunities to spend quality time with their children.

3 **A** cause **B** effect

Because of recently inheriting a large amount of money, I have decided to take a trip around the world.

I recently inherited a large amount of money, so I have decided to take a trip around the world.

4 **A** effect **B** cause

Many people think the zoos are cruel places since zoo animals are kept locked up in cages.

Zoo animals are kept locked in cages. For this reason, many people think zoos are cruel places.

5 **A** effect **B** cause

I would like to find a new job as soon as possible because my current job is boring and the salary is low.

My current job is boring, and the salary is low. Therefore, I would like to find a new job as soon as possible.

PRACTICE 10 (PAGE 173)

1   Buses can carry many passengers at one time, while cars can only carry a few.

2   Taking a walk every day can help you stay strong and healthy. Likewise, bike riding is a good way to get exercise.

3   Unlike cities, small towns generally offer limited job opportunities.

4   Many people find small towns boring. However, others enjoy a small town's slow pace of life.

5   Like beach resorts, lakeside resorts offer families the opportunity to enjoy all kinds of water sports.

PRACTICE 11 (PAGE 173)

Possible answers. Answers will vary.

1   Contrast

Exercise is important for maintaining health, but many people don't exercise regularly.

Even though exercise is important for maintaining health, many people don't exercise regularly.

2 Contrast

While some people feel that it is cruel to keep animals in zoos, other people believe that zoos provide important opportunities for research and education.

Some people feel that it is cruel to keep animals in zoos. However, other people believe that zoos provide important opportunities for research and education.

3 Compare

The price of milk rose sharply in 2020. There was also a significant increase in the price of bread.

Like the price of bread, the price of milk rose sharply in 2020.

4 Compare

Many adults struggle with weight gain. Similarly, obesity is a problem for many children.

Many adults struggle with weight gain. In the same way, obesity is a problem for many children.

5 Contrast

Children in small families get a lot of adult attention. In contrast, children in large families may not get all the adult attention they need.

Children in small families get a lot of adult attention. Children in large families, however, may not get all the adult attention they need.

PRACTICE 12 (PAGE 175)

1 Telecommuting is very convenient for employees. It has advantages for employers as well.

2 That store has a really nice selection of merchandise. Furthermore, the staff is very helpful and courteous.

3 Meals cooked at home are less expensive than restaurant meals. They are also usually more nutritious.

Or

Meals cooked at home are less expensive than restaurant meals. They are usually more nutritious also.

Or

Meals cooked at home are less expensive than restaurant meals. Also, they are usually more nutritious.

4 Electric cars don't cause air pollution. In addition, they are easy and inexpensive to maintain.

5   This neighborhood has many houses that are affordably priced. Moreover, it is conveniently located close to stores and public transportation.

PRACTICE 13 (PAGE 176)

Possible answers. Answers will vary.

1   Too many private cars on the roads lead to frequent traffic jams. Also, they create high levels of air pollution.

Too many private cars on the roads lead to frequent traffic jams. What's more, they create high levels of air pollution.

2   City life is stressful because of the crowds and noise. Moreover, high levels of crime make cities very dangerous.

City life is stressful because of the crowds and noise. High levels of crime make cities very dangerous, too.

3   Zoos provide scientists with many opportunities for research. They also allow the general public to learn about the habits of wild animals.

Zoos provide scientists with many opportunities for research. In addition, they allow the general public to learn about the habits of wild animals.

4   If you wait until you are 30 to get married, you will have a better idea of the type of person you want to marry. In addition, you will have had more time to establish yourself in your profession.

If you wait until you are 30 to get married, you will have a better idea of the type of person you want to marry. You will have had more time to establish yourself in your profession as well.

5   Telecommuting means that people don't have to spend time and money traveling between work and home. Additionally, it gives them more time to devote to family responsibilities such as cooking, cleaning, and child care.

Telecommuting means that people don't have to spend time and money traveling between work and home. Furthermore, it gives them more time to devote to family responsibilities such as cooking, cleaning, and child care.

PRACTICE 14 (PAGE 178)

1   There are several advantages to living in this neighborhood. For one thing, it is close to two bus routes.

2   Zoos provide the public with important educational opportunities. For example, they can teach people about the importance of preserving native habitat.

3   Traffic problems in cities are due to a number of factors including lack of public transportation and poorly designed roads.

4   Visitors to a zoo can enjoy a variety of fun activities such as seeing the animals, talking with scientists, and visiting the gift shop.

5 People avoid using public transportation for a variety of reasons. For one thing, they may feel that train and bus schedules are not convenient.

PRACTICE 15 (PAGE 179)

Possible answers. Answers will vary.

1 For one thing, you'll meet a wider variety of people in a city.
2 For example, there are more opportunities for outdoor activities.
3 For instance, the neighborhood is noisy and dangerous.
4 such as local tours, boat rides, and snorkeling.
5 including cost, speed, and convenience.

LEXICAL RESOURCE

PRACTICE 1 (PAGE 182)

1 We cannot deny the <u>importance</u> of <u>physical</u> <u>education</u>.
                   noun   *adjective* *noun*

2 <u>Enrollment</u> at the academy increased <u>significantly</u> last semester.
   noun   *adverb*

3 Most people <u>recognize</u> that smoking is <u>dangerous</u> to the health.
          verb   *adjective*

4 I plan to <u>organize</u> a <u>formal</u> party so that we can <u>celebrate</u> the event.
       verb   *adjective*   *verb*

5 Foreign language study should be a <u>requirement</u> in primary schools because
                             noun

   young children learn languages <u>easily</u>.
                    adverb

PRACTICE 2 (PAGE 184)

1 In physical education classes, children learn to *compete* in a healthy way.
2 Team sports are very *competitive*.
3 *Competition* in the job market can make it difficult for people to find employment even if they are highly qualified.
4 These products sold quickly because they were *competitively* priced.
5 Some private schools are quite *selective* about the students they admit.
6 University students can *select* which courses they want to take each semester.
7 I like shopping at this store because they have a wide *selection* of merchandise.
8 Eat desserts *selectively* if you want to avoid weight problems.
9 Some parents make the *decision* to send their children to school at an early age.

10 Many families _decide_ to care for their elderly parents at home.

11 Once you have a plan, act _decisively_ to carry it out.

12 A _decisive_ person does not hesitate to act.

13 _Persistent_ people often achieve their goals.

14 _Persistence_ got me the job I wanted.

15 I finally got a refund after I _persistently_ complained to the manager.

16 A child's learning problems will _persist_ if they are not dealt with early on.

17 Some people give up smoking _reluctantly_.

18 I was _reluctant_ to complain about the poor service.

19 The _reluctance_ to follow a regular exercise plan can make weight loss very difficult.

20 We will _beautify_ the city by planting trees along the street.

21 The entire cast performed the play _beautifully_.

22 I know that the _beauty_ of this place will impress you.

23 We had a _beautiful_ view from our room.

24 I can write _authoritatively_ about this issue since I have studied it in depth.

25 Dr. Smith is a leading _authority_ on this subject.

26 This tour book is the _authoritative_ guide to this region of the country.

27 Your professor will have to _authorize_ your absence from class on exam day.

28 I appreciate the _efficiency_ of the hotel staff.

29 Spending on heating fuel has gone down because of more _efficient_ heating systems.

30 Nursing homes can care for patients more _efficiently_.

PRACTICE 3 (PAGE 186)

Noun	Verb	Adjective	Adverb
demonstration	demonstrate	demonstrative	demonstratively
popularity	popularize	popular	popularly
intensity	intensify	intense	intensely
ability		able	ably
recognition	recognize	recognizable	recognizably
dependence	depend	dependable	dependably
emotion		emotional	emotionally
width	widen	wide	widely

PRACTICE 4 (PAGE 186)

Answers will vary.

PRACTICE 5 (PAGE 187)

1 pick, select
2 chilly, frosty, wintry,
3 focus on, pay attention to
4 delectable, scrumptious, tasty
5 breakfast, dine, have a meal
6 decrease, drop, go down
7 quick, rapid, speedy
8 acquire, obtain
9 decent, excellent, wonderful
10 clean, tidy
11 calm, peaceful
12 climb, go up, increase
13 explain, inform

PRACTICE 6 (PAGE 188)

Possible answers. Answers will vary.

A

The weather in Springfield was very cold last winter. Temperatures fell in December, and they **1** _dropped_ again in January. Because of the **2** _wintery_ weather, schools were closed for three days. Temperatures rose slightly in February and March. In April they continued to **3** _climb_.

B

I recommend that you eat at the Three Feathers Restaurant during your stay in the city. I always have a good experience when I **4** _dine_ there. It is a very good restaurant. The food is **5** _wonderful_, and the service is **6** _excellent_. The menu is long and there are many delicious dishes to choose from. Sometimes it is hard to know what to **7** _pick_ because everything looks so **8** _tasty_.

C

Different people need different kinds of study conditions. For example, I study best in a quiet environment. Noise really bothers me, and I can't study well unless I am in a **9** _peaceful_ place. Neatness is also important to me because a messy room distracts me. I really need to study in a **10** _tidy_ place in order to be able to concentrate on my work.

PRACTICE 7 (PAGE 190)

1 expects
2 matches
3 buzzes
4 dismisses
5 decisions
6 suffixes
7 animals
8 entries
9 essays
10 cashes
11 satisfies
12 delays
13 discussed
14 increased
15 admitted
16 hardened
17 relied
18 referred
19 helped
20 apologized
21 strayed
22 notified
23 insisted
24 offered
25 stronger, strongest
26 cleaner, cleanest
27 dimmer, dimmest
28 wealthier, wealthiest
29 cheaper, cheapest
30 hotter, hottest
31 muddier, muddiest
32 luckier, luckiest
33 bigger, biggest
34 higher, highest
35 dirtier, dirtiest
36 shorter, shortest

PRACTICE 8 (PAGE 191)

1 powerful<u>ly</u>
2 lucki<u>ly</u>
3 terrib<u>ly</u>
4 safe<u>ly</u>
5 energetic<u>ally</u>
6 reasonab<u>ly</u>
7 traditional<u>ly</u>
8 cautious<u>ly</u>
9 fantastic<u>ally</u>
10 responsib<u>ly</u>
11 satisfactori<u>ly</u>

PRACTICE 9 (PAGE 192)

1 Sad movies always <u>affect</u> me.

2 The waiter was happy to <u>accept</u> our generous tip.

3 The bad weather has had a serious <u>effect</u> on agriculture.

4 There was over 75 percent enrollment during every month <u>except</u> December.

5 Everyone at the meeting indicated their <u>assent</u> to the plan.

6 He followed his doctor's <u>advice</u> to get more exercise.

7 The teacher might <u>advise</u> the parents to get extra help for their child.

8 The <u>ascent</u> of the mountain took over six hours.

9 Her <u>aide</u> answers her phone calls and takes messages.

10 We were interested to see the variety of cactus growing in the <u>desert</u>.

11 I would like your <u>aid</u> in choosing a new apartment.

12 A small dish of fruit is a more healthful <u>dessert</u> than a large slice of cake.

13 More tourists visited the area <u>later</u> in the year.

14 She owns both a car and a bicycle. The <u>latter</u> is her preferred form of transportation.

15 I have vacationed in the area several times in the <u>past</u>.

16 He studied hard and <u>passed</u> all his exams.

17 Driving a car is more convenient <u>than</u> riding a bicycle.

18 They chose this <u>site</u> for their new office building.

19 We ate at a restaurant, and <u>then</u> we went to the movies.

20 Sunset over the ocean is a beautiful <u>sight</u>.

PRACTICE 10 (PAGE 195)

A

The charts show the ~~percentag~~ percentage of homes that were heated with solar power in two ~~diffrent~~ different years, as well as the reasons why people chose this method of heating ~~there~~ their homes. Most people reported that they chose solar power because they are concerned about protecting the ~~enviroment~~ environment. Some people chose solar power because they ~~recieved~~ received money from the ~~goverment~~ government to help pay for the installation.

B

I am writing to tell you that I will be visiting Springfield next month. I know you are ~~familar~~ familiar with that city as you have been there several times. ~~Therefor~~ Therefore, I hope you can ~~reccomend~~ recommend some interesting things to see and do during my visit. You know I am very interested in ~~modren~~ modern art, so I would like to take the ~~oppotunity~~ opportunity to visit some art galleries. And I would ~~definitly~~ definitely like to do some shopping, so I hope you can give me the names of some of the best stores. I would also like to know about the weather so I can decide what clothes to pack. Are the ~~temparitures~~ temperatures high or low at this time of year? I won't finalize my plans ~~untill~~ until I hear from you, so please answer as soon as ~~posible~~ possible.

C

People have different ideas of what ~~sucess~~ success is. Some ~~beleive~~ believe that it means making a lot of money. Others feel that it means the ~~achievment~~ achievement of something important. In my ~~opinon~~ opinion, it means finding happiness. ~~Nowdays~~ Nowadays, people feel that they have to work long hours to make a lot of money. This makes them look successful in the eyes of ~~soceity~~ society. However, I don't think that it is ~~necassary~~ necessary to make a lot of money. Of course, money is nice, but there are other things that are more important.

D

The only way to ~~acheive~~ achieve success in anything is to work hard. Natural ability isn't enough. The most talented musician has to practice a lot in order to become an ~~exellent~~ excellent performer. The smartest student has to complete all ~~assinements~~ assignments well and answer all test questions correctly. Even smart and talented people may fail to reach ~~thier~~ their goals sometimes and feel ~~disapointment~~ disappointment. But if they keep working hard, they can become ~~successfull~~ successful. So you should ~~lisen~~ listen to your parents and teachers when they tell you to work hard. You won't regret it.

GRAMMATICAL RANGE AND ACCURACY

PRACTICE 1 (PAGE 198)

1 _Ø_ oranges make delicious **2** _Ø_ juice. After harvesting, **3** _the_ oranges are placed in **4** _a_ washer. **5** _The_ washer uses **6** _Ø_ water and **7** _Ø_ soap to clean **8** _the_ oranges. **9** _The_ soap is special food-grade soap. Next, **10** _the_ oranges go to **11** _an_ extractor, and **12** _the_ extractor squeezes **13** _the_ fruit.

PRACTICE 2 (PAGE 199)

Sample answer. Answers will vary.

First, fill a sink with warm water. Add soap to the water. Put dirty dishes in the water and let them soak for a few minutes. Next, scrub the dishes with a sponge and then rinse them in clean water. Let the dishes dry on a rack.

PRACTICE 3 (PAGE 201)

1 Speedy Talk Systems <u>manufactures</u> cell phones.

2 Most of the stores on the first floor of the mall <u>sell</u> clothing.

3 I thought that two hundred dollars <u>was</u> a low price for these shoes.

4 All the animals at City Zoo <u>have</u> been well cared for.

5 Everybody <u>enjoys</u> working at this place.

6 Bad news always <u>spreads</u> quickly.

7 The view from these windows <u>is</u> spectacular.

8 Prices always <u>rise</u> during the tourist season.

9 Eating at restaurants <u>costs</u> more than eating at home.

10 Pink sand <u>covers</u> the beaches of the island.

11 All of the people in this class <u>are</u> first-year students.

12 Chocolate <u>comes</u> from cacao beans.

13 Everything <u>seems</u> to happen at once.

14 Nobody <u>was</u> at the office last Saturday.

15 Ten dollars <u>doesn't</u> buy much these days.

16 Regular exercise <u>helps</u> you stay healthy.

17 Measles <u>is</u> an infectious disease.

18 The rents in this city <u>have</u> risen a lot in the past year.

19 Ice cream <u>was</u> my favorite dessert when I was young.

20 Collecting stamps <u>is</u> a hobby of mine.

PRACTICE 4 (PAGE 202)

A

In my opinion, talking on a cell phone while driving is dangerous. Therefore, it should be illegal for drivers to use cell phones. If it **1** <u>is</u> (be) illegal, then people **2** <u>will have</u> (have) to stop this dangerous habit. If some people **3** <u>continue</u> (continue) to use cell phones while driving, they **4** <u>will have</u> (have) to pay a fine. Nobody likes to pay a fine. I also think there should be education about the risks of this habit. People **5** <u>will stop</u> (stop) using cell phones while driving if they **6** <u>understand</u> (understand) how dangerous it is.

B

I think parents should send their children to preschool. There are many advantages to it. If a child **7** <u>starts</u> (start) school young, she **8** <u>will learn</u> (learn) to socialize with other children. She **9** <u>won't have</u> (not have) this opportunity if she **10** <u>stays</u> (stay) at home all day. Also, she **11** <u>will learn</u> (learn) many important skills if she **12** <u>goes</u> (go) to preschool. She will listen to stories, draw pictures, and have fun with blocks and other toys. These activities aren't just games. They help the child's brain develop. If a child **13** <u>does</u> (do) these things in school every day, it **14** <u>will help</u> (help) her later when it's time to learn to read and write.

PRACTICE 5 (PAGE 203)

I live in a small town. If I **1** <u>lived</u> (live) in a city, I **2** <u>would have</u> (have) many more opportunities. For example, cities have museums. If I **3** <u>were</u> (be) able to go to museums frequently, I **4** <u>would learn</u> (learn) a lot about history, science, and art. I also **5** <u>would have</u> (have) the chance to meet a wider variety of people if I **6** <u>lived</u> (live) in a city. In general, my life **7** <u>would be</u> (be) a lot more interesting if I **8** <u>had</u> (have) a home in the city.

PRACTICE 6 (page 204)

I didn't make my hotel reservation early. If I **1** <u>had made</u> (make) my reservation early, they **2** <u>would have given</u> (give) me a better room. As it was, the room they gave me was small, and the bed was lumpy. If the bed **3** <u>had been</u> (be) more comfortable, I **4** <u>would have slept</u> (sleep) better. Since I didn't sleep well, I got up late. I **5** <u>would have had</u> (have) time for breakfast if I **6** <u>had gotten</u> (get) up early. But, I didn't have time for breakfast, and I was hungry all morning. Next time, I will make my hotel reservation early.

PRACTICE 7 (PAGE 204)

Answers will vary.

PRACTICE 8 (PAGE 206)

1   The waiter (who) served us was very polite.
<u>Restrictive</u>

2   Houses (that) are well insulated burn less heating fuel.
<u>Restrictive</u>

3   My apartment, (which) is on the top floor, gets a lot of sunlight.
<u>Nonrestrictive</u>

4   School is fun for children (whose) <u>teachers provide them with interesting activities</u>.
<u>Restrictive</u>

5   The front desk clerk, (who) <u>was very busy at the time</u>, forgot to give me my room key.
<u>Nonrestrictive</u>

6   Public transportation is convenient for commuters (who) <u>travel during rush hour</u>.
<u>Restrictive</u>

7   You should avoid eating snacks (that) <u>are high in fat and sugar</u>.
<u>Restrictive</u>

8   The local zoo, (which) <u>is open 365 days a year</u>, is always crowded on holidays.
<u>Nonrestrictive</u>

PRACTICE 9 (PAGE 206)

People **1** <u>whose</u> elderly parents are unable to care for themselves have a difficult choice to make. Will they care for their parents at home? Or will they put their parents in the hands of nursing home workers **2** <u>who</u> can provide them with care 24 hours a day? People **3** <u>who</u> have full-time jobs often don't have the time or energy to provide the needed care. On the other hand, nursing homes can be quite expensive, and nursing homes **4** <u>which</u> charge less may not provide excellent care. It is a difficult decision **5** <u>that</u> requires a lot of thought and discussion. If a family decides to use a nursing home, they should choose a home **6** <u>that</u> is pleasant, comfortable, and convenient to visit. And they should visit frequently. Nursing home residents **7** <u>whose</u> families visit them often live longer, happier lives.

PRACTICE 10 (PAGE 208)

1 We really enjoyed the meal (that) you prepared for us last night.
<u>Restrictive</u>

2 Our house, (which) we bought just three years ago, is too small for our growing family.
<u>Nonrestrictive</u>

3 I don't have a phone number for the woman (whose) purse I found.
<u>Restrictive</u>

4 The sales manager, (whom) I spoke with about my problem, was very helpful.
<u>Nonrestrictive</u>

5 This is not the bus (that) I usually ride to work.
<u>Restrictive</u>

6 I have not yet met the staff members (who) we hired last week.
<u>Restrictive</u>

7 Our city's subway system, (which) transports thousands of commuters daily, should be expanded.
<u>Nonrestrictive</u>

8 The man (whose) ideas we heard last night is an experienced city planner.
<u>Restrictive</u>

PRACTICE 11 (PAGE 208)

Acme Fashions, **1** <u>which</u> many people name as their favorite store, has some of the most stylish clothes in town. Unfortunately, the quality is not very high. The dress **2** <u>that</u> I bought there yesterday had a hole in the back and a stain near the hem. When I tried to return the dress to the store, the man **3** <u>who</u> I asked to assist me was very rude. He said I had damaged the dress myself. In my opinion, it is not good policy to treat your customers, **4** <u>who</u> you rely on to keep your business going, in this way. I cannot wear the damaged dress and I expect the store to return the money **5** <u>that</u> I spent on it. Otherwise, I will have to do my shopping somewhere else.

PRACTICE 12 (PAGE 210)

1	passive	3	passive	5	active	7	passive
2	active	4	passive	6	passive	8	active

PRACTICE 13 (PAGE 210)

1   were pruned

2   were sprayed

3   are harvested

4   are packed

5   are taken

6   is crushed

7   is collected

PRACTICE 14 (PAGE 212)

1   Work and play are both important things to include in your life.

2   I like traveling, writing, and meeting new people.

3   Children learn foreign languages quickly and easily.

4   The teacher told the students to study hard, rest well before a test, and come to class on time.

5   At the zoo, they feed the animals once a day and bathe them once a week. (or At the zoo, the animals are fed once a day and bathed once a week.)

6   A subway carries many passengers, travels rapidly, and costs little to ride.

7   At my company, telecommuters are asked to check in with their boss daily and to submit a report at the end of the week.

8   The last time I took my car to the mechanic, the oil was changed, and the brakes were checked.

PRACTICE 15 (PAGE 214)

Sample answers. Answers will vary.

1   I enjoy reading, cooking, and gardening.

2   People shouldn't smoke because it causes cancer, harms the environment, and costs money.

3   People should use public transportation because it reduces air pollution and traffic congestion.

4   Some people don't use public transportation because they think it is inconvenient and expensive.

5   Zoos provide the public with the opportunity to see wild animals up close, learn about their habits, and understand the importance of protecting them.

6   Zoos take animals away from their life of freedom and lock them up in cages.

7 Teachers ask their students to pay attention in class, turn in their homework on time, and do their best.

8 I like my job because I can be creative and work on interesting projects.

PRACTICE 16 (PAGE 217)

1	compound-complex	**5**	complex
2	simple	**6**	compound
3	compound-complex	**7**	compound
4	simple	**8**	complex

PRACTICE 17 (PAGE 217)

1 Some neighborhoods are noisy and crowded, but others are quiet and clean.

2 I enjoy water sports, so I always spend my vacation at the beach.

3 You can have dinner alone, or I can cook for you.

4 I will move to a new apartment if I can find one closer to my job.

5 This neighborhood was quiet and peaceful before they built a large shopping mall nearby.

6 I usually eat at restaurants because I don't like to cook.

7 People like living in this city even though rents are high and crime is a growing problem.

8 Life in a small town is peaceful and quiet, but many young people move away because they can't find jobs.

PRACTICE 18 (PAGE 219)

Sample answers. Answers will vary.

1 **Simple:** You can see animals from all over the world in a zoo.
Compound: Some people don't like zoos, so they never visit them.
Complex: Scientists can study animals more easily when they study them in a zoo.
Compound-complex: Zoos are popular places, but I never visit them because I don't like to see animals in cages.

2 **Simple:** Physical education classes are part of the curriculum in many schools.
Compound: Physical education classes are important, but academic classes are more important.
Complex: Physical education classes are important because they teach children about competition.
Compound-complex: When children take physical education classes, they learn how to follow rules, and they get exercise at the same time.

3 **Simple:** I prefer life in a city to life in a small town.
Compound: Some people like city life, and others prefer small town life.
Complex: If I lived in a city, my life would be busy and stressful.
Compound-complex: Life in a small town is peaceful, but it can also be boring because there isn't much to do.

PRACTICE 19 (PAGE 221)

1 Telecommuting, which has become an increasingly popular way to work, is not favored by many supervisors.

2 When children start school at an early age, do they learn better?

3 Some people feel that physical education isn't as important as academics.

4 Children's interests change as they grow up.

5 After I got home, I noticed the stains on the jacket.

6 Clearly, people's ideas are influenced by things they see on TV and the Internet.

7 Some houses were heated with solar power, and others were heated with oil or gas.

8 What is the best age to begin foreign language study?

9 We had to go along with our parents' decision even though we didn't agree with it.

10 When I was a child, I wanted either a dog, a cat, or a parrot as a pet, but my parents wouldn't let me have one.

11 London, one of the biggest cities in the world, is a fascinating place to visit.

12 In the evening, you can visit one of our city's famous theaters.